DEDICATION

TO MY MOTHER. IF IT WASN'T FOR HER CARE, LOVE,
AND NURTURING I PROBABLY WOULD HAVE BEEN AN
AXE WIELDING HOMICIDAL MANIAC.

–STEPHEN

MADE IN THE USA

FOURTH EDITION

ACKNOWLEDGMENTS

Special Thanks!

To Mom and Dad, Stuart and Cindy, and all the rest of my
relatives whom I do not see often enough.
To Castle Hill Foundation, The 1640 Hart House, The Choate
Bridge Pub, Ipswich; the Peabody Marriott; CHF Inc. Salem, NH;
everyone I served with at Combat support 3/18th Inf.; Scott
Blanchette, Paul Masiello, Kelly and Jay Cappelli, Kurt Welter,
Will Norris, Bryan Miller, Frankie at the Hog's Breath Saloon, Key
West; Jacob Marley's, Joe Tecce's, The Black Cow, Brad Parker,
Matthew Olga, Mike Shaw, Randy Rollins, Cara, Brittany and
Jacquie Howe, Walter Hall, Joe Kaszuba, Amy Diamond, Maria
Hickey, Mike Hamori, Ipswich Clam Bake Company, Frank
Sullivan, Larry Cabana, and Wally Faber.

Publisher's Cataloging-in-Publication
(Provided by Quality Books, Inc.)

Cunningham, Stephen Kittredge.
  The bartender's black book/ Stephen Kittredge Cunningham.
-- 4th ed.
    p. cm.
    Includes index.
    ISBN: 0-9657746-0-0

  1. Bartending–Handbooks, manuals, etc. 2. Cocktails.
I. Title.

TX951.C86 1998   641.8'74
                        QBI98-275

ISBN 0-9657746-0-0

THE BARTENDER'S BLACK BOOK
TABLE OF CONTENTS:

NEW!

MIXING

Glassware
In recent years the trend of establishments to have specialized glassware has changed. Multi-purpose glassware has taken over. Many busy businesses have made it using only shaker glasses and snifters. The choice is yours.

Flaming
Any alcohol concentration of 87 proof or greater will ignite if exposed to a direct flame. Many liquors and liqueurs of lesser proof will ignite if heated first and then exposed to a direct flame. *CAUTION*, people have been maimed drinking flaming shots.

Floating
To make floating drinks, layered drinks, pousse-café, one must pour the heaviest liqueurs or liquors first, then slowly pour the lighter ones on top over the back of a spoon. If you have time to make drinks ahead of time you can refrigerate, and the individual ingredients will separate themselves in an hour or so.

Frosting and Chilling glasses
To frost a glass simply run cold water all over glass and place in freezer. Allow 5-10 minutes for ample frosting.

To chill a glass, if time allows just place in a refrigerator for 5 to 10 minutes. If time does not permit, fill glass with ice and let set a minute or two.

Shaking
Most bars have in their arsenal metal or plastic shaker cups which fit over their glasses. If no shaker cups are available you can pour from one glass to another until mixed.

Stirring
Stir with spoon in a home atmosphere. In an establishment it is more appropriate to stick a straw or a stirrer into drinks and let the patron stir their own drink. Be careful not to over stir drinks containing Champagne, sodas or other sparkling ingredients.

Straining
The easiest way to strain a drink is to acquire a metal mixing cup and a drink strainer which fits over the cup. In a bind you can place straws or a knife over cup, and pour very gently.

GARNISHES

Wash fresh fruit and vegetables thoroughly. Many are grown in foreign soil and may have been exposed to harmful insecticides.

BANANAS: Ripe yellow cross sections of bananas make a colorful and stylish garnish. Before peeling and adding fresh banana to a blended drink, cut a 1/2-3/4 inch cross section from the middle. Then cut from the center through the peel. This should make it fit nicely onto the rim of a glass.

CELERY: Always wash celery thoroughly. Cut off the base as well as the tips of the leaves, so that there is no discoloration, just healthy light green celery. When making a drink calling for celery as a garnish, make sure you leave room to accommodate the stick of celery. Keep celery in ice water, in a refrigerator until needed.

CHERRIES: Red Maraschino cherries are essential for adult drinks, as well as children's drinks. After opening the jar be sure to refrigerate.

CINNAMON: Ground cinnamon as well as cinnamon sticks are used in many recipes. It is easy to overpower a drink with cinnamon. Use ground cinnamon sparingly. Drinks calling for cinnamon sticks, leave whole unless specified. Long sticks can make excellent stirrers.

COCKTAIL SHRIMP: Shrimp make delicious exotic garnish for drinks such as a Bloody Mary or a Red Snapper. Cook them as if they were for a shrimp cocktail, removing the black vein in the back. If shrimp, after cooking and waiting to be used become slimy, throw them away.

COFFEE BEANS: Coffee Beans are a traditional garnish for Sambuca drinks. Three beans represent Health, Wealth and Happiness.

CUCUMBER: Cut either into spears or wheels, cucumbers are a great garnish instead of, or in addition to celery for a Virgin Mary and other drinks of that nature. Wash thoroughly. Peeling is optional.

LEMONS: *Wedges.* Cut off the ends of a lemon, then cut down the middle from flat end to flat end making two halves. Make a 1/4 inch incision in the center of the halves against the grain, then cut 3 or 4 equal sized wedges from the half. The tiny incision was made so your wedge will fit snugly on rim of glass.
    Twists. Cut off the ends of a lemon, then make 4 long lengthwise cuts into the rind (Be careful not to cut into the meat of the lemon). Soak lemon in hot tap water for 5 minutes. Separate the rind from the meat, and cut the rind into long 1/4 inch strips. When a twist is called for a drink, it should be twisted over the drink, then rubbed around the lip of the glass.

LIMES: *Wedges*. Cut off the ends of a lime, then cut down the middle from flat end to flat end making two halves. Make a 1/4 inch incision in the center of the halves against the grain. Cut 3 or 4 equal sized wedges from the half. The tiny incision was made so your wedge will fit snugly on the rim of a glass.

     Wheels. Cut off the ends. Cut 1/6th inch cross sections. Cut the rind to allow a place to sit on the glass.

OLIVES: Green olives (with or without pimentos) are essential for martinis. Refrigerate after opening a fresh container.

ONIONS: Cocktail onions are the distinguishing difference between a Martini and a Gibson. They can be found in most grocery stores. Refrigerate after opening.

ORANGES: Cut the ends off an orange. Cut down the middle from flat end to flat end. Cut half wheels across the grain approximately 1/6th inch thick. A slight pull on the the ends will allow you to sit it on the rim of the glass.

PINEAPPLES: *Sticks*. Cut off the top, bottom and sides, making a solid block of pineapple meat. Cut this into equal sized sticks.

     Wedges. Cut off the top and bottom, then quarter the pineapple the long way. Cut off pointed part of quarter. Slice straight down flat side about 1/4 inch deep. Cut into 1/2 inch wedges.

SALT (KOSHER): Salt is primarily used to rim glasses by moistening the glass with either water or fruit juice from a cut piece of fruit (lemon, lime, orange) and dipping the glass into the salt (which should be laid out in a dish or any contained flat surface).

SHAVED ALMONDS: Commonly found in a cook's arsenal, they make a very appealing decoration for drinks with traces of Almond Liqueurs (Amaretto, Creme De Nouyax). Sprinkle them on whipped cream or float them on a creamy drink's surface.

SHAVED CHOCOLATE: A favorite at fancy establishments is freshly shaved dark chocolate. Just buy a block of chocolate and introduce it to your friendly cheese grater, and you're in business.

SPRINKLES or JIMMIES: Pleasant to the eye as well as the palate, they do justice to hot coffee drinks and many frozen concoctions. They are available at most convenience stores.

STRAWBERRIES: Fresh ripe strawberries enhance any drink containing berries or strawberry liqueur. Wash berries thoroughly. Cut large ones in two; leave small ones whole. Simply push a berry onto the rim of a glass until it fits snugly.

WHIPPED CREAM: You can use either fresh or canned. Whipped cream is expected to top many hot drinks. If fresh whipped cream is used, you may want to add 1/2 tsp of sugar to your drink due to the fact that processed whipped cream is sweetened.

ABBY ROAD
Fill glass with ice.
1 oz Amaretto
1 oz Black Raspberry Liqueur
1 oz Coffee Liqueur
Stir.

ABBY ROAD COFFEE
1 oz Amaretto
1 oz Black Raspberry Liqueur
1 oz Coffee Liqueur
Fill with hot Black Coffee.
Top with Whipped Cream.
Drizzle with Chocolate Syrup.

ABC (floater)
1/2 oz Amaretto (bottom)
1/2 oz Irish Cream
1/2 oz Orange Liqueur (top)

ACAPULCO
Fill glass with ice.
1 oz Brandy
1 oz Gin
Dash of Grenadine
Dash of Sour Mix
Dash of Orange Juice
Fill with Ginger Ale.
Garnish with Orange and Cherry.

ACAPULCO GOLD
Fill glass with ice.
1 oz Tequila
1 oz Amber Rum
1 oz Cream of Coconut
1 oz Pineapple Juice
1 oz Grapefruit Juice
Shake.

ADIOS MOTHER aka CODE BLUE
Fill glass with ice.
1/2 oz Vodka
1/2 oz Rum
1/2 oz Tequila
1/2 oz Gin
1/2 oz Blue Curacao
Fill with Sour Mix.
Shake.

ADULT HOT CHOCOLATE aka PEPPERMINT KISS, COCOANAPPS, SNUGGLER
2 oz Peppermint Schnapps
Fill with Hot Chocolate.
Stir.
Top with Whipped Cream.
Sprinkle with Shaved
Chocolate or Sprinkles.

AFTERBURNER
Fill glass with ice.
1 oz Peppered Vodka
1 oz Cinnamon Schnapps
1 oz Coffee Liqueur
Shake.
Strain into shot glass.

AFTERBURNER 2
Fill glass with ice.
1/2 oz 151-Proof Rum
1/2 oz Jaegermeister
1/2 oz Coffee Liqueur
Stir.
Strain into chilled glass.

AFTER EIGHT (floater)
1/2 oz Coffee Liqueur (bottom)
1/2 oz White Creme De Menthe
1/2 oz Irish Cream (top)

AFTER FIVE (floater)
1/2 oz Coffee Liqueur (bottom)
1/2 oz Irish Cream
1/2 oz Peppermint Schnapps (top)

AFTER FIVE COFFEE
1/2 oz Coffee Liqueur
1/2 oz Irish Cream
1/2 oz Peppermint Schnapps
Fill with hot Black Coffee.
Top with Whipped Cream.
Sprinkle with Shaved
Chocolate or Sprinkles.

AGENT O.
Fill glass with ice.
1/2 oz Vodka
1/2 oz Orange Liqueur
Fill with Orange Juice.
Shake.
Garnish with Orange.

AGGRAVATION aka TEACHER'S PET
Fill glass with ice.
1 oz Scotch
1 oz Coffee Liqueur
Fill with Milk or Cream.
Shake.

ALABAMA SLAMMER
Fill glass with ice.
3/4 oz Vodka
3/4 oz Southern Comfort
3/4 oz Amaretto
Dash of Sloe Gin or Grenadine
Fill with Orange Juice.
Shake.
Garnish with Orange.

ALABAMA SLAMMER 2
Fill glass with ice.
1 oz Vodka
1 oz Southern Comfort
Dash of Sloe Gin or Grenadine
Fill with Orange Juice.
Shake.
Garnish with Orange.

ALABAMA SLAMMER 3
Fill glass with ice.
1 oz Southern Comfort
1 oz Amaretto
Dash of Sloe Gin or Grenadine
Fill with Orange Juice.
Shake.
Garnish with Orange.

ALABAMA SLAMMER 4
Fill glass with ice.
1/2 oz Southern Comfort
1/2 oz Triple Sec
1/2 oz Galliano
1/2 oz Sloe Gin
Fill with Orange Juice.
Shake.
Garnish with Orange.

ALABAMA SLAMMER 5
Fill glass with ice.
1/2 oz Whiskey
1/2 oz Southern Comfort
1/2 oz Amaretto
1/2 oz Sloe Gin
Fill with Orange Juice.
Shake.
Garnish with Orange.

ALABAMA SLAMMER (frozen)
In Blender:
1/2 cup of Ice
1 oz Vodka
1 oz Southern Comfort
Dash of Sloe Gin or Grenadine
Scoop of Orange Sherbet
Blend until smooth.
If too thick add Orange Juice.
If too thin add ice or sherbet.
Garnish with Orange.

ALASKAN ICED TEA
Fill glass with ice.
1/2 oz Vodka
1/2 oz Gin
1/2 oz Rum
2 oz Blue Curacao
2 oz Sour Mix
Fill with Lemon-Lime Soda.
Garnish with Lemon.

ALBATROSS (frozen)
In Blender:
1 cup of Ice
1 oz Gin
1 oz Melon Liqueur
1 Egg White
1 oz Lime Juice
Blend until smooth.

ALEXANDER
Fill glass with ice.
1 oz Gin
1 oz White or Dark Creme De Cacao
Fill with Milk or Cream.
Shake.

ALEXANDER THE GREAT
Fill glass with ice.
1 1/2 oz Greek Brandy
1/2 oz Dark Creme De Cacao
2 oz Milk or Cream
Shake.
Strain into chilled glass.

ALEXANDER'S SISTER
Fill glass with ice.
1 oz Gin
1 oz Green Creme De Menthe
Fill with Milk or Cream.
Shake.

ALGONQUIN
Fill glass with ice.
1 1/2 oz Whiskey
1 oz Dry Vermouth
1 oz Pineapple Juice
Shake.
Strain into chilled glass.

ALICE IN WONDERLAND aka DALLAS ALICE
Fill glass with ice.
3/4 oz Tequila
3/4 oz Orange Liqueur
3/4 oz Coffee Liqueur
Shake.
Strain into shot glass.

ALIEN SECRETION
Fill glass with ice.
1 oz Coconut Rum
1 oz Melon Liqueur
Fill with Pineapple Juice.
Shake.
Garnish with Cherry.

ALMOND ENJOY
Fill glass with ice.
1 oz Amaretto
1 oz Dark Creme De Cacao
1 oz Cream of Coconut
Fill with Cream or Milk.
Shake.

ALMOND KISS aka COCOETTO
2 oz Amaretto
Fill with Hot Chocolate.
Stir.
Top with Whipped Cream.
Place Chocolate Kiss on top
or Shaved Chocolate.

ALMOND MOCHA COFFEE
1 oz Amaretto
1 oz Creme De Cacao
Fill with hot Black Coffee.
Top with Whipped Cream.
Sprinkle with Shaved Almonds
and/or Shaved Chocolate.

AMARETTO *(type liqueur)*
Bring 2 cups of Water mixed with 1 1/2 cups of Brown Sugar and 1 cup of Granulated Sugar to a boil.
Stir often.
Lower heat and let simmer 5 minutes.
Let cool 2 minutes.
Pour mixture into glass container.
Add 1 qt Vodka, 6 tsp vanilla, 8 tsp almond extract.
Stir and pour into bottles with screw top.
Place in a dark cool place for 1 week.

AMARETTO SOUR
Fill glass with ice.
2 oz Amaretto
Fill with Sour Mix.
Shake.
Garnish with Orange and Cherry.

AMARIST
1 oz Amaretto
1 oz Orange Liqueur
Microwave for 10-15 seconds.

AMBER CLOUD
1 1/2 oz Cognac
1/2 oz Galliano
Microwave for 10 seconds.

AMBROSIA
Fill glass with ice.
1 oz Brandy
1/4 oz Triple Sec
Fill with Champagne.

AMBUSH COFFEE
1 oz Irish Whiskey
1 oz Amaretto
Fill with hot Black Coffee.
Top with Whipped Cream.
Sprinkle with Shaved Almonds.
Dribble 4-5 drops of Green Creme De Menthe on top.

AMERICAN GRAFFITI
Fill glass with ice.
1/2 oz Light Rum
1/2 oz Dark Rum
1/2 oz Southern Comfort
1/2 oz Sloe Gin
Dash of Lime Juice
Fill with equal parts Sour Mix and Pineapple Juice.
Shake.
Garnish with Lime.

AMERICAN SOUR
Fill glass with ice.
2 oz Bourbon
Dash of Orange Curacao or Triple Sec
Dash of Orange Juice
Fill with Sour Mix.
Shake.

AMIGO aka WHITE BULL
Fill glass with ice.
1 oz Tequila
3/4 oz Coffee Liqueur
Fill with Milk or Cream.
Shake.

ANGEL FACE
Fill glass with ice.
1 oz Gin
1/2 oz Apricot Brandy
1/2 oz Apple Brandy
Shake.
Strain into chilled glass.

ANGEL KISS (floater)
1 oz Dark Creme De Cacao (bottom)
1 oz Milk or Cream (top)

ANGEL WING (floater)
1 1/2 oz White Creme De Cacao (bottom)
1/2 oz Irish Cream (top)

ANGEL WING 2 (floater)
1 oz White Creme De Cacao (bottom)
1 oz Brandy
1/2 oz Milk or Light Cream (top)

ANGEL'S TIT (floater)
1 oz Dark Creme De Cacao (bottom)
1 oz Milk or Cream (top)
Garnish with Cherry on toothpick across top of glass.

ANISETTE *(type liqueur)*
Bring 2 cups of Water and 2 cups of Granulated Sugar to a boil.
Simmer 10 minutes, stirring often.
Add 1 tsp Vanilla, 1 1/2 tsp Anise Extract, 1 qt Vodka.

ANKLE BREAKER
Fill glass with ice.
1 1/2 oz 151-Proof Rum
1 oz Cherry Brandy
1 oz Lime Juice
1 tsp Sugar Syrup
Shake.

ANNA'S BANANA (frozen)
In Blender:
1/2 cup of Ice
2 oz Vodka
1/2 fresh ripe Banana
1 tsp Honey
Dash of Lime Juice
Blend until smooth.
If too thick add fruit.
If too thin add ice.
Garnish with Banana.

ANTI-FREEZE
Fill glass with ice.
1 oz Vodka
1 oz Green Creme De Menthe or
Melon Liqueur
Shake.
Strain into shot glass.

ANTI-FREEZE 2
Fill glass with ice.
1 oz Mentholated Schnapps
1 oz Blue Curacao
Shake.
Strain into chilled glass.
Top with Lemon-Lime Soda.

ANTIQUAN KISS
Fill glass with ice.
1/2 oz Light Rum
1/2 oz Dark Rum
1/2 oz Apricot Brandy
1/2 oz Peach Schnapps
Dash of Cranberry Juice
Fill with Orange Juice.
Shake.

ANTIQUAN SMILE
Fill glass with ice.
1 1/2 oz Dark Rum
1/2 oz Banana Liqueur
Pinch of Powdered Sugar
Fill with Orange Juice.
Shake.
Garnish with Lime.

APOLLO COOLER
Fill glass with ice.
1 1/2 oz Metaxa
1/2 oz Lemon Juice
Shake.
Fill with Ginger Ale.

APPENDECTOMY aka
APPENDICITIS
Fill glass with ice.
1 oz Gin
1/2 oz Orange Liqueur
1 oz Sour Mix
Shake.
Strain into chilled glass.

APPETIZER
4 oz Red Wine
Fill with Orange Juice.
Dash of Bitters (optional)

APPLE COOLER
Fill glass with ice.
1 oz Light Rum
1 oz Brandy
Fill with Apple Cider or Juice.
Shake.
Strain into chilled glass.
Float 1/2 oz Dark Rum on top.

APPLE MARGARITA (frozen)
In Blender:
1 cup of Ice
1 oz Tequila
1 oz Apple Brandy
2 Tbsp Applesauce
1 oz Sour Mix
Blend until smooth.
If too thick add applesauce
or Sour Mix.
If too thin add ice.
Rim glass with Cinnamon and
Sugar.

APPLE PIE
Fill glass with ice.
1 1/2 oz Vodka
1/2 oz Apple Cider or Juice
Strain into chilled glass.
Sprinkle with Cinnamon.

APPLE PIE (floater)
3/4 oz Apple Brandy (bottom)
3/4 oz Cinnamon Schnapps
3/4 oz Irish Cream (top)

APPLE POLISHER
2 oz Southern Comfort
Fill with hot Apple Cider.
Garnish with Cinnamon Stick.

APRES SKI
Fill glass with ice.
1 oz Peppermint Schnapps
1 oz Coffee Liqueur
1 oz White Creme De Cacao
Shake.

APRES SKI 2
1 oz Brandy
1 oz Apple Brandy
Fill with Apple Cider.
Garnish with Cinnamon Stick.

APRICOT FRAPPE
Fill large stemmed glass (Red Wine
glass, Champagne saucer) with
crushed ice.
1 oz Brandy
1 oz Apricot Brandy

APRICOT SOUR
Fill glass with ice.
2 oz Apricot Brandy
Fill with Sour Mix.
Shake.
Garnish with Orange and Cherry.

APRIL IN PARIS
1 oz Orange Liqueur
Fill with Champagne.
Garnish with Orange Slice.

ARIZONA LEMONADE
Fill glass with ice.
2 oz Tequila
2 tsp Powdered Sugar
Fill with fresh Lemon Juice.
Shake until sugar dissolves.
Garnish with Lemon.

AROUND THE WORLD
Fill glass with ice.
1 1/2 oz Gin
1 1/2 oz Green Creme De Menthe
1 1/2 oz Pineapple Juice
Shake.

ARTIFICIAL INTELLIGENCE
Fill glass with ice.
1/2 oz Dark Rum
1/2 oz Light Rum
1/2 oz Coconut Rum
Dash of Lime Juice
3 oz Pineapple Juice
Shake.
Strain into chilled glass.
Float 1/2 oz Melon Liqueur
on top.

ASPEN COFFEE
3/4 oz Coffee Liqueur
or Orange Liqueur
3/4 oz Irish Cream
3/4 oz Hazelnut Liqueur
Fill with hot Black Coffee.
Top with Whipped Cream.
Sprinkle with Shaved
Chocolate.

ASPEN HUMMER
1 oz 151-Proof Rum
1 oz Coffee Liqueur
Fill with hot Black Coffee.
Top with Whipped Cream.

ATOMIC WASTE
Fill glass with ice.
3/4 oz Vodka
3/4 oz Melon Liqueur
1/2 oz Peach Schnapps
1/2 oz Banana Liqueur
Fill with Milk.
Shake.
Strain into chilled glass.

AUGUST MOON
Fill glass with ice.
1 oz Amaretto
1 oz Triple Sec
1 oz Orange Juice
Shake.
Strain into chilled glass.

AUNT JEMIMA (floater)
1/2 oz Brandy (bottom)
1/2 oz White Creme De Cacao
1/2 oz Benedictine (top)

AVALANCHE (floater)
1/2 oz Coffee Liqueur (bottom)
1/2 oz White Creme De Cacao
1/2 oz Southern Comfort (top)

B & B
1 oz Brandy
1 oz Benedictine
Stir gently.

B-51 aka CONCORD (floater)
1/2 oz Coffee Liqueur (bottom)
1/2 oz Irish Cream
1/2 oz 151-Proof Rum (top)

B-52 (floater)
1/2 oz Coffee Liqueur (bottom)
1/2 oz Irish Cream
1/2 oz Orange Liqueur (top)

B-52 (frozen)
In Blender:
1/2 cup of Ice
3/4 oz Coffee Liqueur
3/4 oz Irish Cream
3/4 oz Orange Liqueur
Scoop of Vanilla Ice Cream
Blend until smooth.
If too thick add Milk or Cream.
If too thin add ice or ice cream.
Garnish with Chocolate
shavings or Sprinkles.

B-52 (rocks)
Fill glass with ice.
1 oz Coffee Liqueur
1 oz Irish Cream
1 oz Orange Liqueur
Shake.

B-52 COFFEE
1/2 oz Coffee Liqueur
1/2 oz Irish Cream
1/2 oz Orange Liqueur
Fill with hot Black Coffee.
Top with Whipped Cream.
Garnish with Orange.

B-52 ON A MISSION (floater)
1/2 oz Coffee Liqueur (bottom)
1/2 oz Irish Cream
1/2 oz Orange Liqueur
1/2 oz 151-Proof Rum (top)

B-52 WITH BOMBAY DOORS
(floater)
1/2 oz Coffee Liqueur
1/2 oz Irish Cream
1/2 oz Orange Liqueur
1/2 oz Dry Gin (top)

B-54 aka DC-10 (floater)
1/2 oz Coffee Liqueur (bottom)
1/2 oz Irish Cream
1/2 oz Amaretto (top)

B-57 (floater)
1/2 oz Coffee Liqueur (bottom)
1/2 oz Amaretto
1/2 oz Cognac or Brandy (top)

BABBIE'S SPECIAL
Fill glass with ice.
1 oz Gin
3/4 oz Apricot Brandy
Fill with Milk or Cream.
Shake.

BACARDI COCKTAIL
Fill glass with ice.
2 oz Rum
Dash of Grenadine
Fill with Sour Mix.
Shake.
Garnish with Orange and Cherry.

BAD ATTITUDE
Fill glass with ice.
1 oz Coconut Rum
1 oz Spiced Rum
2 oz Pineapple Juice
Shake.
Strain into chilled glass.
John Couture

BAHAMA MAMA
Fill glass with ice.
1 oz Light Rum
1 oz Dark Rum
1 oz Amber Rum
2 oz Sour Mix
2 oz Orange Juice
2 oz Pineapple Juice
Shake.
Put dash of Grenadine in second
glass and fill with mixture.
Garnish with Orange and Cherry.

BAHAMA MAMA 2
Fill glass with ice.
1 oz Light Rum
1 oz Coconut Rum
1 oz Amaretto
Dash of Grenadine
Fill with equal parts Orange and
Pineapple Juice.

BAILEY'S AND COFFEE
2 oz Irish Cream
Fill with hot Black Coffee.
Top with Whipped Cream.

BAILEY'S COMET
Fill glass with ice.
1 1/2 oz Vodka
1/2 oz Irish Cream

BAILEY'S FIZZ
Fill glass with ice.
2 oz Irish Cream
Fill with Soda Water.

BALALAIKA
Fill glass with ice.
1 1/2 oz Vodka
1/2 oz Triple Sec
2 oz Sour Mix
Shake.
Strain into chilled glass.
Garnish with Lime.

BAMBINI ARUBA
Fill glass with ice.
1 oz Vodka
1 oz Rum
1 oz Bourbon
Dash of Grenadine
Fill with equal parts Sour Mix,
Orange and Pineapple Juice.
Shake.
Garnish with Orange and Cherry.

BANANA BOAT
Fill glass with ice.
1 oz Coconut Rum
1 oz Banana Liqueur
2 oz Pineapple Juice
Shake.
Strain into chilled glass.

BANANA COLADA (frozen)
In Blender:
1/2 cup of Ice
2 oz Light Rum
2 Tbsp Cream of Coconut
1 whole peeled ripe Banana
1 Tbsp Vanilla Ice Cream
Blend until smooth.
If too thick add more fruit.
If too thin add ice or ice cream.
Garnish with Banana.

BANANA COW (frozen)
In Blender:
1/2 cup of Ice
1 1/2 oz Dark Rum
1/2 oz Banana Liqueur
1/2 peeled ripe Banana
Scoop of Vanilla Ice Cream
Blend until smooth.
If too thick add Milk.
If too thin add ice or ice cream.
Garnish with Banana.

BANANA CREAM PIE (frozen)
In Blender:
1/2 cup of Ice
1 oz Vodka
1/2 oz Irish Cream
1/2 oz Banana Liqueur
1/2 peeled ripe Banana
Scoop of Vanilla Ice Cream
Blend until smooth.

BANANA DAIQUIRI (frozen)
In Blender:
1 cup of Ice
1 1/2 oz Rum
1/2 oz Banana Liqueur
Dash of Lime Juice
1 whole peeled ripe Banana
Blend until smooth.
If too thick add more fruit.
If too thin add ice.
Garnish with Banana.

BANANA FROST (frozen)
In Blender:
1/2 cup of Ice
1 1/2 oz Amaretto
1/2 oz Banana Liqueur
Scoop of Banana
or Vanilla Ice Cream
1/2 peeled ripe Banana
Blend until smooth.
If too thick add Milk.
If too thin add ice or ice cream.
Garnish with Banana.

BANANA POPSICLE (frozen)
In Blender:
1/2 cup of Ice
1 oz Vodka
1 oz Banana Liqueur
1/2 scoop Orange Sherbet
1/2 scoop Vanilla Ice Cream
1/2 peeled ripe Banana
Blend until smooth.
If too thick add Orange Juice or
Milk.
If too thin add ice or ice cream.

BANANA SANDWICH (floater)
1/2 oz Coffee Liqueur (bottom)
1/2 oz Banana Liqueur
1/2 oz Rum Cream (top)

BANANA SOMBRERO
Fill glass with ice.
2 oz Banana Liqueur
Fill with Milk or Cream.
Shake.

BANANA SPLIT
Fill glass with ice.
2 oz Banana Liqueur
Fill with Milk or Cream.
Top with Whipped Cream.
Dribble Coffee Liqueur on top.
Garnish with Cherry.
Joe Sugden

BANANA SPLIT 2
Fill glass with ice.
1 1/2 oz Vodka
1/2 oz Banana Liqueur
1/2 oz Strawberry Liqueur
1/2 oz Dark Creme De Cacao
Fill with Milk.
Shake.

BANANA SPLIT (frozen)
In Blender:
1/2 cup of Ice
1 oz Rum
1 oz Coffee Liqueur
1 Tbsp Cream of Coconut
1/2 peeled ripe Banana
Scoop of Vanilla Ice Cream
1 Tbsp Chocolate Syrup
1/4 cup fresh or canned Pineapple
2 Maraschino Cherries (no stems)
Blend until smooth.
Top with Whipped Cream.
Garnish with Cherry.
Hurricane Jayne

**BANANA STRAWBERRY
DAIQUIRI** (frozen)
In Blender:
1 cup of Ice
1 oz Rum
1/2 oz Banana Liqueur
1/2 oz Strawberry Liqueur
1/2 cup fresh or frozen
Strawberries
1/2 peeled ripe Banana
Blend until smooth.
If too thick add fruit.
If too thin add ice.
Garnish with Banana and
Strawberry.

**BANGING THE CAPTAIN 3 WAYS
ON THE COMFORTER**
Fill glass with ice.
1 oz Spiced Rum
1 oz Southern Comfort
Fill with equal parts Orange,
Pineapple and Cranberry Juice.
Shake.

BANSHEE aka CAPRI
Fill glass with ice.
1 oz Banana Liqueur
1/2 oz White Creme De Cacao
Fill with Milk or Cream.
Shake.

BANSHEE (frozen)
In Blender:
1/2 cup of Ice
1 oz Banana Liqueur
1/2 oz White Creme De Cacao
Scoop of Vanilla Ice Cream
1 whole peeled ripe Banana
Blend until smooth.
If too thick add Milk.
If too thin add ice or ice cream.
Garnish with Banana.

BARBARELLA aka BARBELLS
Fill glass with ice.
2 oz Orange Liqueur
1 oz Sambuca
Shake.
Serve or strain into chilled glass.

B

BARBARY COAST
Fill glass with ice.
1/2 oz Rum
1/2 oz Gin
1/2 oz Scotch
1/2 oz White Creme De Cacao or
White Creme De Menthe
Fill with Cola.
Shake.
Serve or strain into chilled glass.

BARRACUDA
Fill glass with ice.
1 oz Amber Rum
1 oz Light Rum
1/2 oz Galliano
Dash of Lime Juice
1/2 tsp Powdered Sugar
2 oz Pineapple Juice
Shake.
Top with Champagne.

BART SIMPSON
Fill glass with ice.
1/2 oz Vodka
1/2 oz Coconut Rum
1/2 oz Melon Liqueur
Shake.
Strain into chilled glass.

BARTMAN
Fill glass with ice.
1 oz Light Rum
1 oz Apple Brandy
Dash of Grenadine
Dash of Sour Mix
Fill with Orange Juice.
Shake.
Garnish with Orange and Cherry.

BAT BITE
Fill glass with ice.
2 oz Rum
Fill with Cranberry Juice.
Garnish with Lime.

BAY BREEZE aka HAWAIIAN SEA BREEZE, DOWNEASTER
Fill glass with ice.
2 oz Vodka
Fill with equal parts Cranberry and
Pineapple Juice.
Garnish with Lime.

BBC
1 oz Brandy
1 oz Irish Cream
Fill with hot Black Coffee.
Top with Whipped Cream.

BEACH HUT MADNESS (floater)
1/2 oz Irish Cream (bottom)
1/2 oz Amaretto
1/2 oz Sambuca (top)

BEACON HILL BLIZZARD
Fill glass with ice.
1 oz Dark Rum
1 oz Coconut Rum
Fill with equal parts
Cranberry and Grapefruit Juice.
Garnish with Lime.

BEAM ME UP SCOTTI
Fill glass with ice.
1 oz Vodka
1 oz Irish Cream
1 oz Banana Liqueur
Shake.
Strain into shot glass.

BEAM ME UP SCOTTI (floater)
1/2 oz Coffee Liqueur (bottom)
1/2 oz Banana Liqueur
1/2 oz Irish Cream (top)
Dash of Vodka or Hazelnut Liqueur
(optional).

BEARHUG (Floater)
1/2 oz Coffee Liqueur (bottom)
1/2 oz Sambuca
1/2 oz Orange Liqueur (top)

BEAUTIFUL THING
Fill glass with ice.
1 oz Peppermint Schnapps
1 oz Irish Cream
Stir.

BEE STING
Fill glass with ice.
1 oz Jaegermeister
1 oz Bärenjäger

BEE'S KNEES
Fill glass with ice.
1 1/2 oz Rum
1 tsp of Honey
1 oz Sour Mix
Shake.
Strain into chilled glass.

BEEHIVE
Fill glass with ice.
2 oz Bourbon
1 tsp Honey
Fill with Grapefruit Juice.
Shake.

BEER BUSTER
In chilled beer glass:
2 oz chilled 100-Proof Vodka
3 dashes of Tabasco Sauce
Fill with Beer.

BELLINI
In Blender:
1 fresh Peach (no pit or skin)
or 1/2 cup canned Peaches (no
juice)
Blend.
Pour pureed peach into glass.
Fill with cold Champagne.

14

BELLY BUTTON SHOT
Find an attractive desirable belly button (inny).
Ask permission to use it.
If yes, lay owner of belly button on their back
(totally nude if possible).
Fill belly button with favorite straight liquor or liqueur (be careful not to spill any or you'll have to clean it up with a rag or your tongue).
Place lips over belly button and slurp out drink as loudly as possible. Take turns and repeat process until interests change.

BEND ME OVER
Fill glass with ice.
1 oz Vodka
or 1/2 oz Vodka and 1/2 oz Whiskey
1 oz Amaretto
1 oz Sour Mix
Shake.
Strain into chilled glass.

BERLIN WALL
Fill glass with ice.
1 1/2 oz Vodka
1/2 oz Irish Cream
Stir.

BERMUDA TRIANGLE
Fill glass with ice.
1 oz Spiced Rum
1 oz Peach Schnapps
Fill with Orange Juice.
Shake.

BETSY ROSS
Fill glass with ice.
1 oz Brandy
1 oz Port
1/2 oz Triple Sec
Dash of Bitters
Stir.
Strain into chilled glass.

BETWEEN THE SHEETS
Fill glass with ice.
1 oz Rum
1 oz Cognac or Brandy
1 oz Triple Sec
Dash of Sour Mix
Shake.
Strain into chilled glass.

BEVERLY HILL (floater)
1 oz 100-Proof Cinnamon Schnapps (bottom)
1 oz Jaegermeister (top)

BIBLE BELT
Fill glass with ice.
2 oz Bourbon
or Southern Comfort
1 oz Triple Sec
2 oz Lime Juice
2 oz Sour Mix
Shake.
Rim glass with Powdered Sugar.
Garnish with a Lemon.

BIG BAMBOO
Fill glass with ice.
2 oz 151-Proof Rum
1 oz Dark Rum
1/4 oz Triple Sec
2 oz Orange Juice
2 oz Pineapple Juice
1/2 oz Sugar Syrup
Dash of Bitters
Shake.
Strain into 3 or 4 shot glasses.

BIKINI LINE
Fill glass with ice.
3/4 oz Vodka
3/4 oz Coffee Liqueur
3/4 oz Raspberry Liqueur

BIKINI LINE (floater)
1/2 oz Strawberry Liqueur (bottom)
1/2 oz Orange Liqueur
1/2 oz Vodka (top)

BIMINI ICE-T
Fill glass with ice.
1/2 oz Vodka
1/2 oz Gin
1/2 oz Rum
1/2 oz Tequila
1/2 oz Blue Curacao
1 oz Sour Mix
1 oz Orange Juice
1 oz Pineapple Juice
Shake.
Top with Cola.
Garnish with Lemon.

BIRD OF PARADISE
Fill glass 3/4 full with ice.
Fill 3/4 with Champagne.
Fill with Pineapple Juice.
Dash of Grenadine

BIT OF HONEY (frozen)
In Blender:
1/2 cup of Ice
1/2 oz Scotch
1 Tbsp Honey
Scoop of Vanilla Ice Cream
Blend until smooth.
Float 1/2 oz of B&B on top.

BLACK AND TAN
Fill glass 1/2 with Amber Ale.
Fill glass 1/2 with Stout.

BLACK BARRACUDA
Fill glass with ice.
1 oz Dark Rum
1/2 oz Banana Liqueur
1/2 oz Blackberry Brandy
Dash of Lime Juice
Dash of Grenadine
Fill with Orange Juice.
Shake.
Garnish with Lime and Orange.

BLACK CAT
Fill glass with ice.
1 oz Vodka
1 oz Cherry Liqueur
Fill glass with equal parts
Cranberry Juice and Cola.

BLACK COW
In glass:
Scoop of Vanilla Ice Cream
Fill with Root Beer.
Serve with straw and spoon.

BLACK COW 2
Fill glass with ice.
1 oz Vodka or Vandermint
1 oz Dark Creme De Cacao
Fill with Cream or Milk.
Shake.

BLACK EYE
Fill glass with ice.
1 1/2 oz Vodka
1/2 oz Blackberry Brandy
Stir.

BLACK-EYED SUSAN aka KENTUCKY SCREWDRIVER, YELLOW JACKET
Fill glass with ice.
2 oz Bourbon
Fill with Orange Juice.

BLACK FOREST (floater)
1/2 oz Coffee Liqueur (bottom)
1/2 oz Black Raspberry Liqueur
1/2 oz Irish Cream
1/2 oz Vodka (top)

BLACK FOREST (frozen)
In Blender:
1/2 cup of Ice
3/4 oz Vodka
3/4 oz Coffee Liqueur
3/4 oz Black Raspberry Liqueur
Scoop of Chocolate Ice Cream
Blend until smooth.
If too thick add Milk.
If too thin add ice or ice cream.
Garnish with Shaved Chocolate or Sprinkles.

BLACK HAWK
Fill glass with ice.
1 1/2 oz Whiskey
1 1/2 oz Sloe Gin
Stir.
Strain into chilled glass.
Garnish with Cherry.

BLACK ICED TEA
Fill glass with ice.
3/4 oz Dark Rum
3/4 oz Brandy
3/4 oz Triple Sec
1 oz Orange Juice
Fill with Cola.
Garnish with Orange.

BLACK JAMAICAN
Fill glass with ice.
1 1/2 oz Rum
1/2 oz Coffee Liqueur
Stir.

BLACK LADY
Fill glass with ice.
2 oz Orange Liqueur
1/2 oz Coffee Liqueur
1/2 oz Brandy
Shake.
Strain into chilled glass.

BLACK MAGIC
Fill glass with ice.
1 1/2 oz Vodka
1 oz Coffee Liqueur
Dash of Sour Mix
Stir.
Garnish with Lemon Twist.

BLACK MAGIC 2
3/4 oz Amaretto
3/4 oz Irish Cream
3/4 oz Coffee Liqueur
Fill with Hot Chocolate.
Top with Whipped Cream.
Sprinkle with Shaved Chocolate.

BLACK MARTINI
Fill glass with ice.
2 oz Gin or Rum
1/2 oz Blackberry Brandy
or Black Raspberry Liqueur
Stir.
Strain into chilled glass
or pour contents (with ice) into
short glass.
Garnish with Lemon Twist
or Black Olive.

BLACK PRINCE
1 oz Blackberry Brandy
Dash of Lime Juice
Fill with Champagne.

BLACK ROSE
Fill glass with ice.
2 oz Rum
1 tsp Sugar
Fill with cold Black Coffee.
Shake.

BLACK ROSE (frozen)
In Blender:
1 cup of Ice
1/2 oz Gold Tequila
1/2 oz Coffee Liqueur
1/2 oz Black Raspberry Liqueur
1/2 cup fresh or frozen
Strawberries
1/2 oz Cream or Milk
Blend until smooth.
If too thick add cream or milk.
If too thin add ice.

BLACK RUSSIAN
Fill glass with ice.
1 1/2 oz Vodka
1 oz Coffee Liqueur
Stir.

BLACK RUSSIAN (frozen)
In Blender:
1/2 cup of Ice
1 1/2 oz Vodka
1 oz Coffee Liqueur
Scoop of Chocolate Ice Cream
Blend until smooth.
If too thick add milk or cream.
If too thin add ice or ice cream.
Garnish with Chocolate
shavings or Sprinkles.

BLACK SHEEP
Fill glass with ice.
1 oz Blackberry Brandy
1 oz Black Raspberry Liqueur
1/2 oz Lime Juice
Stir.
Strain into chilled glass.
Garnish with Lime.

BLACK TIE (floater)
1/2 oz Amaretto (bottom)
1/2 oz Drambuie
1/2 oz Scotch (top)

BLACK VELVET
Fill glass 1/2 with Champagne.
Fill glass 1/2 with Stout.

BLACK VELVETEEN
Fill glass 3/4 with Hard Cider.
Fill glass with Stout.

BLACK WATCH
Fill glass with ice.
1 1/2 oz Scotch
1/2 oz Coffee Liqueur
Stir.

BLACK WITCH
Fill glass with ice.
1 1/2 oz Amber Rum
1/4 oz Dark Rum
1/4 oz Apricot Brandy
1/2 oz Pineapple Juice
Shake.
Strain into chilled glass.

BLACKBERRY SWIZZLE
Fill glass with ice.
1 1/2 oz Gin
1/2 oz Black Raspberry Liqueur
Fill with Blackberry Flavored Spring
Water.

BLACKJACK
Fill glass with ice.
1 oz Brandy
1 oz Blackberry Brandy
1 oz Cream
Shake.
Serve or strain into chilled glass.

BLAST
Fill glass with ice.
1 oz Rum
1 oz Brandy
Dash of Sour Mix
Fill with equal parts Orange and
Pineapple Juice.
Shake.

BLEACHER CREATURE
Fill glass with ice.
1/3 oz Vodka
1/3 oz Tequila
1/3 oz Rum
1/3 oz Triple Sec
1/3 oz Melon Liqueur
1/3 oz Green Creme De Menthe
Fill with Sour Mix.
Shake.

BLINKER
Fill glass with ice.
2 oz Whiskey
Dash of Grenadine
Fill with Grapefruit Juice.
Shake.

BLIZZARD
Fill glass with ice.
2 oz Vodka
Fill with Lemon-Lime Soda.
Garnish with Lemon or Lime.

BLIZZARD (frozen)
In Blender:
1/2 cup of Ice
1/2 oz Dark Rum
1/2 oz Brandy
1/2 oz Coffee Liqueur
1/2 oz Irish Cream
Scoop of Vanilla Ice Cream
Blend until smooth.

BLOOD AND SAND
Fill glass with ice.
1 oz Scotch
3/4 oz Cherry Brandy
1/2 oz Sweet Vermouth
1 oz Orange Juice
Stir.
Strain into chilled glass.

BLOOD CLOT (floater)
1 1/2 oz 151-Proof Rum
Dash of Grenadine
Float 1/4 oz Cream on top.

BLOODY BASTARD
Fill glass 1/2 with ale.
1 tsp Horseradish
Fill with Bloody Mary Mix.
Rub rim of second glass with Lime
and dip into Kosher Salt.
Pour drink into second glass.

BLOODY BRAIN
1 oz Strawberry Liqueur
Dash of Grenadine
1/2 oz Irish Cream

BLOODY BREW
1 1/2 oz Vodka
2 oz Tomato Juice
Fill with Beer or Malt Liquor.
Dash of Salt

BLOODY BULL
Fill glass with ice.
2 oz Vodka
1 oz Beef Bouillon
1 tsp Horseradish
3 dashes of Tabasco Sauce
3 dashes of Worcestershire Sauce
Dash of Lime Juice
3 dashes of Celery Salt
3 dashes of Pepper
1 oz Clam Juice (optional)
Dash of Sherry (optional)
Fill with Tomato Juice.
Pour from one glass to
another until mixed.
Garnish with Lemon and/or Lime,
Celery and/or Cucumber and/or
Cocktail Shrimp.

BLOODY CAESAR
Fill glass with ice.
2 oz Vodka
1 tsp Horseradish
3 dashes of Tabasco Sauce
3 dashes of Worcestershire Sauce
Dash of Lime Juice
3 dashes of Celery Salt
3 dashes of Pepper
Dash of Sherry (optional)
1 tsp Dijon Mustard (optional)
Fill with equal parts tomato and
Clam Juice.
Pour from one glass to
another until mixed.

Garnish with Lemon and/or Lime,
Celery and/or Cucumber and/or
Cocktail Shrimp.

BLOODY HOLLY aka
DANISH MARY
Fill glass with ice.
2 oz Aquavit
1 tsp Horseradish
3 dashes of Tabasco Sauce
3 dashes of Worcestershire Sauce
Dash of Lime Juice
3 dashes of Celery Salt
3 dashes of Pepper
1 oz Clam Juice (optional)
Dash of Sherry (optional)
1 tsp Dijon Mustard (optional)
Fill with Tomato Juice.
Pour from one glass to
another until mixed.
Garnish with Lemon and/or Lime,
Celery and/or Cucumber and/or
Cocktail Shrimp.

BLOODY JOSEPHINE
Fill glass with ice.
2 oz Scotch
1 tsp Horseradish
3 dashes of Tabasco Sauce
3 dashes of Worcestershire Sauce
Dash of Lime Juice
3 dashes of Celery Salt
3 dashes of Pepper
1 oz Clam Juice (optional)
Dash of Sherry (optional)
1 tsp Dijon Mustard (optional)
Fill with Tomato Juice.
Pour from one glass to
another until mixed.
Garnish with Lemon and/or Lime,
Celery and/or Cucumber and/or
Cocktail Shrimp.

BLOODY MARIA
Fill glass with ice.
2 oz Tequila
1 tsp Horseradish
3 dashes of Tabasco Sauce
3 dashes of Worcestershire Sauce
Dash of Lime Juice
3 dashes of Celery Salt
3 dashes of Pepper
1 oz Clam Juice (optional)
Dash of Sherry (optional)
1 tsp Dijon Mustard (optional)
Fill with Tomato Juice.
Pour from one glass to
another until mixed.
Garnish with Lemon and/or Lime,
Celery and/or Cucumber and/or
Cocktail Shrimp.

BLOODY MARISELA
Fill glass with ice.
2 oz Light Rum
1 tsp Horseradish
3 dashes of Tabasco Sauce
3 dashes of Worcestershire Sauce
Dash of Lime Juice
3 dashes of Celery Salt
3 dashes of Pepper
1 oz Clam Juice (optional)
Dash of Sherry (optional)
1 tsp Dijon Mustard (optional)
Fill with Tomato Juice.
Pour from one glass to
another until mixed.
Garnish with Lemon and/or Lime,
Celery and/or Cucumber and/or
Cocktail Shrimp.

BLOODY MARY
Fill glass with ice.
2 oz Vodka
1 tsp Horseradish
3 dashes of Tabasco Sauce
3 dashes of Worcestershire Sauce
Dash of Lime Juice
3 dashes of Celery Salt
3 dashes of Pepper
1 oz Clam Juice (optional)
Dash of Sherry (optional)
1 tsp Dijon Mustard (optional)
Fill with Tomato Juice.
Pour from one glass to
another until mixed.
Garnish with Lemon and/or Lime,
Celery and/or Cucumber and/or
Cocktail Shrimp.

BLOODY MOLLY
Fill glass with ice.
2 oz Irish Whiskey
1 tsp Horseradish
3 dashes of Tabasco Sauce
3 dashes of Worcestershire Sauce
Dash of Lime Juice
3 dashes of Celery Salt
3 dashes of Pepper
1 oz Clam Juice (optional)
Fill with Tomato Juice.
Pour from one glass to
another until mixed.
Garnish with Lemon and/or Lime,
Celery and/or Cucumber and/or
Cocktail Shrimp.

B. J. (floater)
1/2 oz Cream (bottom)
1/2 oz White Creme De Cacao
1/2 oz Vodka (top)
Contents should mix slightly.
To drink, place hands behind back
and pick up using only mouth.

B. J. 2 (floater)
Fill glass with ice.
3/4 oz Coffee Liqueur
3/4 oz Orange Liqueur
3/4 oz Banana Liqueur
Top with Whipped Cream.
To drink, place hands behind back
and pick up using only mouth.

B. J. 3 (floater)
1 oz Irish Cream (bottom)
1 oz Orange Liqueur (top)
Top with Whipped Cream.

BLUE BAYOU (frozen)
In Blender:
1 cup of Ice
1 1/2 oz Vodka
1/2 oz Blue Curacao
1/2 cup fresh or canned Pineapple
2 oz Grapefruit Juice
Blend until smooth.
If too thick add juice.
If too thin add ice.
Garnish with Pineapple.

BLUE BIJOU 2 (frozen)
In Blender:
1 cup of Ice
1 1/4 oz Rum
1 oz Blue Curacao
3 oz Orange Juice
3 oz Pineapple Juice
3 or 4 drops of Lime Juice
Blend on low speed for 3-5
seconds.

BLUE HAWAIIAN
Fill glass with ice.
1 oz Rum
1 oz Blue Curacao
1 oz Cream of Coconut
Fill with Pineapple Juice.
Shake.
Garnish with Pineapple.

BLUE HAWAIIAN 2
Fill glass with ice.
1 1/2 oz Vodka
1/2 oz Blue Curacao
Fill with equal parts Orange and
Pineapple Juice.
Shake.
Garnish with Pineapple.

BLUE KAMIKAZE
Fill glass with ice.
2 oz Vodka
1/2 oz Blue Curacao
1 oz Lime Juice
Shake.
Serve or strain into chilled glass.
Garnish with Lime.

BLUE LADY
Fill glass with ice.
1 1/2 oz Gin
1/4 oz Blue Curacao
1 oz Sour Mix
Stir.

BLUE LEMONADE
1 oz Citrus Vodka
1 oz Blue Curacao
Dash of Sour Mix
Dash of Lemon-Lime Soda
Stir.

BLUE MARGARITA
Fill glass with ice.
2 oz Tequila
1 oz Blue Curacao
Dash of Lime Juice
3 oz Sour Mix
Shake.
Rub rim of second glass with Lime
and dip rim into Kosher Salt. Either
pour contents (with ice) or strain
into salted glass.
Garnish with Lime.

BLUE SHARK
Fill glass with ice.
1 oz Vodka
1 oz Tequila
3/4 oz Blue Curacao
Shake.
Strain into chilled glass.

BLUE TAIL FLY
Fill glass with ice.
1 oz Blue Curacao
1 oz White Creme De Cacao
Fill with Milk or light Cream.
Shake.

BLUE VALIUM
Fill glass with ice.
2/3 oz 151-Proof Rum
3/4 oz Whiskey
3/4 oz Blue Curacao
Dash of Sour Mix
Shake.
Strain into chilled glass.
Dash of Lemon-Lime Soda

BLUE WHALE
Fill glass with ice.
1 oz Blue Curacao
1 oz Blueberry Schnapps
Fill with Pineapple Juice.
Shake.
Garnish with Orange.
Joe Sugden

B. M. P.
Fill glass with ice.
1 3/4 oz Amber Rum
1/2 oz Light Rum
3 oz Pineapple Juice
1 oz Lime Juice
Dash of Bitters
Shake.
Strain into glass.

BOA CONSTRICTOR
Fill glass with ice.
1 oz Galliano
1/2 oz Rum
1/2 oz Banana Liqueur
Dash of Pineapple Juice
Dash of Orange Juice
Dash of Cranberry Juice
Shake.
Scott Bernstein

BOARDWALK BREEZER
Fill glass with ice.
1 1/2 oz Dark Rum
1/2 oz Banana Liqueur
1/2 oz Lime Juice
Fill with Pineapple Juice.
Shake.
Top with dash of Grenadine.
Garnish with Orange and Cherry.

BOB MARLEY
Fill glass with ice.
1 oz Dark Rum
1 oz Tia Maria
Dash of Cream of Coconut
Dash of Milk or Cream
Dash of Pineapple Juice
Shake.
Strain into chilled glass.

BOCCI BALL
Fill glass with ice.
1 1/2 oz Vodka
1/2 oz Amaretto
Fill with Orange Juice.
Splash with Soda Water.
Garnish with Orange.

BODY SHOT
Pour shot of Tequila.
Lick unclothed area of favorite
person.
Sprinkle dampened area with salt.
Place Lime in favorite person's
mouth.
Lick salted area. Drink shot.
Suck Lime from friend's mouth.
Take turns.

BOG FOG aka
RUM MADRAS
Fill glass with ice.
2 oz Rum
Fill with equal parts Orange and
Cranberry Juice.
Garnish with Lime.

BOILERMAKER
Fill shot glass with Whiskey.
Fill chilled glass with Beer.
Either drink shot and chase with
beer or mix together and drink.

BOMB
Fill glass with ice.
1/2 oz Scotch
1/2 oz Bourbon
1/2 oz 151-Proof Rum
1/2 oz Dark Rum
Dash of Grenadine
Fill with equal parts Orange and Pineapple Juice.
Shake.

BON BON
Fill glass with ice.
3/4 oz Irish Cream
3/4 oz Black Raspberry Liqueur
3/4 oz Truffles Liqueur
Shake.
Strain into chilled glass.

BONGO
Fill glass with ice.
1 1/2 oz Rum
1/2 oz Blackberry Brandy
Fill with Pineapple Juice.
Shake.

BOP THE PRINCESS
Fill glass with ice.
2 oz Premium Whiskey
Fill with equal parts Cranberry Juice and Lemon-Lime Soda.
Garnish with Cherry and Lemon.

BOS'N MATE
Fill glass with ice.
1 oz Light Rum
1 oz Dark Rum
Dash of Triple Sec
Dash of Grenadine
Fill with equal parts Lime and Pineapple Juice.
Garnish with Lime and Pineapple.

BOSOM CARESSER
1 1/2 oz Brandy
1/2 oz Curacao
Dash of Grenadine
1 Egg Yolk
Shake.

BOSS
Fill glass with ice.
3/4 oz Bourbon
1/2 oz Amaretto
Stir.

BOSSA NOVA
Fill glass with ice.
1 oz Galliano
1 oz Amber Rum
1/4 oz Apricot Brandy
Dash of Sour Mix
1/2 Egg White
Fill with Pineapple Juice.
Shake.
Garnish with Orange and Cherry.

BOSTON ICED TEA
Fill glass with ice.
1/2 oz Vodka
1/2 oz Gin
1/2 oz Rum
1/2 oz Coffee Liqueur
1/2 oz Amaretto
2 oz Sour Mix
Fill with Cola.
Garnish with Lemon.

BOSTON MASSACRE
Fill glass with ice.
Dash of Irish Cream
Dash of Orange Liqueur
Dash of Coffee Liqueur
Dash of Hazelnut Liqueur
Dash of Irish Whiskey
Dash of Amaretto
Dash of Dark Creme De Cacao
Fill with Cream.
Shake.
Sharon L. Foster

BOSTON MASSACRE (frozen)
In Blender:
1/2 cup of Ice
Dash of Irish Cream
Dash of Orange Liqueur
Dash of Coffee Liqueur
Dash of Hazelnut Liqueur
Dash of Irish Whiskey
Dash of Amaretto
Dash of Dark Creme De Cacao
Scoop of Vanilla Ice Cream
Blend until smooth.
If too thick add milk or cream.
If too thin add ice or ice cream.
Pour into glass. Insert straw in glass against side and dribble Grenadine into straw. It should run down inside of glass and look like dripping blood.

BOTTOM LINE
Fill glass with ice.
2 oz Gin
1/2 oz Lime Juice
Fill with Tonic Water.
Stir.
Garnish with Lime.

BOURBON MANHATTAN
Fill glass with ice.
2 oz Bourbon
Dash of Sweet Vermouth
Stir.
Strain into chilled glass or pour contents (with ice) into short glass and serve.
Garnish with Cherry.
CAUTION: SWEET means extra Sweet Vermouth.
DRY can mean either use Dry Vermouth instead of Sweet Vermouth, or less Sweet Vermouth than usual and garnish with a Lemon Twist or Cherry.

BOURBON OLD FASHIONED
Muddle together in short glass:
stemless Maraschino Cherry,
Orange Slice,
1/2 tsp of Sugar, and
3 dashes of Bitters.
Fill glass with ice.
2 oz Bourbon
Dash of Soda Water
Stir.

BOURBON SATIN
Fill glass with ice.
1 1/2 oz Bourbon
1 oz White Creme De Cacao
2 oz Milk or Cream
Shake.
Strain into chilled glass.

BOX CAR
Fill glass with ice.
1 1/2 oz Rum
1/2 oz Triple Sec
Fill with Sour Mix.
Shake.
Garnish with Orange and Cherry.

BRAHMA BULL
Fill glass with ice.
1 1/2 oz Gold Tequila
1/2 oz Coffee Liqueur
Stir.

BRAIN
1 oz Strawberry Liqueur
or Peach Schnapps
1/4 oz Grenadine
1/2 oz Irish Cream.
Put in drop by drop.

BRAIN (floater)
Fill glass with ice.
1 oz Coffee Liqueur (bottom)
1 oz Peach Schnapps
1 oz Irish Cream (top)

BRAIN ERASER
Fill glass with ice.
1 oz Vodka
1/2 oz Coffee Liqueur
1/2 oz Amaretto
Splash with Club Soda.
Supposed to be drunk in one shot
through a straw.

BRAIN TUMOR
Fill glass with ice.
2 oz Irish Cream
5 or 6 drops of Strawberry Liqueur

BRAIN WAVE (floater)
1 1/4 oz Irish Cream (bottom)
3/4 oz Vodka (top)
Place a drop of Grenadine into
center of drink.

BRANDY ALEXANDER
Fill glass with ice.
1 1/2 oz Brandy
1/2 oz Dark Creme De Cacao
3 oz Cream or Milk
Shake.
Serve or strain into chilled glass.
Sprinkle Nutmeg on top.

BRANDY ALEXANDER (frozen)
In Blender:
1/2 cup of Ice
1 1/2 oz Brandy
1/2 oz Dark Creme De Cacao
Scoop of Vanilla Ice Cream
Blend until smooth.
If too thick add milk or cream.
If too thin add ice or ice cream.
Sprinkle Nutmeg on top.

BRANDY ALMOND MOCHA
1 oz Brandy
1 oz Amaretto
Fill with equal parts Hot
Chocolate and hot Coffee.
Stir.
Top with Whipped Cream.
Sprinkle with Shaved Almonds.

BRANDY GUMP
Fill glass with ice.
2 oz Brandy
Dash of Grenadine
Fill with Sour Mix.
Shake.
Serve or strain into chilled glass.
Garnish with Orange and Cherry.

BRANDY MILK PUNCH
2 oz Brandy
1 tsp Sugar or Sugar Syrup
Fill with Milk or Cream.
Shake.

BRASS KNUCKLES
Fill glass with ice.
1 1/2 oz Bourbon
1/2 oz Triple Sec
Fill with Sour Mix.
Shake.

BRASS MONKEY
Fill glass with ice.
1 oz Vodka
1 oz Rum
Fill with Orange Juice.
Garnish with Orange.

BRAVE BULL
Fill glass with ice.
1 1/2 oz Tequila
1/2 oz Coffee Liqueur
Stir.
Strain into shot glass.

BRAVE COW
Fill glass with ice.
1 1/2 oz Gin
1/2 oz Coffee Liqueur
Stir.
Serve or strain into chilled glass.

BRAZILIAN COFFEE
3/4 oz Coffee Liqueur
3/4 oz Brandy
3/4 oz Orange Liqueur
Fill with hot Black Coffee.
Top with Whipped Cream.
Sprinkle Brown Sugar on top.

BRONCO COCKTAIL
Fill glass with ice.
1 oz Orange Liqueur
2 oz Orange Soda
Fill with Champagne.
Garnish with Orange.

BROWN COW
Fill glass with ice.
2 oz Dark Creme De Cacao
Fill with Milk or Cream.
Shake.

BROWN DERBY
Fill glass with ice.
2 oz Vodka
Fill with Cola.

BROWN SQUIRREL
1 oz Amaretto
1 oz Dark Creme De Cacao
1 oz Cream or Milk
Shake.
Strain into chilled glass.

BROWN SQUIRREL (frozen)
In Blender:
1/2 cup of Ice
1 oz Amaretto
3/4 oz Dark Creme De Cacao
Scoop of Vanilla Ice Cream
Dash of Milk
Blend until smooth.
If too thick add milk.
If too thin add ice or ice cream.

BRUT AND BOGS aka CHAM CRAN CHAM, SCARLET LETTER
Fill glass 3/4 with ice.
Fill glass 3/4 with Champagne.
Dash of Black Raspberry Liqueur
Fill with Cranberry Juice.

B-STING
Fill glass with ice.
1 1/2 oz B&B
1/2 oz White Creme De Menthe

BUBBLE GUM
Fill glass with ice.
1 oz Vodka
1 oz Southern Comfort
1 oz Banana Liqueur
Dash of Grenadine
1 oz Cream
Shake.
Strain into chilled glass.
Garnish with Bubble Gum Stick.

BUBBLE GUM 2
Fill glass with ice.
1 oz Melon Liqueur
1 oz Amaretto
or Creme De Nouyax
1 oz Milk or Cream
Dash of Grenadine (optional)
Shake.
Strain into chilled glass.
Garnish with Bubble Gum Stick.

BUCK
Fill glass with ice.
2 oz desired Liquor
Fill with Ginger Ale.
Garnish with Lemon.

BUCKAROO
Fill glass with ice.
2 oz Rum
Fill with Root Beer.

BUCKHEAD ROOT BEER
Fill glass with ice.
2 oz Jaegermeister
Fill with Club Soda.
Garnish with Lime and Orange.

BUCKING BRONCO (floater)
1 oz Southern Comfort (bottom)
1 oz Tequila (top)

BUFFALO PISS
Fill glass with ice.
2 oz Tequila
Fill with equal parts Grapefruit
Juice and Lemon-Lime Soda.

BUFFALO SWEAT
2 oz Bourbon
Dash of Tabasco Sauce
Stir.

BULL SHOT
1 oz Vodka
1 oz Beef Bouillon
Dash of Worcestershire Sauce
Dash of Salt
Dash of Pepper

BULL'S MILK
Fill glass with ice.
1 1/2 oz Brandy
1/2 oz Dark Rum
1/2 tsp Sugar
Fill with Milk.
Shake.
Sprinkle with Cinnamon.

BULLDOG
Fill glass with ice.
1 oz Vodka or Rum
1 oz Coffee Liqueur
Fill with equal parts Cream and Cola.

BULLFROG aka KAMIKAZE
Fill glass with ice.
2 oz Vodka
1/2 oz Triple Sec
1 oz Lime Juice
Shake.
Serve or strain into chilled glass.
Garnish with a Lime.

BULLFROG 2
Fill glass with ice.
2 oz Vodka
Fill with equal parts Sour Mix and Grapefruit Juice.

BUMBLE BEE
Fill glass with ice.
2 oz Tia Maria
Fill with Milk.
Shake.
Top with Peach Schnapps.

BUNGEE JUMPER
Fill glass with ice.
2 oz Irish Mist
Dash of Cream
Fill with Orange Juice.
Shake.
Top with Amaretto.

BURNING BUSH aka PRAIRIE FIRE
2 oz Tequila
Add Tabasco Sauce until pink.

BURNT ALMOND aka, ROASTED TOASTED ALMOND, ORGASM
Fill glass with ice.
1 oz Vodka
1 oz Coffee Liqueur
1 oz Amaretto
Fill with Milk or Cream.
Shake.

BURNT ALMOND (frozen)
In Blender:
1/2 cup of Ice
1 oz Vodka
1 oz Coffee Liqueur
1 oz Amaretto
Scoop of Vanilla Ice Cream
Blend until smooth.
If too thick add milk or cream.
If too thin add ice or ice cream.

BUSHWACKER aka SHILLELAGH
Fill glass with ice.
1 oz Irish Whiskey or Irish Mist
1 oz Irish Cream
Stir.

BUSHWACKER 2
Fill glass with ice.
1 1/2 oz Dark Rum
1/2 oz Coffee Liqueur
1/2 oz Dark Creme De Cacao
1 oz Cream of Coconut
Fill with Cream or Milk.
Shake.

BUSTED CHERRY (floater)
1/2 oz Coffee Liqueur (bottom)
1/2 oz Cream
1/2 oz Cherry Brandy (top)

BUSTED RUBBER (floater)
1/2 oz Raspberry Liqueur (bottom)
1/2 oz Irish Cream
1/2 oz Orange Liqueur (top)

BUTTAFINGER
Fill glass with ice.
1/2 oz Vodka
1 oz Cookies and Cream Liqueur
1 oz Butterscotch Schnapps
Fill with Cream or Milk.
Shake.

BUTTER BALL (floater)
1 1/2 oz Butterscotch Schnapps (bottom)
1/2 oz Irish Cream or Orange Liqueur (top)

BUTTER SHOT (floater)
1 oz Butterscotch Schnapps (bottom)
1/2 oz Vodka
1/2 oz Irish Cream (top)

C & B
1 oz Cognac
1 oz Benedictine

CABLEGRAM
Fill glass with ice.
2 oz Whiskey
1/2 oz Sour Mix
1 tsp Sugar Syrup
Shake.
Fill glass with Ginger Ale.
Garnish with Lemon.

CACTUS BANGER aka FREDDY FUDPUCKER
Fill glass with ice.
1 1/2 oz Tequila
Fill with Orange Juice.
Top with Galliano.
Garnish with Orange.

CACTUS JUICE
Fill glass with ice.
1/2 oz Spiced Rum
1/2 oz Tequila
1/2 oz Triple Sec
1/2 oz Amaretto
Fill with equal parts Cranberry Juice, Pineapple Juice and Sour Mix.
Shake.
Scott Bernstein

CACTUS JUICE 2
Fill glass with ice.
1 1/2 oz Tequila
1/2 oz Amaretto
Fill with Sour Mix.
Shake.

CADIZ
Fill glass with ice.
3/4 oz Blackberry Brandy
3/4 oz Dry Sherry
1/2 oz Triple Sec
1/4 oz Cream
Shake.

CAFÉ AMORE
1 oz Cognac
1 oz Amaretto
Fill with hot Black Coffee.
Top with Whipped Cream.
Sprinkle with Shaved Almonds.

CAFÉ DIABLO
3/4 oz Cognac or Brandy
3/4 oz Sambuca
3/4 oz Orange Liqueur
Fill with hot Black Coffee.
Sprinkle with grated Orange Rind,
Allspice and Brown Sugar.
Garnish with Orange.

CAFÉ FOSTER
1 oz Dark Rum
3/4 oz Banana Liqueur
Fill with hot Black Coffee.
Top with Whipped Cream.
Garnish with Banana.

CAFÉ GATES
3/4 oz Tia Maria
3/4 oz Orange Liqueur
3/4 oz Dark Creme De Cacao
Fill with hot Black Coffee.
Top with Whipped Cream.
Sprinkle with Shaved Chocolate or
Sprinkles.

CAFÉ ITALIA
1 1/2 oz Tuaca
1 tsp Sugar or Sugar Syrup
Fill with hot Black Coffee.
Top with Whipped Cream.
Sprinkle with Cinnamon.

CAFÉ MAGIC
3/4 oz Amaretto
3/4 oz Irish Cream
3/4 oz Coffee Liqueur
Fill with hot Black Coffee.
Top with Whipped Cream.
Sprinkle with Shaved Chocolate.

CAFÉ MARSEILLES
3/4 oz Hazelnut Liqueur
3/4 oz Black Raspberry Liqueur
3/4 oz Coffee Liqueur
Fill with hot Black Coffee.
Top with Whipped Cream.

CAFÉ ORLEANS
1 oz Coffee Liqueur
1 oz Praline Liqueur
Fill with hot Black Coffee.
Top with Whipped Cream.
Sprinkle with crushed Peanut
Brittle.

CAFÉ REGGAE
3/4 oz Dark Rum
3/4 oz Coffee Liqueur
3/4 oz Dark Creme De Cacao
Fill with hot Black Coffee.
Top with Whipped Cream.

CAFÉ ROYALE
2 oz Cognac or Brandy
Fill with hot Black Coffee.
Garnish with Lemon Twist.

CAFÉ THEATRE
1/2 oz Irish Cream
1/2 oz White Creme De Cacao
Fill with hot Black Coffee.
Dash of Hazelnut Liqueur
Dash of Dark Creme De Cacao
Top with Whipped Cream.

CAFÉ VENITZIO
3/4 oz Amaretto
3/4 oz Brandy
3/4 oz Galliano
Fill with hot Black Coffee.

CAJUN COFFEE
2 oz Praline Liqueur
Fill with hot Black Coffee.
Top with Whipped Cream.
Garnish with crushed Peanut
Brittle.

CAJUN MARTINI aka CREOLE MARTINI
Fill glass with ice.
2 oz Peppered Vodka
1/2 oz Dry Vermouth
Stir.
Strain into chilled glass.
Garnish with a Jalapeno Pepper.

CALIFORNIA BREEZE aka MADRAS
Fill glass with ice.
2 oz Vodka
Fill with equal parts Orange and
Cranberry Juice.
Stir.
Garnish with Orange or Lime.

CALIFORNIA COOL AID
Fill glass with ice.
2 oz Rum
Fill with equal parts Orange Juice
and Milk.
Shake.

CALIFORNIA DRIVER
Fill glass with ice.
2 oz Vodka
Fill with equal parts Orange and
Grapefruit Juice.

CALIFORNIA ICED TEA
Fill glass with ice.
1/2 oz Vodka
1/2 oz Gin
1/2 oz Rum
1/2 oz Tequila
1/2 oz Triple Sec
2 oz Grapefruit Juice
Top with Cola.
Garnish with Lemon.

CALIFORNIA LEMONADE
Fill glass with ice.
1/2 oz Vodka
1/2 oz Gin
1/2 oz Brandy
2 oz Sour Mix
2 oz Orange Juice
Dash of Grenadine
Shake.
Garnish with a Lemon.

CALIFORNIA LEMONADE 2
Fill glass with ice.
2 oz Blended Whiskey
1 oz Sour Mix
Dash of Lime Juice
Dash of Grenadine
Fill with Soda Water.
Garnish with Orange and Cherry.

CALIFORNIA MOTHER
Fill glass with ice.
1 oz Brandy
1 oz Coffee Liqueur
Fill with equal parts Milk or Cream
and Cola.

CALIFORNIA ROOT BEER
Fill glass with ice.
1 oz Coffee Liqueur
Fill with Soda Water.
Top with 1/2 oz Galliano.
Dash of Cola or Beer or Milk
(optional).

CALYPSO COFFEE
1 oz Tia Maria
or Dark Creme De Cacao
1 oz Rum
Fill with hot Black Coffee.
Top with Whipped Cream.
Sprinkle with Shaved Chocolate.

CANADA COCKTAIL
Fill glass with ice.
1 1/2 oz Canadian Whiskey
1/2 oz Triple Sec
2 dashes of Bitters
1 tsp Sugar
Shake.
Strain into chilled glass.
Garnish with Orange.

CANADIAN CIDER (frozen)
In Blender:
1/2 cup of Ice
1 oz Canadian Whiskey
1/2 oz Cinnamon Schnapps
3 oz Apple Cider
1/4 ripe Red Apple
Blend until smooth.

CANADIAN COFFEE
2 oz Yukon Jack
Fill with hot Black Coffee.
Top with Whipped Cream.
Dribble 5-6 drops of Creme De
Nouyax on top.

CANCUN (frozen)
In Blender:
1/2 cup ice
3/4 oz Coffee Liqueur
3/4 oz Sambuca
3/4 oz Irish Cream
3 oz cold espresso
Scoop of Vanilla Ice Cream.
Blend until smooth.

CANDY APPLE
Fill glass with ice.
1 oz Apple Brandy
1 oz Cinnamon Schnapps
Fill with Cranberry Juice.
Stir.

CANDY ASS
Fill glass with ice.
1 oz Black Raspberry Liqueur
1 oz Chocolate Liqueur
Stir.

CANDY CANE
Fill glass with ice.
2 oz Peppermint Schnapps
Fill with Milk.
Shake.
Float 1/2 oz Cherry Brandy
on top.

CANDY CANE (floater)
1 1/2 oz Peppermint Schnapps
(bottom)
1/2 oz Creme De Nouyax (top)

CANYON QUAKE
Fill glass with ice.
1 oz Brandy
1 oz Irish Cream
Fill with Milk or Cream.
Shake.

CAPE CODDER
Fill glass with ice.
2 oz Vodka
Fill with Cranberry Juice.
Garnish with Lime.

CAPRI aka BANSHEE
Fill with ice.
1 oz Banana Liqueur
1/2 oz White Creme De Cacao
Fill with Milk or Cream.
Shake.

CAPTAIN MARINER
Fill glass with ice.
1 1/2 oz Spiced Rum
1/2 oz Orange Liqueur
Dash of Grenadine
Fill with Orange Juice.
Shake.
Garnish with Orange.

CARIBBEAN CHAMPAGNE
1 oz Light Rum
1 oz Banana Liqueur
Stir.
Fill with Champagne.
Garnish with Banana and Cherry.

CARIBBEAN DREAM COFFEE
3/4 oz Dark Rum
3/4 oz Dark Creme De Cacao
3/4 oz Banana Liqueur
Fill with hot Black Coffee.
Garnish with Banana.

CARROLL COCKTAIL
Fill glass with ice.
1 1/2 oz Brandy
3/4 oz Sweet Vermouth
Stir.
Strain into chilled glass.

CARTEL BUSTER (floater)
1 oz Coffee Liqueur (bottom)
1 oz Orange Liqueur
1 oz Gold Tequila (top)

CASABLANCA
Fill glass with ice.
2 oz Rum
1 1/2 tsp Triple Sec
1 1/2 tsp Cherry Liqueur
1 1/2 oz Lime Juice
Shake.
Strain into chilled glass.

CATFISH
Fill glass with ice.
1 1/2 oz Rum
1/2 oz Triple Sec
Fill with Cola.
Garnish with Lime.

CEMENT MIXER
Fill shot glass with Irish Cream.
Add dash of Lime Juice.
Let set 30 seconds.

CEREBRAL HEMORRHAGE
(floater)
Fill glass with ice.
1 oz Coffee Liqueur (bottom)

1 oz Peach Schnapps
1 oz Irish Cream (top)
Add several drops of Grenadine.

CHAM CRAN CHAM aka BRUT AND BOGS, SCARLET LETTER
Fill glass 3/4 with ice.
Fill glass 3/4 with Champagne.
Dash of Black Raspberry Liqueur
Fill with Cranberry Juice.

CHAMPAGNE COCKTAIL
1/2 tsp Sugar
2 dashes of Bitters
Fill with Champagne.
Garnish with Lemon Twist.

CHAMPAGNE SUPER NOVA
Fill glass with ice.
1/2 oz Vodka
1/2 oz Gin
1/2 oz Blue Curacao
Dash of Cranberry Juice
Dash of Sour Mix
Fill with Champagne.

CHANNEL
2 oz Blackberry Brandy
Fill with Beer.
Matt Olga

CHAOS
Fill glass with ice.
1/2 oz 151-Proof Rum
1/2 oz Gin
1/2 oz Sloe Gin
1/2 oz Orange Liqueur
1/2 oz Lime Juice
Shake.
Strain into chilled glass.

CHEAP SHADES
Fill glass with ice.
1 oz Vodka
1/2 oz Peach Schnapps
1/2 oz Melon Liqueur
Dash of Sour Mix
Dash of Pineapple Juice
Fill with Lemon-Lime Soda.
Garnish with Pineapple.

CHEAP SUNGLASSES
Fill glass with ice.
2 oz Vodka
Fill with equal parts Cranberry
Juice and Lemon-Lime Soda.
Garnish with Lime.

CHERRY BLOSSOM
Fill glass with ice.
1 oz Rum or Brandy
1 oz Cherry Brandy
1 tsp Grenadine
1 tsp Lemon Juice
Shake.
Garnish with Cherry.

CHERRY BOMB aka EAT THE CHERRY
Place pitted, stemless Cherry in shot glass.
1 tsp Cherry Juice
Fill with Grain Alcohol or Vodka.

CHERRY COLA
Fill glass with ice.
1 1/2 oz Cherry Brandy
Fill with Cola.
Garnish with Cherry.

CHERRY LIFE-SAVOR
Fill glass with ice.
2 oz Amaretto
Fill with Cranberry Juice.

CHERRY SCREW
Fill glass with ice.
2 oz Cherry Brandy
Fill with Orange Juice.
Shake.
Garnish with Orange and Lime.

CHERRY SWIZZLE
Fill glass with ice.
2 oz Gin
Dash of Cherry Brandy
Fill with Cherry Flavored Spring Water.
Stir.
Garnish with Cherry.

CHICAGO
Fill glass with ice.
1 1/2 oz Brandy
Dash of Curacao or Triple Sec
Dash of Bitters
Shake.
Strain into glass rimmed with sugar.
Fill with Champagne.

CHI-CHI
Fill glass with ice.
1 1/2 oz Rum
1/2 oz Blackberry Brandy
Fill with Pineapple Juice.
Shake.
Garnish with Pineapple.

CHI-CHI (frozen)
In Blender:
1/2 cup of Ice
2 oz Vodka
1/2 oz Blue Curacao
1/2 oz Cream of Coconut
1/2 cup fresh or canned Pineapple
Scoop of Vanilla Ice Cream
Blend until smooth.
If too thick add juice.
If too thin add ice or ice cream.
Garnish with Pineapple.

CHILES FRITOS
Fill glass with ice.
2 oz Tequila
Dash of Lime Juice
Dash of Celery Salt
Dash of Tabasco Sauce
Dash of Worcestershire Sauce
Dash of Pepper
Dash of Grenadine
Dash of Orange Juice
Shake.
Garnish with 2 Chili Peppers.

CHINA BEACH
Fill glass with ice.
1 oz Vodka
1 oz Ginger Liqueur
Fill with Cranberry Juice.
Stir.

CHINESE COCKTAIL
Fill glass with ice.
1 1/2 oz Dark Rum
1 tsp Triple Sec
1 tsp Cherry Liqueur
1 tsp Grenadine
Dash of Bitters
Shake.
Strain into chilled glass.

CHINESE TORTURE (floater)
1 1/2 oz Ginger Liqueur (bottom)
1/2 oz 151-Proof Rum (top)
Ignite.

CHIQUITA
Fill glass with ice.
1/2 oz Banana Liqueur
1/2 oz Orange Liqueur or Triple Sec
Fill with equal parts Orange Juice and Milk.
Shake.

CHOCOLATE BANANA FREEZE (frozen)
In Blender:
1/2 cup of Ice
1 oz Vodka
1 oz Dark Creme De Cacao
1/2 oz Banana Liqueur
1 Tbsp Chocolate Syrup
1/2 fresh peeled ripe Banana
Scoop of Chocolate Ice Cream
Blend until smooth.
If too thick add fruit or Milk.
If too thin add ice or ice cream.
Garnish with Banana.
Top with Whipped Cream.

CHOCOLATE COLADA (frozen)
In Blender:
1/2 cup of Ice
2 oz Rum
2 Tbsp Cream of Coconut
1 oz Chocolate Syrup
Dash of Milk or Cream
Blend until smooth.

CHOCOLATE COVERED CHERRY
Fill glass with ice.
1/2 oz Coffee Liqueur
1/2 oz Amaretto
1/2 oz White Creme De Cacao
Shake.
Strain into chilled glass.
Add 1 drop of Grenadine.

CHOCOLATE COVERED CHERRY
(frozen)
In Blender:
1/2 cup of Ice
1 1/2 oz Vodka
1/2 oz Dark Creme De Cacao
Dash of Cherry Brandy
4 Maraschino Cherries (no stems)
Scoop of Chocolate Ice Cream
Blend until smooth.
If too thick add Milk.
If too thin add ice or ice cream.

CHOCOLATE IRISH
RASPBERRY
1 oz Irish Cream
1 oz Black Raspberry Liqueur
Fill with Hot Chocolate.
Top with Whipped Cream.
Sherry Brown

CHOCOLATE KISS
1 1/2 oz Peppermint Schnapps
1/2 oz Coffee Liqueur
Fill with Hot Chocolate.
Top with Whipped Cream.
Sprinkle with Shaved Chocolate or
Sprinkles.

CHOCOLATE SQUIRREL
Fill glass with ice.
3/4 oz Amaretto
3/4 oz Hazelnut Liqueur
3/4 oz Dark Creme De Cacao
Fill with Milk.
Shake.
Serve or strain into chilled glass.

CHOCOLATE THUNDER
2 oz Vodka
Fill with Ovaltine.

CLAM DIGGER
Fill glass with ice.
2 oz Vodka or Gin
Dash of Tabasco Sauce
Dash of Worcestershire Sauce
Dash of Lime Juice or Sour Mix
Dash of Salt
Dash of Pepper
Dash of Tomato Juice
2 oz Clam Juice
Shake.

CLIMAX
Fill glass with ice.
1/2 oz Vodka
1/2 oz Triple Sec
1/2 oz Amaretto
1/2 oz White Creme De Cacao
1/2 oz Banana Liqueur
Fill with Milk or Cream.
Shake.

CLIMAX 2
Fill glass with ice.
1/2 oz Brandy
1/2 oz Coffee Liqueur
1/2 oz Amaretto
1/2 oz Triple Sec
Fill with Milk or Cream.
Shake.

CLOUDS OVER SCOTLAND
(floater)
1 1/2 oz Green Creme De Menthe
or Melon Liqueur
(bottom)
1/2 oz Irish Cream (top)

CLOUDY NIGHT
Fill glass with ice.
1 1/2 oz Vodka
1/2 oz Tia Maria
Stir.

COBRA
Fill glass with ice.
2 oz Coffee Liqueur
Fill with Soda Water.
Garnish with Lime.

COCA
Fill glass with ice.
3/4 oz Vodka
3/4 oz Southern Comfort
3/4 oz Black Raspberry Liqueur
1 oz Orange Juice
1 oz Cranberry Juice
Shake.
Strain into chilled glass.

COCA 2 aka GRAPE CRUSH
Fill glass with ice.
1 1/2 oz Vodka
1/2 oz Black Raspberry Liqueur
Dash of Sour Mix
Shake.
Fill with Lemon-Lime Soda.

COCA LADY
Fill glass with ice.
1/2 oz Vodka
1/2 oz Rum
1/2 oz Coffee Liqueur
1/2 oz Amaretto
Fill with Milk or Cream.
Shake.
Dash of Cola

C

COCO LOCO
Fill glass with ice.
1 oz Dark Rum
1 oz Light Rum
1/2 oz Vodka
1/2 oz Banana Liqueur
1/2 oz Pineapple Juice
1/2 oz Sugar Syrup
1/2 oz Cream of Coconut
Shake.
Strain into chilled glass.

COCOANAPPS aka
ADULT HOT CHOCOLATE,
PEPPERMINT KISS,
SNUGGLER
2 oz Peppermint Schnapps
Fill with Hot Chocolate.
Stir.
Top with Whipped Cream.
Sprinkle with Shaved
Chocolate or Sprinkles.

COCOETTO aka
ALMOND KISS
2 oz Amaretto
Fill with Hot Chocolate.
Stir.
Top with Whipped Cream.
Sprinkle with Shaved Almonds or
Chocolate.

COCONUT CREAM FRAPPE
Fill glass with ice.
1 oz Rum
1 oz Irish Cream
1 tsp Cream of Coconut
Fill with Milk.
Shake.

COCOPUFF
1 oz Coffee Liqueur
1 oz Irish Cream
Fill with Hot Chocolate.
Stir.
Top with Whipped Cream.
Sprinkle with Shaved
Chocolate or Chocolate Syrup.

CODE BLUE aka
ADIOS MOTHER
Fill glass with ice.
1/2 oz Vodka
1/2 oz Gin
1/2 oz Rum
1/2 oz Tequila
1/2 oz Blue Curacao
Fill with Sour Mix.
Shake.

COFFEE ALEXANDER
1 oz Brandy
1 oz Dark Creme De Cacao
Fill with hot Black Coffee.
Top with Whipped Cream.
Sprinkle with Nutmeg.

COFFEE COLADA (frozen)
In Blender:
1/2 cup of Ice
2 oz Coffee Liqueur
1 oz Rum
2 Tbsp Cream of Coconut
1/2 cup fresh or canned Pineapple
1 Tbsp Vanilla Ice Cream
Blend until smooth.
If too thick add fruit or juice.
If too thin add ice or ice cream.

COFFEE LIQUEUR
(type liqueur)
Bring 3 cups water and 4 cups
Granulated Sugar to a boil.
Simmer 20 minutes.
Let cool.
Mix together 2 oz Instant Coffee
and 1 cup boiling Water.
Let cool.
Mix syrups.
Add 1 qt Vodka.
Add 1 Vanilla Bean (cut
lengthwise).
Store in glass container for two
weeks.
Shake for 1 minute everyday.

COFFEE SOMBRERO
Fill glass with ice.
2 oz Coffee Brandy
Fill with Milk or Cream.
Shake.

COLLINS
Fill glass with ice.
2 oz desired Liquor or Liqueur
Fill with Sour Mix.
Shake.
Splash with Soda Water.
Garnish with Orange and Cherry.

COLORADO BULLDOG
Fill glass with ice.
1 oz Vodka
1 oz Coffee Liqueur
Fill with equal parts Milk or Cream
and Cola.
Shake.

COLORADO MOTHER
Fill glass with ice.
3/4 oz Vodka
3/4 oz Coffee Liqueur
3/4 oz Tequila
Fill with Milk or Cream.
Shake.
Top with Galliano.

COLORADO MOTHER 2
Fill glass with ice.
1 oz Tequila
1 oz Coffee Liqueur
Fill with equal parts Milk or Cream
and Cola.

COMMANDO FIX
1 oz Irish Whiskey
Dash of Triple Sec
Dash of Raspberry Schnapps
Dash of Lime Juice
Stir.

CONCORD aka B-51 (floater)
1/2 oz Coffee Liqueur (bottom)
1/2 oz Irish Cream
1/2 oz 151-Proof Rum (top)

COOKIE MONSTER (floater)
1/2 oz Coffee Liqueur (bottom)
1/2 oz Irish Cream
1/2 oz 100-Proof Peppermint
Schnapps (top)

**COOKIES AND CREAM aka
OR-E-OH COOKIE** (frozen)
In Blender:
1/2 cup of Ice
1 oz Vodka
3/4 oz Dark Creme De Cacao
2 Oreo Cookies
Scoop of Vanilla Ice Cream
Blend until smooth.
If too thick add milk or cream. If too
thin add ice or ice cream.
Garnish with cookie.

COOL AID
Fill glass with ice.
3/4 oz Vodka
3/4 oz Melon Liqueur or Peach
Schnapps
3/4 oz Amaretto
Fill with Cranberry Juice.
Shake.

COOL AID 2
Fill glass with ice.
1 oz Southern Comfort
1/2 oz Amaretto
1/2 oz Melon Liqueur
Dash of Orange Juice
Dash of Cranberry Juice
Shake.
Fill with Lemon-Lime Soda.

COOL BREEZE
Fill glass with ice.
2 oz Vodka
Fill with equal parts Cranberry and
Grapefruit Juice.
Top with Ginger Ale.
Garnish with Lime.

**COPENHAGEN
POUSSE-CAFÉ** (floater)
1/2 oz Banana Liqueur (bottom)
1/2 oz Cherry Brandy
1/2 oz Cognac or Brandy (top)

COPPERHEAD
Fill glass with ice.
2 oz Vodka
Fill with Ginger Ale.
Garnish with Lime.

CORAL SEA (frozen)
In Blender:
1 cup of Ice
1 1/2 oz Rum
1/2 oz Triple Sec
1 Egg White
1/2 cup fresh or canned
Pineapple
1 tsp Grenadine
Blend until smooth.
If too thick add juice or fruit.
If too thin add ice.
Garnish with Pineapple and Cherry.

CORKSCREW
Fill glass with ice.
1 oz Rum
1/2 oz Peach Schnapps
1/2 oz Dry Vermouth
Stir.
Strain into chilled glass.

CORPSE REVIVER
Fill glass with ice.
3/4 oz Apple Brandy
3/4 oz Cognac or Brandy
1/2 oz Sweet Vermouth
Stir.
Strain into chilled glass.

COSMOPOLITAN
Fill glass with ice.
2 oz Vodka
1/2 oz Triple Sec
1/2 oz Lime Juice
Dash of Cranberry Juice
Stir.
Strain into chilled glass.
Garnish with Lime.

COUGH DROP
Fill glass with ice.
1 oz Mentholated Schnapps
1 oz Blackberry Brandy
Stir.

COWBOY
Fill glass with ice.
2 oz Bourbon
Fill with Milk.
Shake.

CRAMP RELIEVER
1 oz Blackberry Brandy

CRANAPPLE COOLER
Fill glass with crushed ice.
1 oz Vodka or Rum
1 oz Apple Brandy
Fill with Cranberry Juice.
Stir.
Garnish with Lime.

CRANBERRY LIQUEUR
(type liqueur)
Cook 1 lb Cranberries with
2 cups Sugar and
1 cup Water until berries pop.
Strain out the liquid and mix with 1
qt Vodka.
Store 1 week.
Then add 2 more cups of Sugar.
Store 1 more week.

CRANES BEACH PUNCH
1 gallon Cherry Cool Aid
1 liter cheap Red Wine
1 500ml bottle of Vodka

CRANKIN' WANKER
Fill glass with ice.
3/4 oz Vodka
3/4 oz Southern Comfort
3/4 oz Drambuie
Fill with equal parts Orange and
Pineapple Juice.

CREAM DREAM
1 1/2 oz Dark Creme De Cacao
1 oz Hazelnut Liqueur
Fill with Cream.
Shake.
Tom Lewis

CREAMSICLE
Fill glass with ice.
1 oz Rum
1/2 oz Triple Sec
1/2 oz Licor 43
Fill with equal parts Orange Juice
and Cream.
Shake.

CREAMSICLE 2
Fill glass with ice.
1 oz Banana Liqueur
1 oz Triple Sec
Fill with equal parts Orange Juice
and Milk.
Shake.

CREAMSICLE (frozen)
In Blender:
1/2 cup ice
1 oz Rum
1/2 oz Triple Sec
1/2 oz Licor 43
1/2 scoop Vanilla Ice Cream
1/2 scoop Orange Sherbet
Blend until smooth.
If too thick add Milk or Orange
Juice.
If too thin add ice or ice cream or
sherbet.
Garnish with popsicle stick.

CREATURE FROM THE BLACK
LAGOON (floater)
1 oz Jaegermeister (bottom)
1 oz Black Sambuca (top)

CREME DE MENTHE
(type liqueur)
Bring 2 cups water and 2 cups
Sugar to a boil.
Simmer 5 minutes and let cool.
Stir in 1 1/3 cups Vodka,
1/2 tsp Peppermint Extract,
2 tsp of Vanilla Extract,
7 drops of Green Food Coloring
(optional)
Store in glass bottle in dark place
for 1 week.

CREOLE MARTINI aka CAJUN
MARTINI
Fill glass with ice.
2 oz Peppered Vodka
1/2 oz Dry Vermouth
Stir.
Strain into chilled glass.
Serve with Jalapeno Peppers.

CRICKET
Fill glass with ice.
1 oz Rum
3/4 oz White Creme De Menthe
3/4 oz Dark Creme De Cacao
Fill with Milk or Cream.
Shake.
Serve or strain into chilled glass.

CRUISE CONTROL
Fill glass with ice.
1 oz Rum
1/2 oz Apricot Brandy
1/2 oz Orange Liqueur or Triple Sec
1/2 oz Sour Mix
Shake.
Fill with Soda Water.
Garnish with Lemon and Orange.

CUBA LIBRA
Fill glass with ice.
2 oz Light Rum
Fill with Cola.
Garnish with Lime.

CUBAN PEACH
Fill glass with ice.
1 1/2 oz Light Rum
1 1/2 oz Peach Schnapps
1/2 oz Lime Juice
Dash of Sugar Syrup
Shake.
Strain into chilled glass.
Garnish with Mint Sprig.

CUDDLER
1 oz Irish Cream
3/4 oz Amaretto
Heat in microwave for 7-8 seconds.

CUPID'S POTION
Fill glass with ice.
1 1/2 oz Amaretto
1/2 oz Triple Sec
Dash of Grenadine
Fill with equal parts Orange Juice
and Sour Mix.
Shake.

CURE-ALL
Fill glass with ice.
1 oz Peppermint Schnapps
1/2 oz Blackberry Brandy
Stir.

CURLEY'S DELIGHT COFFEE
3/4 oz Irish Whiskey
3/4 oz Irish Cream
3/4 oz Orange Liqueur
Fill with hot Black Coffee.
Top with Whipped Cream.
Linda Graham

DAIQUIRI
Fill glass with ice.
2 oz Rum
2 oz Lime Juice
Dash of Sour Mix
1/2 tsp Sugar
Shake.
Garnish with Lime.

DAIQUIRI (frozen)
In Blender:
1 cup of Ice
2 oz Rum
2 oz Lime Juice
Dash of Sour Mix
1/2 tsp Sugar
Blend until smooth.
Garnish with Lime.

DAISY
Fill glass with ice.
2 oz desired Liquor or Liqueur
1/2 tsp Powdered Sugar
1 tsp Raspberry Syrup
or Grenadine
Shake.
Strain into chilled glass.

DALLAS ALICE aka
ALICE IN WONDERLAND
FIll glass with ice.
3/4 oz Tequila
3/4 oz Orange Liqueur
3/4 oz Coffee Liqueur
Shake.
Strain into shot glass.

DAMN-THE-WEATHER
Fill glass with ice.
1 oz Gin
1/2 oz Sweet Vermouth
1/4 oz Triple Sec
1/2 oz Orange Juice
Shake.
Garnish with Cherry.

DANISH MARY aka
BLOODY HOLLY
Fill glass with ice.
2 oz Aquavit
1 tsp Horseradish
3 dashes of Tabasco Sauce
3 dashes of Worcestershire Sauce
Dash of Lime Juice
3 dashes of Celery Salt
3 dashes of Pepper
1 oz Clam Juice (optional)
Dash of Sherry (optional)
1 tsp Dijon Mustard (optional)
Fill with Tomato Juice.
Pour from one glass to
another until mixed.
Garnish with Lemon and/or Lime,
Celery and/or Cucumber and/or
Cocktail Shrimp.

DARB
Fill glass with ice.
1 oz Gin
1 oz Dry Vermouth
1 oz Apricot Brandy
1/2 oz Sour Mix
1 tsp Sugar
Shake.
Strain into chilled glass.

DARK AND STORMY
Fill glass with ice.
2 oz Dark Rum
Fill with Ginger Beer.
Garnish with Lime.

DARK EYES
Fill glass with ice.
1 1/2 oz Vodka
1/4 oz Blackberry Brandy
2 tsp Lime Juice
Shake.
Strain into chilled glass.

DARK SECRET
Fill glass with ice.
1 1/4 oz Black Sambuca
Fill with Club Soda.
Stir.

DC-10 aka B-54 (floater)
1/2 oz Coffee Liqueur (bottom)
1/2 oz Irish Cream
1/2 oz Amaretto (top)

DEAD NAZI aka
SCREAMING NAZI
Fill glass with ice.
1 oz Jaegermeister
1 oz 100-Proof Peppermint
Schnapps
Stir.
Strain into chilled glass.

DEATH IN THE AFTERNOON
1 oz Pernod
9 oz Champagne

DEATH MINT
1 oz Green Chartreuse
1 oz 100-Proof Peppermint
Schnapps
Stir.

DEATHWISH
Fill glass with ice.
1/2 oz 151-Proof Rum
1/2 oz 100-Proof Bourbon
1/2 oz 100-Proof Peppermint
Schnapps
1/2 oz Grenadine
Shake.
Strain into chilled glass.

DEAUVILLE
Fill glass with ice.
1 1/2 oz Apple Brandy
1/2 oz Triple Sec
Dash of Grenadine
2 oz Sour Mix
Shake.
Strain into chilled glass.

DECEIVER
Fill glass with ice.
1 1/2 oz Tequila
1/2 oz Galliano
Stir.

DEEP SEA
Fill glass with ice.
1/2 oz Gin
1/2 oz Blue Curacao
1/2 oz Pineapple Juice
1/2 oz Lime Juice
1/2 oz Sugar Syrup
Shake.

DEEP THROAT (floater)
1 oz Coffee Liqueur (bottom)
1 oz Vodka (top)
Top with Whipped Cream.
To drink, place hands behind back
and pick up using only mouth.

DELMONICO
Fill glass with ice.
2 oz Brandy
1/2 oz Sweet Vermouth
Dash of Bitters (optional)
Stir.
Strain into chilled glass or pour
contents (with ice) into short glass.
Garnish with Cherry.

DEPTH BOMB
Fill glass with ice.
1 1/2 oz Apple Brandy
1 1/2 oz Brandy
1/4 tsp Grenadine
1/4 tsp Sour Mix
Shake.
Strain into chilled glass.

DEPTH CHARGE
Fill shot glass with Whiskey
or Peppermint Schnapps
or Drambuie.
Fill chilled glass with Beer leaving 1
inch from top.
Drop shot glass into beer glass.

DE RIGUEUR
Fill glass with ice.
1 1/2 oz Whiskey
3/4 oz Grapefruit Juice
1 tsp Honey
Shake.
Strain into chilled glass.

DESERT SUNRISE
Fill glass with ice.
2 oz Tequila
Dash of Sour Mix
Fill with Orange Juice.
Top with 1/2 oz Blue Curacao.

DESIGNER JEANS
Fill glass with ice.
1/2 oz Dark Rum
1/2 oz Irish Cream
1/2 oz Raspberry Schnapps
Shake.
Strain into chilled glass.

DEVIL'S TAIL (frozen)
In Blender:
1/2 cup ice
1 1/2 oz Rum
1 oz Vodka
1/2 oz Apricot Brandy
1 oz Lime Juice
1/2 oz Grenadine
Blend 4-5 seconds.
Garnish with Lime.

DIABLO
Fill glass with ice.
1 1/2 oz Brandy
1/2 oz Triple Sec
1/2 oz Dry Vermouth
2 dashes of Bitters
Stir.
Strain into chilled glass.
Garnish with Lemon Twist.

DIAMOND FIZZ
Fill glass with ice.
1 1/2 oz Gin
Dash of Sour Mix
1 tsp Powdered Sugar
Shake.
Strain into chilled glass.
Fill with Champagne.

DIAMOND HEAD
Fill glass with ice.
1 1/2 oz Gin
1/2 oz Curacao or Triple Sec
2 oz Pineapple Juice
1 tsp Sweet Vermouth
Shake.
Strain into chilled glass.
Garnish with Pineapple.

DIKI DIKI

Fill glass with ice.
1 1/2 oz Apple Brandy
3/4 oz Gin
1 oz Grapefruit Juice
Shake.
Strain into chilled glass.

DIRE STRAITS aka
DIRTY M. F.

Fill glass with ice.
1 1/2 oz Brandy
1/2 oz Coffee Liqueur
1/2 oz Galliano
1/2 oz Milk or Cream
Shake.

DIRTY ASHTRAY

Fill glass with ice.
1/2 oz Vodka
1/2 oz Gin
1/2 oz Rum
1/2 oz Tequila
1/2 oz Blue Curacao
Dash of Grenadine
Fill with equal parts Pineapple
Juice and Sour Mix.
Shake.
Garnish with Lemon.

DIRTY BANANA

Fill glass with ice.
1 oz Dark Creme de Cacao
1 oz Banana Liqueur
1 oz Cream or Milk
Shake.
Strain into chilled glass.

DIRTY BIRD

Fill glass with ice.
1 oz Vodka or Tequila
1 oz Coffee Liqueur
Fill with Milk or Cream.
Shake.

DIRTY G. S.

Fill glass with ice.
1 oz Vodka
1/2 oz Coffee Liqueur
1/2 oz Peppermint Schnapps
Fill with Milk or Cream.
Shake.

DIRTY HARRY

Fill glass with ice.
1 oz Orange Liqueur
1 oz Coffee Liqueur
Shake.
Strain into shot glass.

DIRTY MONKEY (frozen)

In Blender:
1/2 cup of Ice
3/4 oz Vodka
3/4 oz Coffee Liqueur
3/4 oz Banana Liqueur
1/2 scoop Vanilla Ice Cream
Blend until smooth.

DIRTY MOTHER aka
SEPARATOR

Fill glass with ice.
1 1/2 oz Brandy
3/4 oz Coffee Liqueur
1 oz Cream (optional)
Stir.

DIRTY MOTHER 2

Fill glass with ice.
3/4 oz Tequila
3/4 oz Vodka
3/4 oz Coffee Liqueur
Fill with Milk or Cream.
Shake.

DIRTY M. F. aka DIRE STRAITS

Fill glass with ice.
1 1/2 oz Brandy
1/2 oz Coffee Liqueur
1/2 oz Galliano
1/2 oz Milk or Cream
Shake.

DIRTY WATER

Fill glass with ice.
2 oz Currant Vodka
Dash of Cranberry Juice
Fill with Tonic Water.
Garnish with Lemon.
Maryann Bakaj

DIRTY WHITE MOTHER

Fill glass with ice.
1 1/2 oz Brandy
1/2 oz Coffee Liqueur
Float Cream on top.

DOCTOR'S ELIXIR

Fill glass with ice.
1 oz Mentholated Schnapps
1 oz Black Raspberry Liqueur
Stir.

DOG SLED

Fill glass with ice.
2 oz Canadian Whiskey
1 tsp Grenadine
1 Tbsp Sour Mix
Fill with Orange Juice.
Shake.

DOUBLE-D (D-D)

Fill glass with ice.
3/4 oz Brandy
3/4 oz Southern Comfort
3/4 oz Cherry Brandy
Dash of Sour Mix
Dash of Cranberry Juice
Shake.
Strain into chilled glass.

D

DOWNEASTER aka HAWAIIAN SEABREEZE, BAYBREEZE
Fill glass with ice.
2 oz Vodka
Fill with equal parts Cranberry and Pineapple Juice.
Garnish with Lime.

DR. FUNK
Fill glass with ice.
1 1/2 oz Dark Rum
2 oz Sour Mix
2 oz Pineapple Juice
Dash of Grenadine
Shake.
Top with 1/2 oz Triple Sec.

DR. FUNK 2
Fill glass with ice.
1/2 oz Light Rum
1/2 oz Dark Rum
1/2 oz Galliano
1/2 oz Triple Sec
1/2 oz Sour Mix
Fill with equal parts Orange and Pineapple Juice.
Shake.
Garnish with Orange and Cherry.
Float 1/2 oz Cherry Brandy on top.

DR. J
1 oz Mentholated Schnapps
1 oz Jaegermeister

DR. P.
1/2 oz Amaretto
1/2 oz Light Rum or Brandy
Fill with cold Beer.

DR. P. FROM HELL
In shot glass pour:
3/4 oz 151-Proof Rum
3/4 oz Amaretto
Ignite.
Drop into glass of Beer 3/4 filled.

DRAGOON
Fill glass with ice.
1/2 oz Coffee Liqueur
1/2 oz Irish Cream
1/2 oz Black Sambuca
Stir.

DRAMBUIE *(type liqueur)*
Mix 1 qt Scotch, 2 cups Honey, and 2 Tbsp Coriander Seeds.
Store 1 month and shake for 1 minute each week.

DREAM COCKTAIL
Fill glass with ice.
1 1/2 oz Brandy
1/2 oz Orange Liqueur or Triple Sec
1/2 tsp Anisette
Stir.
Strain into chilled glass.

DREAMSICLE
Fill glass with ice.
2 oz Amaretto or Licor 43
Fill with equal parts Milk or Cream and Orange Juice.
Float 1/2 oz Galliano on top (optional).

DRUNKEN WAITER
Fill glass with ice.
Fill with equal parts Red Wine and cola.

DRY ARROYO
Fill glass with ice.
1 oz Black Raspberry Liqueur
1 oz Coffee Liqueur
1 oz Sour Mix
1 oz Orange Juice
Shake.
Strain into chilled glass.
Fill with Champagne.
Garnish with Orange Twist.

DRY MANHATTAN
(*CAUTION:* DRY can mean make drink with Dry Vermouth or less Sweet Vermouth than usual.)
Fill glass with ice.
2 oz Whiskey
1/2 oz Dry Vermouth
or 1/4 oz Sweet Vermouth
Stir.
Strain into chilled glass, or pour contents (with ice) into short glass.
Garnish with Lemon Twist.

DRY MARTINI
(Caution: DRY means less Dry Vermouth than usual.
EXTRA DRY means even less or no Vermouth at all).
Fill glass with ice.
2 oz Gin or Vodka
1/4 oz Dry Vermouth
Stir.
Strain into chilled glass or pour contents (with ice) into short glass.
Garnish with Lemon Twist or Olives or Cocktail Onions.

DRY ROB ROY
Fill glass with ice.
2 oz Scotch
1/4 oz Dry Vermouth
Stir.
Strain into chilled glass, or pour contents (with ice) into short glass.
Garnish with Lemon Twist.

DUBLIN COFFEE
3/4 oz Irish Whiskey
3/4 oz Irish Mist
3/4 oz Coffee Liqueur
Fill with hot Black Coffee.
Top with Whipped Cream.
Drizzle with Green Creme de Menthe.

DUBONNET COCKTAIL
Fill glass with ice.
1 1/2 oz Gin or Vodka
3/4 oz Dubonnet Rouge
Stir.
Strain into chilled glass.
Garnish with Lemon Twist.

DUBONNET MANHATTAN
Fill glass with ice.
1 1/2 oz Whiskey
3/4 oz Dubonnet Rouge
Shake.
Strain into chilled glass.
Garnish with Cherry.

DUCHESS
Fill glass with ice.
1 oz Pernod
3/4 oz Sweet Vermouth
3/4 oz Dry Vermouth
Shake.
Strain into chilled glass or pour
contents (with ice) into short glass.
Garnish with Cherry.

DUCK FART (floater)
1/2 oz Coffee Liqueur (bottom)
1/2 oz Irish Cream
1/2 oz Blended Whiskey (top)

DUDE
Fill glass with ice.
2 oz Scotch
Dash of Grenadine
Stir.
Float 1/2 oz Sherry on top.

DUNDEE
Fill glass with ice.
1 oz Gin
1/2 oz Drambuie
1/2 oz Scotch
1/2 oz Sour Mix
Shake.
Garnish with Lemon Twist or
Cherry.

DUSTY ROAD (frozen)
In Blender:
1/2 cup of Ice
1 oz Irish Cream
1 oz Black Raspberry Liqueur
1/2 scoop of Vanilla Ice Cream
Blend until smooth.
If too thick add milk or cream.
If too thin add ice or ice cream.

DUSTY ROSE
Fill glass with ice.
1 oz Irish Cream
1 oz Black Raspberry Liqueur
Stir.
Serve or strain into chilled glass.

DUTCH COFFEE
2 oz Vandermint
Fill with hot Black Coffee.
Top with Whipped Cream.
Sprinkle with Chocolate
shavings or Sprinkles.

DUTCH PIRATE
Fill glass with ice.
1 1/2 oz Vodka
1 oz Vandermint
1/2 oz Dark Rum
Shake.
Strain into chilled glass.
Garnish with Orange.

DUTCH TREAT
2 oz Brandy
Fill with Hot Chocolate.
Top with Whipped Cream.
Sprinkle with Chocolate
shavings or Sprinkles.

DYING NAZI FROM HELL
Fill glass with ice.
1 oz Vodka
1 oz Irish Cream
1 oz Jaegermeister
Strain into shot glass.

EAST INDIA
Fill glass with ice.
1 1/2 oz Brandy
1/2 oz Curacao or Triple Sec
1 oz Pineapple Juice
Dash of Bitters
Shake.
Strain into chilled glass.

EAST SIDE
Fill glass with ice.
3/4 oz Rum
3/4 oz Amaretto
3/4 oz Coconut Rum
Fill with Milk or Cream.
Shake.

EAT THE CHERRY aka
CHERRY BOMB
Place pitted, stemless Cherry in
shot glass.
1 tsp Cherry Juice
Fill with Grain Alcohol or Vodka.

ECLIPSE
Place Cherry or ripe Olive in chilled
Martini glass and cover with 1/4 oz
Grenadine.
Fill separate glass with ice.
1 oz Gin
1 1/2 oz Sloe Gin
Dash of Sour Mix
Shake.
Strain gently into second glass so
as not to disturb fruit or Grenadine.

ECLIPSE 2
Fill glass with ice.
2 oz Black Sambuca
Dash of Cream
Stir.
Strain into chilled glass.

ECSTACY
Fill glass with ice.
1 1/2 oz Vodka
1/2 oz Black Raspberry Liqueur
1/2 oz Pineapple Juice
1/2 Cranberry Juice
Shake.
Strain into chilled glass.

EDEN
Fill glass with ice.
2 oz Vodka
Fill with Apple Juice.
Garnish with Cherry.

EDEN ROC FIZZ
Fill glass with ice.
1 1/2 oz Whiskey
Dash of Pernod
Dash of Sugar Syrup
Dash of Sour Mix
1/2 Egg White
Shake.
Fill with Soda Water.

EGGHEAD (frozen)
In Blender:
1/2 cup of Ice
2 oz Vodka
1 Egg
Scoop of Orange Sherbet
Blend until smooth.

EGGNOG
Separate 12 Eggs.
Beat Yolks and 2 cups of Superfine
Sugar until thick.
Stir in 2 cups of Cognac or Brandy,
2 cups of Dark Rum,
2 cups of Cream and 6 cups of
Milk.
Refrigerate mixture.
When thoroughly chilled, beat the
Egg Whites until stiff.
Carefully fold them into mixture.
Garnish with Nutmeg.

EL CID
Fill glass with ice.
1 1/2 oz Tequila
1/2 oz Orgeat Syrup
1 oz Lime Juice
Shake.
Fill with Tonic Water.
Top with dash of Grenadine.
Garnish with Lime.

EL DIABLO
Fill glass with ice.
1 oz Tequila
1/2 oz Creme De Cassis
Dash of Lime Juice
Fill with Ginger Ale.

EL SALVADOR
Fill glass with ice.
1 1/2 oz Rum
3/4 oz Hazelnut Liqueur
Dash of Grenadine
1/2 oz Lime Juice
Shake.
Strain into chilled glass.

ELECTRIC COOL AID
Fill glass with ice.
1/2 oz Amaretto
1/2 oz Triple Sec
1/2 oz Southern Comfort
1/2 oz Melon Liqueur
1/2 oz Cherry Brandy
1/2 oz Sour Mix
1/2 oz Cranberry juice
Dash of Grenadine
Shake.
Strain into chilled glass.

ELECTRIC WATERMELON
Fill glass with ice.
1/2 oz Vodka
1/2 oz Rum
1/2 oz Triple Sec
1/2 oz Melon Liqueur
1 oz Orange Juice
1 oz Grenadine
Fill glass with Lemon-Lime Soda.
Shake.

ELMER FUDPUCKER
Fill glass with ice.
1 oz Vodka
1 oz Tequila
Fill with Orange Juice.
Top with Apricot Brandy.
Garnish with Orange.

ELVIRA
Fill glass with ice.
1 1/2 oz Vodka
1/2 oz Blackberry Brandy
Fill with Sour Mix.
Shake.

ELYSEE PALACE
Fill glass with ice.
1 oz Cognac or Brandy
1/2 oz Black Raspberry Liqueur
Fill with Champagne.
Float 1/4 oz Black Raspberry
Liqueur on top.

EMPIRE STATE SLAMMER
Fill glass with ice.
1 oz Canadian Whiskey
1/2 oz Sloe Gin
1/2 oz Banana Liqueur
2 oz Orange Juice
Shake.
Strain into chilled glass.

ENGLISH SCREWDRIVER
Fill glass with ice.
2 oz Gin
Fill with Orange Juice.
Garnish with Orange.

ERIE CANAL
Fill glass with ice.
1 1/2 oz Irish Whiskey
1/2 oz Irish Mist
1/2 oz Irish Cream
Stir.

E. T. (floater)
1/2 oz Irish Cream (bottom)
1 oz Melon Liqueur
1 oz Vodka (top)

EVERGLADES SPECIAL
Fill glass with ice.
3/4 oz Rum
3/4 oz White Creme De Cacao
1/2 oz Coffee Liqueur
1 oz Cream or Milk
Shake.

EXPRESS
Fill glass with ice.
1 1/2 oz Orange Liqueur
1/2 oz Vodka
Shake.
Strain into chilled glass.
Garnish with Orange.

EYE-OPENER
Fill glass with ice.
1 oz Rum
1/3 oz Triple Sec
1/3 oz White Creme De Cacao
1/3 oz Pernod
1 tsp Sugar Syrup
or Powdered Sugar
1 Egg Yolk
Shake.
Serve or strain into chilled glass.

F-16 (floater)
1 oz Coffee Liqueur (bottom)
1 oz Irish Cream
1 oz Hazelnut Liqueur (top)

FACE ERASER
Fill glass with ice.
1 oz Vodka
1 oz Coffee Liqueur
Fill with Lemon-Lime Soda.
Supposed to be drunk in one shot through straw.

FACE ERASER 2
Fill glass with ice.
1 1/2 oz Vodka
1/2 oz Coffee Liqueur
1/2 oz Irish Cream
Fill with Soda Water.
Supposed to be drunk in one shot through straw.

FAHRENHEIT 5
Coat inside of shot glass with hot sauce.
1 oz Peppered Vodka
1 oz Cinnamon Schnapps

FAIR AND WARMER
Fill glass with ice.
1 1/2 oz Rum
Dash of Triple Sec or Curacao
1/2 oz Sweet Vermouth
Shake.
Serve or strain into chilled glass.
Garnish with Lemon.

FAIRCHILD (floater)
1 oz Melon Liqueur (bottom)
1/2 oz Orange Juice
1/2 oz Irish Whiskey (top)

FALLEN ANGEL
Fill glass with ice.
2 oz Gin
Dash of White Creme De Menthe
Dash of Bitters
2 oz Sour Mix
Shake.
Serve or strain into chilled glass.
Garnish with Cherry.

FANTASIO
Fill glass with ice.
1 1/2 oz Brandy
3/4 oz Dry Vermouth
1 tsp White Creme De Cacao
1 tsp Cherry Liqueur
Shake.
Serve or strain into chilled glass.

FARE-THEE-WELL
Fill glass with ice.
1 1/2 oz Gin
1 oz Dry Vermouth
1/2 oz Triple Sec or Curacao
2 dashes of Sweet Vermouth
Shake.
Strain into chilled glass.

FASCINATION
Fill glass with ice.
1 1/2 oz Dark Rum
3/4 oz Orange Liqueur
1/2 tsp Sugar
1/2 Egg White
Fill with Sour Mix.
Shake.
Strain into chilled glass.

FAT CAT (frozen)
In Blender:
1/2 cup of Ice
3/4 oz Cognac
3/4 oz Galliano
3/4 oz White Creme de Cacao
Scoop of Vanilla Ice Cream
Blend until smooth.
If too thick add Milk.
If too thin add ice or ice cream.

FATHER SHERMAN
Fill glass with ice.
1 1/2 oz Brandy
1/2 oz Apricot Brandy
1 oz Orange Juice
Shake.
Strain into chilled glass.

FAVORITE
Fill glass with ice.
3/4 oz Gin
3/4 oz Apricot Brandy
3/4 oz Dry Vermouth
1/4 tsp Sour Mix
Shake.
Strain into chilled glass.

FEDORA
Fill glass with ice.
3/4 oz Dark Rum
3/4 oz Bourbon
3/4 oz Brandy
Dash of Triple Sec
1 oz Sour Mix
Shake.
Strain into chilled glass.
Garnish with Lemon.

F.E.D.X.
Fill glass with ice.
1 1/2 oz Amaretto
1 oz Black Raspberry Liqueur
2 oz Sour Mix
Shake.
Strain into chilled champagne
glass.
Fill with Champagne.
Garnish with Lemon Twist.

FERN GULLY
Fill glass with ice.
1 oz Dark Rum
1 oz Light Rum
1/2 oz Creme De Nouyax
or Amaretto
1 oz Orange Juice
1/2 oz Cream of Coconut
1/2 oz Lime Juice
Shake.
Garnish with Lime and Orange.

FERRARI
Fill glass with ice.
1 oz Amaretto
2 oz Dry Vermouth
Stir.
Garnish with Lemon Twist.

FESTERING SLOBOVIAN
HUMMER
Fill glass with ice.
1/2 oz 151-Proof Rum
1/2 oz Galliano
1/2 oz Peppermint Schnapps
Shake.
Strain into shot glass.

FESTIVAL
Fill glass with ice.
3/4 oz Dark Creme De Cacao
1 oz Apricot Brandy
1 tsp Grenadine
3/4 oz Cream
Shake.

FIFTH AVENUE aka
LAYER CAKE (floater)
3/4 oz Dark Creme De Cacao
(bottom)
3/4 oz Apricot Brandy
1/2 oz Milk (top)

FIFTY FIFTY (Martini)
Fill glass with ice.
1 1/2 oz Gin
1 1/2 oz Dry Vermouth
Stir.
Strain into chilled glass.
Garnish with Olive.

57 CHEVY
Fill glass with ice.
1 oz Vodka
1 oz White Creme De Cacao
Stir.

57 CHEVY 2
Fill glass with ice.
1/2 oz Vodka
1/2 oz Rum
1/2 oz Amaretto
1/2 oz Southern Comfort
1/2 oz Orange Liqueur
Fill with equal parts Pineapple
Juice and Sour Mix.
Shake.
Serve or strain into chilled glass.

57 T-BIRD
Fill glass with ice.
3/4 oz Rum or Vodka
or Southern Comfort
3/4 oz Amaretto
3/4 oz Orange Liqueur
Fill with equal parts Pineapple,
Cranberry and Orange Juice.
Shake.

57 T-BIRD
(with California Plates)
Fill glass with ice.
3/4 oz Rum or Vodka
or Southern Comfort
3/4 oz Amaretto
3/4 oz Orange Liqueur
Fill with Grapefruit Juice.
Shake.

57 T-BIRD
(with Florida Plates)
Fill glass with ice.
3/4 oz Rum or Vodka
or Southern Comfort
3/4 oz Amaretto
3/4 oz Orange Liqueur
Fill with Orange Juice.
Shake.

57 T-BIRD
(with Hawaiian Plates)
Fill glass with ice.
3/4 oz Rum or Vodka
or Southern Comfort
3/4 oz Amaretto
3/4 oz Orange Liqueur
Fill with Pineapple Juice.
Shake.

57 T-BIRD
(with Massachusetts Plates)
Fill glass with ice.
3/4 oz Rum or Vodka
or Southern Comfort
3/4 oz Amaretto
3/4 oz Orange Liqueur
Fill with Cranberry juice.
Shake.

FIJI FIZZ
Fill glass with ice.
1 1/2 oz Dark Rum
1/2 oz Bourbon
1 tsp Cherry Brandy
3 dashes of Orange Bitters
Shake.
Fill with Cola.
Garnish with Lime.

FILBY
Fill glass with ice.
2 oz Gin
3/4 oz Amaretto
1/2 oz Dry Vermouth
1/2 oz Campari
Stir.
Garnish with Orange.

FINE AND DANDY
Fill glass with ice.
1 1/2 oz Gin
3/4 oz Orange Liqueur or Triple Sec
3/4 oz Sour Mix
Dash of Bitters
Shake.
Strain into chilled glass.
Garnish with Cherry.

FIREBALL
Fill shot glass with Cinnamon
Schnapps.
Add 4-5 drops of Tabasco Sauce.
Stir.

FIREBALL 2
Fill glass with ice.
1/2 oz Vodka
1/2 oz Cinnamon Schnapps
1/2 oz Cherry Brandy
4-5 drops Tabasco Sauce
Stir.
Strain into shot glass.

FIREBIRD
Fill glass with ice.
2 oz Peppered Vodka
Fill with Cranberry Juice.
Stir.

FIRECRACKER
Fill glass with ice.
2 oz Spiced Rum
1/2 oz Sloe Gin or Grenadine
Fill with Orange Juice
Shake.
Float 1/2 oz 151-Proof Rum on top.
Garnish with Orange.

FIREFLY
Fill glass with ice.
2 oz Vodka
Dash of Grenadine
Fill with Grapefruit Juice.
Shake.

FIRE-IN-THE-HOLE
Fill shot glass with Ouzo or
Sambuca
Add 3-5 dashes of Tabasco Sauce.

FIRESIDE
2 oz Dark Rum
1 tsp Sugar
Fill with hot tea.
Stir.

FISH HOUSE PUNCH
Dissolve 3/4 lb Sugar in 1 qt Spring
Water (non-carbonated).
1 1/2 cups Lemon Juice
1/2 cup Peach Schnapps
1 qt Cognac
2 qt Dark Rum
Pour mixture into cold bowl
containing cake of ice.

FIZZ
Fill glass with ice.
2 oz desired Liquor or Liqueur
1 oz Lemon Juice or Sour Mix
1 tsp Powdered Sugar
Shake.
Strain into chilled glass.
Fill with Soda Water.

FJORD
Fill glass with ice.
1 oz Brandy
1/2 oz Aquavit
1 oz Orange Juice
1/2 oz Lime Juice
1 tsp Grenadine
Shake.
Strain into chilled glass.

FLAMING BLUE J.
Fill glass with ice.
1 oz Southern Comfort
1/2 oz Blue Curacao
1/2 oz Peppermint Schnapps
Strain into chilled glass.
Float 1/2 oz 151-Proof Rum on top.
Ignite.

F

FLAMING NORIEGA (floater)
1/2 oz Strawberry Liqueur
(bottom)
1/2 oz Green Creme De Menthe
1/2 oz Sugar Syrup
1/2 oz 151-Proof Rum (top)
Ignite.

FLAMINGO
Fill glass with ice.
1 1/2 oz Gin
1/2 oz Apricot Brandy
1/2 oz Lime Juice
Dash of Grenadine
Shake.
Strain into chilled glass.

FLAMINGO 2
Fill glass with ice.
2 oz Rum or Vodka
Fill with equal parts Sour Mix,
Pineapple Juice and Orange Juice.
Add Grenadine while stirring until
desired pink color.

FLIM FLAM
Fill glass with ice.
1 1/2 oz Rum
3/4 oz Triple Sec
1/2 oz Sour Mix
1/2 oz Orange Juice
Shake.
Serve or strain into chilled glass.

FLIP
Fill glass with ice.
2 oz desired Liquor or Liqueur
1 raw egg
1 tsp Powdered Sugar
Shake.
Strain into glass.
Garnish with Nutmeg.

FLORIDA
Fill glass with ice.
1/2 oz Gin
1/4 oz Kirschwasser
1/4 oz Triple Sec
2 oz Orange Juice
1/4 oz Sour Mix
Shake.
Serve or strain into chilled glass.
Garnish with Orange.

FLORIDA 2
Fill glass with ice.
1 1/2 oz Light Rum
1/2 oz Green Creme De Menthe
1/2 oz Sugar Syrup
or 1/2 tsp Sugar
1/2 oz Lime Juice
1/2 oz Pineapple Juice
Shake.
Strain into chilled glass.
Fill with Soda Water.
Garnish with mint sprig.

FLORIDA ICED TEA
Fill glass with ice.
1/2 oz Vodka
1/2 oz Gin
1/2 oz Rum
1/2 oz Tequila
1/2 oz Triple Sec
2 oz Orange Juice
Top with Cola.
Garnish with Orange.

FLORIDA SUNRISE
Fill glass with ice.
2 oz Rum
Dash of Grenadine
Fill with Orange Juice.
Shake.

FLYING GRASSHOPPER
Fill glass with ice.
1 oz Vodka
3/4 oz Green Creme De Menthe
3/4 oz White Creme De Cacao
Fill with Milk or Cream.
Shake.
Serve or strain into chilled glass.

FLYING GRASSHOPPER (frozen)
In Blender:
1/2 cup of Ice
1 oz Vodka
3/4 oz Green Creme De Menthe
3/4 oz White Creme De Cacao
Scoop of Vanilla Ice Cream
Blend until smooth.
If too thick add milk or cream. If too
thin add ice or ice cream.

FLYING KANGAROO (frozen)
In Blender:
1/2 cup of Ice
3/4 oz Vodka
3/4 oz Rum
3/4 oz Galliano
2 Tbsp Vanilla Ice Cream
Blend until smooth.
If too thick add milk or cream.
If too thin add ice or ice cream.
Garnish with Pineapple and Cherry.

FLYING MADRAS aka
RUSSIAN NIGHTS
Fill glass with ice.
2 oz Vodka
2 oz Cranberry Juice
2 oz Orange Juice
Fill with Champagne.
Garnish with Orange.

FLYING SCOT
Fill glass with ice.
1 oz Scotch
1 oz Sweet Vermouth
1/4 oz Sugar Syrup
2-4 dashes of Bitters
Shake.

FOG CUTTER
Fill glass with ice.
1 oz Rum
1 oz Brandy
1 oz Gin
Dash of Creme De Nouyax
or Triple Sec
Dash of Sour Mix
Fill with equal parts Orange and
Pineapple Juice.
Top with 1/2 oz Sherry.
Shake.

FOG HORN
Fill glass with ice.
2 oz Gin
Fill with Ginger Ale or Ginger Beer.
Garnish with Lemon.

FORESTER
Fill glass with ice.
1 1/2 oz Bourbon
3/4 oz Cherry Liqueur
1 tsp Sour Mix
Shake.

.44 MAGNUM
Fill glass with ice.
1/2 oz Vodka
1/2 oz Light Rum
1/2 oz Dark Rum
1/2 oz Triple Sec
Dash of Sour Mix
Dash of Pineapple Juice
Shake.
Fill with Lemon-Lime Soda.

FOX RIVER
Fill glass with ice.
1 1/2 oz Whiskey
1/2 oz Dark Creme De Cacao
2 or 3 dashes of Bitters
Stir.
Serve or strain into chilled glass.
Garnish with Lemon Twist.

FOXY LADY
Fill glass with ice.
1 oz Amaretto
1 oz Dark Creme De Cacao
Fill with Cream or Milk.
Shake.

FOXHOUND
Fill glass with ice.
1 1/2 oz Brandy
1 tsp Kummel
Dash of Sour Mix
Dash of Cranberry Juice
Shake.
Garnish with a Lemon.

FRANKENBERRY
Fill glass with ice.
1 oz Currant Vodka
1 oz Black Raspberry Liqueur
Fill with equal parts Sour Mix and
Pineapple Juice.
Shake.
*Frankie Gaul, Hog's Breath Saloon,
Key West*

FRANKENJACK
Fill glass with ice.
1 oz Gin
1/2 oz Triple Sec
1/2 oz Apricot Brandy
1/2 oz Dry Vermouth
Shake.

FRAPPE
Fill large stemmed glass (Red Wine
glass, Champagne saucer) with
crushed ice.
Add 2 oz desired Liquor or Liqueur

FREDDY FUDPUCKER aka
CACTUS BANGER
Fill glass with ice.
1 1/2 oz Tequila
Fill with Orange Juice.
Top with Galliano.
Garnish with Orange.

FREDDY KRUGER (floater)
1 oz Sambuca (bottom)
1 oz Jaegermeister
1 oz Vodka (top)

FREEDOM FIGHTER (floater)
1 1/2 oz Irish Whiskey (bottom)
1/2 oz Irish Cream (top)

FRENCH COFFEE
2 oz Orange Liqueur or Cognac
Fill with hot Black Coffee.
Top with Whipped Cream.
Garnish with Orange and
Cinnamon.

FRENCH CONNECTION
Fill glass with ice.
1 1/2 oz Cognac or Brandy
1/2 oz Amaretto
or Orange Liqueur
Stir.

FRENCH CONNECTION COFFEE
1 1/2 oz Cognac or Brandy
1/2 oz Amaretto
Fill with hot Black Coffee.
Top with Whipped Cream.
Sprinkle with Shaved Almonds.

FRENCH DRAGON
1 oz Brandy or Cognac
1 oz Green Chartreuse
Stir.

F

FRENCH DREAM
Fill glass with ice.
1 oz Irish Cream
1 oz Black Raspberry Liqueur
1 oz Coffee Liqueur
Stir.

FRENCH ICED COFFEE (frozen)
In Blender:
1/2 cup of Ice
2 oz Cognac or Brandy
Scoop of Vanilla Ice Cream
1/2 cup of Iced Coffee
Blend until smooth.
If too thick add coffee or Milk.
If too thin add ice or ice cream.

FRENCH LIFT
Fill glass 1/2 with Champagne.
Dash of Grenadine
Fill with sparkling water.
Garnish with 3 or 4 blueberries.

FRENCH MARTINI
Fill glass with ice.
1 oz Vodka
1/2 oz Black Raspberry Liqueur
1/2 oz Peach Schnapps
Shake.
Strain into chilled glass.
Garnish with Cherry.

FRENCH 95
Fill glass with ice.
1 1/2 oz Bourbon or Gin
1 oz Sour Mix
1 oz Orange Juice
Fill with Champagne.
Float 1/2 oz Brandy on top.
Garnish with Orange or Cherry.

FRENCH 75
Fill glass with ice.
1 1/2 oz Cognac or Brandy
or Gin
1 oz Lemon Juice or Sour Mix
1/2 oz Sugar Syrup
Shake.
Fill with Champagne.
Garnish with Lemon Twist.

FRENCH SUMMER
Fill glass with ice.
1 oz Black Raspberry Liqueur
Fill with sparkling water
or Soda Water.
Garnish with Orange.

FRIAR TUCK
Fill glass with ice.
2 oz Hazelnut Liqueur
2 oz Lemon Juice or Sour Mix
2 dashes of Grenadine
Shake.
Garnish with Orange and Cherry.

FRISCO SOUR
Fill glass with ice.
1 1/2 oz Whiskey
3/4 oz Benedictine
1/2 oz Lemon Juice or Sour Mix
1/2 oz Lime Juice
Shake.
Strain into chilled glass.
Garnish with Orange.

FROG-IN-A-BLENDER (frozen)
In Blender:
1 cup of Ice
2 oz Vodka
4 oz Cranberry Juice
2 Lime wheels
Blend 3-5 seconds.

FROSTBITE
Fill glass with ice.
1 1/2 oz Tequila
1/2 oz White Creme De Cacao
1/2 oz Blue Curacao
Fill with Cream.
Shake.

FROSTBITE (frozen)
In Blender:
1 cup of Ice
1 1/2 oz Yukon Jack
3/4 oz Peppermint Schnapps
2 oz Sour Mix
Blend until smooth.
If too thin add ice.
If too thick add Sour Mix.

FROSTED ROMANCE (frozen)
In Blender:
1/2 cup of Ice
1 oz Black Raspberry Liqueur
1 oz White Creme De Cacao
Scoop of Vanilla Ice Cream
Blend until smooth.
If too thick add Milk or liqueur.
If too thin add ice or ice cream.

FROUPE
Fill glass with ice.
1 1/2 oz Brandy
1 1/2 oz Sweet Vermouth
1 tsp Benedictine
Stir.
Strain into chilled glass.

FROZEN BIKINI (frozen)
In Blender:
1 cup of Ice
2 oz Vodka
1 oz Peach Schnapps
3 oz Peach Nectar
2 oz Orange Juice
Blend until smooth.
Pour into large glass.
Top with Champagne.

FRU FRU
Fill glass with ice.
1 oz Peach Schnapps
1 oz Banana Liqueur
Dash of Lime Juice
1 oz Pineapple Juice
Shake.
Strain into chilled glass.
Garnish with Lime.

FRUITBAR
Fill glass with ice.
1 oz Peach Schnapps
1 oz Dark Creme de Cacao
Stir.

F. LOOP
Fill glass with ice.
1/2 oz Vodka
1/2 oz Coconut Rum
1/2 oz Blackberry Brandy
1/2 oz Black Raspberry Liqueur
1/2 oz Banana Liqueur
Dash of Cranberry Juice
Dash of Pineapple Juice
Shake.
Strain into chilled glass.
Shawn Ryan

FU MANCHU
Fill glass with ice.
1 1/2 oz Dark Rum
1/2 oz Triple Sec
1/2 oz White Creme De Menthe
1/2 oz Lime Juice
Dash of Sugar Syrup
or 1/4 tsp Sugar
Shake.
Strain into chilled glass.

FUDGESICLE (frozen)
In Blender:
1/2 cup of Ice
1 1/2 oz Vodka
1/2 oz Dark Creme De Cacao
1 Tbsp Chocolate Syrup
Scoop of Chocolate Ice Cream
Blend until smooth.
If too thick add milk or cream.
If too thin add ice or ice cream.
Garnish with a popsicle stick.

FUEL-INJECTION
Fill glass with ice
1 1/2 oz Brandy
1/2 oz Mentholated Schnapps
Shake.
Strain into chilled glass.

FULL MOON
Fill glass with ice.
1 oz Orange Liqueur
1 oz Amaretto
Stir.

FUNKY MONKEY (frozen)
In Blender:
1/2 cup of Ice
3/4 oz Rum
3/4 oz White Creme De Cacao
3/4 oz Banana Liqueur
1/2 fresh ripe peeled Banana
Scoop of Vanilla Ice Cream
Blend until smooth.
If too thick add Milk or fruit.
If too thin add ice or ice cream.
Garnish with Banana.

FUZZY FRUIT
Fill glass with ice.
2 oz Peach Schnapps
Fill with Grapefruit Juice.
Stir.

FUZZY GUPPIE
Fill glass with ice.
1 1/2 oz Vodka
1/2 oz Peach Schnapps
1 oz White Wine
Fill with Ginger Ale.
Originally garnished with a fish.
(I don't condone killing an
innocent animal for garnishes.)

FUZZY KAMIKAZE
Fill glass with ice.
2 oz Vodka
2 oz Peach Schnapps
1 oz Lime Juice
Shake.
Serve or strain into chilled glass.
Garnish with Lime.

FUZZY MONKEY
Fill glass with ice.
1 oz Banana Liqueur
1 oz Peach Schnapps
Fill with Orange Juice.
Stir.
Garnish with Orange or Banana.

FUZZY MOTHER
1 1/2 oz Gold Tequila
Top with 1/4 oz 151-Proof Rum.
Ignite.

FUZZY NAVEL
Fill glass with ice.
1 oz Vodka
or 2 oz Peach Schnapps
1 oz Peach Schnapps
Fill with Orange Juice.
Garnish with Orange.

FUZZY NAVEL WITH LINT
Fill glass with ice.
1 oz Vodka
1 oz Peach Schnapps
Fill with Orange Juice.
Top with 1/2 oz Irish Cream or Milk.

F

G AND C
Fill glass with ice.
1 oz Galliano
1 oz Cognac

GALACTIC GARGLE BLASTER
Fill glass with ice.
3/4 oz Vodka
3/4 oz Rum
3/4 oz Melon Liqueur
Dash of Sour Mix
Dash of Lime Juice
Shake.
Strain into chilled glass.
Fill with Lemon-Lime Soda.

GALE WARNING
Fill glass with ice.
2 oz Scotch
Fill with equal parts Cranberry and
Pineapple Juice.

GALLIANO *(type liqueur)*
Bring 2 cups of Sugar and
2/3 cup water to a boil.
Simmer 10 minutes.
1/2 tsp Anise Extract
1/2 tsp Vanilla Extract
3 tsp Lime Juice
6 drops of Yellow Food Coloring
Let cool.
Add 2 1/2 cups of Vodka.
Put in tightly corked bottle.
Store 6 weeks.

GANDY DANCER
Fill glass with ice.
1 oz Yukon Jack
1 oz Amaretto
1 oz Banana Liqueur
1 oz Pineapple Juice
Shake.
Strain into chilled glass.

GANGRENE
Fill glass with ice.
1 oz Light Rum
1/2 oz Spiced Rum
1/2 oz Melon Liqueur
1/2 oz Blue Curacao
Fill with Sour Mix.
Shake.

GAUGIN or GAUGUIN *(frozen)*
In Blender:
1 cup of Ice
2 oz Rum
1 tsp passion fruit syrup
1 tsp Lime Juice
1 tsp Lemon Juice
Blend until smooth.
Garnish with Cherry and Lemon
Twist.

GENOA
Fill glass with ice.
1 1/2 oz Vodka
3/4 oz Campari
Fill with Orange Juice.
Shake.
Garnish with Orange.

GENTLE BEN
Fill glass with ice.
3/4 oz Vodka
3/4 oz Gin
3/4 oz Rum
Fill with Orange Juice.
Shake.
Garnish with Orange.

GENTLE BULL
Fill glass with ice.
1 1/2 oz Tequila
3/4 oz Coffee Liqueur
Fill with Cream or Milk.
Shake.

GEORGIA PEACH
Fill glass with ice.
2 oz Peach Schnapps
Fill with Cranberry Juice.
Stir.

GHOSTBUSTER
Fill glass with ice.
1 oz Peach Schnapps
1 oz Melon Liqueur
Shake.
Strain into chilled glass.
Add 3-5 drops of Irish Cream into
center of drink.

GIBSON
(Caution: DRY usually means less
Vermouth than usual.
EXTRA DRY can mean even less
Vermouth than usual, or no
Vermouth at all.)
Fill glass with ice.
2 oz Gin
1/2 oz Dry Vermouth
Stir.
Strain into chilled glass or pour
contents (with ice) into short glass.
Garnish with Cocktail Onions.

GILLIGAN'S ISLE
Fill glass with ice.
2 oz Rum
Dash of Amaretto
Dash of Maraschino Cherry juice
Dash of Lime Juice
Dash of Grapefruit Juice
Stir.
Strain into chilled glasses.

GIMLET
Fill glass with ice.
2 oz Gin or Vodka
1 oz Lime Juice
Stir.
Strain into chilled glass or pour
contents (with ice) into short glass.
Garnish with Lime.

GIN AND TONIC
Fill glass with ice.
2 oz Gin
Fill with Tonic Water.
Garnish with Lime.

GIN BUCK
Fill glass with ice.
2 oz Gin
Fill with Ginger Ale.
Stir.
Garnish with Lemon.

GIN CASSIS
Fill glass with ice.
1 1/2 oz Gin
1/2 oz Creme De Cassis
1/2 oz Lemon Juice or Sour Mix
Shake.
Serve or strain into chilled glass.

GIN DAISY
Fill glass with ice.
2 oz Gin
1 tsp Sugar
1 tsp Raspberry Syrup
or Grenadine
1 oz Lemon Juice or Sour Mix
Shake.
Fill with Soda Water.
Garnish with Orange and Lemon.

GIN FIZZ
Fill glass with ice.
2 oz Gin
1/2 tsp Sugar
1 oz Sour Mix
Dash of Lime Juice
Shake.
Fill with Soda Water.
Garnish with Cherry.

GINGERBREAD MAN
Fill glass with ice.
1 oz Cinnamon Schnapps
1 oz Irish Cream
1 oz Butterscotch Schnapps
Shake.
Strain into chilled glass.

GINGER SNAP
Fill glass with ice.
2 oz Ginger Brandy
Fill with Ginger Ale.

GIN RICKEY
Fill glass with ice.
2 oz Gin
1 Tbsp Lime Juice
Fill with Soda Water.
Garnish with Lime.

G. S. COOKIE
Fill glass with ice.
1 oz Vodka
1 oz Coffee Liqueur
1 oz Peppermint Schnapps
Fill with Milk or Cream.
Shake.

G. S. COOKIE (floater)
1/2 oz Coffee Liqueur (bottom)
1/2 oz Irish Cream
1/2 oz Peppermint Schnapps (top)

G. S. COOKIE (frozen)
In Blender:
1/2 cup of Ice
1 oz Vodka
1/2 oz Coffee Liqueur
1/2 oz Peppermint Schnapps
Scoop of Vanilla Ice Cream
Blend until smooth.
If too thick add milk or cream.
If too thin add ice or ice cream.
Garnish with Chocolate shavings or
Sprinkles or a cookie.

GLASS TOWER
Fill glass with ice.
1 oz Vodka
1 oz Light Rum
1/2 oz Triple Sec
1/2 oz Peach Schnapps
1/2 oz Sambuca
Fill with Lemon-Lime Soda.
Garnish with Lime.

GLOOMLIFTER
Fill glass with ice.
1 1/2 oz Whiskey
1/2 oz Brandy
1/2 oz Raspberry Syrup
or Black Raspberry Liqueur
1 tsp Sugar
1/2 oz Lemon Juice or Sour Mix
1/2 Egg White
Shake.

GLUEWEIN
In a sauce pan:
5 oz Dry Red Wine
1 Cinnamon Stick (broken up)
2 whole Cloves
1 tsp Honey
Pinch of ground Nutmeg
Heat without boiling.
Pour into mug.
Garnish with Lemon Twist and
Orange.

G

GODCHILD
Fill glass with ice.
1 1/2 oz Brandy or Cognac
1/2 oz Amaretto

GODFATHER
Fill glass with ice.
1 1/2 oz Scotch
1/2 oz Amaretto
Stir.

GODMOTHER aka
TAWNY RUSSIAN
Fill glass with ice.
1 1/2 oz Vodka
1/2 oz Amaretto
Stir.

GO-GO JUICE
Fill glass with ice.
1/2 oz Vodka
1/2 oz Gin
1/2 oz Rum
1/2 oz Tequila
1/2 oz Blue Curacao
1/2 oz Orange Juice
1 oz Sour Mix
Shake.
Fill with Lemon-Lime Soda.
Garnish with Lemon.

GOLDEN CADDIE (frozen)
In Blender:
1 cup of Ice (or 1/2 cup of Ice if
using Ice Cream)
2 oz White Creme De Cacao
1 oz Galliano
3 oz Cream or Milk or
1/2 scoop of Vanilla Ice Cream
Blend 5 seconds on low speed.
Strain and serve.

GOLDEN CAPPUCCINO
1 1/2 oz Galliano
Fill with Espresso.
Top with Steamed Milk.
Garnish with Lemon Twist.

GOLDEN DAWN
Fill glass with ice.
1 oz Gin
1 oz Apricot Brandy
1 oz Orange Juice
Shake.
Strain into chilled glass.

GOLDEN DAY
Fill glass with ice.
1 1/2 oz Vodka
1/2 oz Galliano
Stir.

GOLDEN DAZE
Fill glass with ice.
1 1/2 oz Gin
1/2 oz Peach or Apricot Brandy
1 oz Orange Juice
Shake.
Strain into chilled glass.

GOLDEN DRAGON
Fill glass with ice.
1 1/2 oz Yellow Chartreuse
1 1/2 oz Brandy
Stir.
Strain into chilled glass.
Garnish with Lemon Twist.

GOLDEN DREAM
Fill glass with ice.
1 oz Galliano
1/2 oz Triple Sec
Fill with equal parts Orange Juice
and Cream or Milk.
Shake.
Serve or strain and serve.
Garnish with Orange.

GOLDEN DREAM
(with Double Bumpers)
Fill glass with ice.
1/2 oz Galliano
1/2 oz Triple Sec
1/2 oz Brandy
1/2 oz Benedictine
Fill with equal parts of Orange Juice
and Cream or Milk.
Shake.
Serve or strain into chilled glass.

GOLDEN FIZZ
Fill glass with ice.
2 oz Gin
1 Egg Yolk
1 1/2 oz Sour Mix
or Lemon Juice
1 tsp Powdered Sugar
Shake.
Fill with Soda Water.
Garnish with Lemon Wedge.

GOLDEN GATE
Fill glass with ice.
1 oz Rum
1/2 oz Gin
1/2 oz White Creme De Cacao
1 tsp 151-Proof Rum
1 tsp Falernum
1 oz Lemon Juice or Sour Mix
Shake.
Garnish with Orange.

GOLDEN MARGARITA
Fill glass with ice.
1 1/2 oz Gold Tequila
1/2 oz Grand Marnier
or Cointreau or Triple Sec
1/2 oz Lime Juice
3 oz Sour Mix
Dash of Orange Juice
(optional)
Shake.
Rub rim of second glass with Lime
and dip in kosher salt.
Strain or pour contents (with ice)
into salted glass.
Garnish with Lime.

GOLDEN MARGARITA (frozen)
In Blender:
1 cup of Ice
1 1/2 oz Golden Tequila
1/2 oz Grand Marnier or Orange
Liqueur or Triple Sec
1/2 oz Lime Juice
3 oz Sour Mix
Dash of Orange Juice
(optional)
Blend until smooth.
If too thick add juice.
If too thin add ice.
Rub rim of second glass with Lime
and dip in kosher salt.
Strain or pour contents (with ice)
into salted glass.
Garnish with Lime.

GOLDEN NAIL
Fill glass with ice.
2 oz Drambuie
Fill with Grapefruit Juice.
Stir.

GOLDEN RUSSIAN
Fill glass with ice.
1 1/2 oz Vodka
1 oz Galliano
Stir.
Garnish with Lime.

GOLDEN SCREW aka
ITALIAN SCREW
Fill glass with ice.
2 oz Galliano
Fill with Orange Juice.
Shake.

GOLDEN SHOWERS
Uncork bottle of chilled
Champagne or Sparkling Wine.
Cover top with thumb and shake.
Face bottle in direction of
unsuspecting friend.
Remove thumb.

GOLDEN TORPEDO
Fill glass with ice.
1 oz Amaretto
1 oz Galliano
Fill with Cream or Milk.
Shake.

GOLDRUSH
Fill glass with ice.
1 oz Gold Tequila
1 oz Goldschlager

GOLDRUSH 2
Fill glass with ice.
1 1/2 oz Gold Tequila
1/2 oz Orange Liqueur
1/2 oz Lime Juice
Rub rim of second glass with Lime
and dip into Kosher Salt.
Strain or pour contents (with ice)
into salted glass.

GOLF
Fill glass with ice.
1 1/2 oz Gin
3/4 oz Dry Vermouth
2 dashes of Bitters
Stir.
Strain into chilled glass.
Garnish with Olive.

GOOD AND PLENT-E
1 oz Ouzo or Anisette
1 oz Coffee Liqueur
or Blackberry Brandy

GOOD AND PLENT-E (frozen)
In Blender:
1/2 cup of Ice
1 oz Vodka
1 oz Coffee Liqueur
1/2 oz Anisette
Scoop of Vanilla Ice Cream
Blend until smooth.
If too thick add milk or cream.
If too thin add ice or ice cream.

GOOD FORTUNE
Fill glass with ice.
1 oz Ginger Liqueur
1 oz Irish Cream
Stir.

GOOMBAY SMASH
Fill glass with ice.
1 oz Rum
1/2 oz Banana Liqueur
1 tsp Cream of Coconut
Dash of Orange Juice
Fill with Pineapple Juice.
Shake.
Top with Dark Rum.

GORILLA
Fill glass with ice.
1 oz Dark Creme De Cacao
1 oz Banana Liqueur
Fill with Orange Juice.

GRADEAL SPECIAL
Fill glass with ice.
1 1/2 oz Gin or Rum
3/4 oz Rum or Gin
3/4 oz Apricot Brandy
1 tsp Sugar Syrup
Shake.
Strain into chilled glass.

GRAND ALLIANCE
1 oz Amaretto
Fill with Champagne.

GRAND APPLE
Fill glass with ice.
1 oz Apple Brandy
1/2 oz Cognac or Brandy
1/2 oz Orange Liqueur
Stir.
Strain into chilled glass.
Garnish with Orange and Lemon
Twist.

G

GRAND MIMOSA
Fill glass with ice.
Fill 3/4 with Champagne.
Dash of Orange Liqueur
Fill with Orange Juice.
Garnish with Orange.

GRAND OCCASION
Fill glass with ice.
1 1/2 oz Rum
1/2 oz Orange Liqueur
1/2 oz White Creme De Cacao
1/2 oz Lemon Juice or Sour Mix
Shake.
Strain into chilled glass.

GRAND PASSION
Fill glass with ice.
2 oz Gin
1 oz Passion Fruit Nectar
2 or 3 dashes of Bitters
Shake.
Serve or strain into chilled glass.

GRAND SLAM
Fill glass with ice.
1 1/2 oz Swedish Punch
3/4 oz Dry Vermouth
3/4 oz Sweet Vermouth
Stir.
Strain into chilled glass.

GRAPE APE
Fill glass with ice.
2 oz Vodka
Fill glass with equal parts
Grape Juice and Lemon-Lime
Soda.

GRAPE CRUSH aka COCA
Fill glass with ice.
1 1/2 oz Vodka
1/2 oz Black Raspberry Liqueur
Dash of Sour Mix
Shake.
Fill with Lemon-Lime Soda.

GRAPE SOUR BALL
Fill glass with ice.
1 oz Vodka
1 oz Blue Curacao
2 oz Sour Mix
Fill with Cranberry Juice.
Shake.
Strain into chilled glass.

GRASSHOPPER
Fill glass with ice.
1 oz White Creme De Cacao
1 oz Green Creme De Menthe
Fill with Milk or Cream.
Shake.
Serve or strain into chilled glass.

GRASSHOPPER (frozen)
In Blender:
1/2 cup of Ice
1 oz White Creme De Cacao
1 oz Green Creme De Menthe
Scoop of Vanilla Ice Cream
Blend until smooth.
If too thick add milk or cream. If too
thin add ice or ice cream.

GREAT SECRET
Fill glass with ice.
1 1/2 oz Gin
1/2 oz Lillet
Dash of Bitters
Shake.
Strain into chilled glass.
Garnish with Orange.

GREATFUL D.
Fill glass with ice.
1/2 oz Vodka
1/2 oz Gin
1/2 oz Rum
1/2 oz Tequila
1/2 oz Triple Sec
1/2 oz Black Raspberry Liqueur
Fill with Sour Mix
Shake.
Jerry, We miss you!

GREEK COFFEE
1 oz Metaxa
1 oz Ouzo
Fill with hot Black Coffee.
Top with Whipped Cream.

GREEN APPLE
Fill glass with ice.
1 oz Apple Brandy
1 oz Melon Liqueur
1 oz Sour Mix
Stir.

GREEN DRAGON
Fill glass with ice.
2 oz Vodka
1 oz Green Chartreuse
Shake.
Strain into chilled glass.

GREEN EYES
Fill glass with ice.
1 1/2 oz Vodka
1/2 oz Blue Curacao
Fill with Orange Juice.
Shake.

GREEN GODDESS
Fill glass with ice.
1 oz Vodka
1/2 oz Melon Liqueur
1/2 oz Cream of Coconut
Shake.

GREEN HORNET aka IRISH STINGER
Fill glass with ice.
1 1/2 oz Brandy
1/2 oz Green Creme De Menthe
Stir.
Serve or strain into chilled glass.

GREEN KAMIKAZE
Fill glass with ice.
2 oz Vodka
1/2 oz Melon Liqueur
1 oz Lime Juice
Shake.

GREEN LIZARD
Fill glass with ice.
1/2 oz 151-Proof Rum
1 oz Green Chartreuse
Shake.
Strain into shot glass.

GREEN MEANY
Fill glass with ice.
1 oz Southern Comfort
1 oz Melon Liqueur
1 oz Pineapple Juice
Stir.
Strain into shot glass.

GREEN MOUNTAIN MELON
Fill glass with ice.
1 oz Vodka
1/2 oz Melon Liqueur
1 oz Lime Juice
Fill with Sour Mix.
Shake.
Garnish with Lime.

GREEN RUSSIAN
Fill glass with ice.
1 1/2 oz Vodka
1/2 oz Melon Liqueur
Stir.

GREEN RUSSIAN 2
Fill glass with ice.
1 1/2 oz Vodka
1/2 oz Melon Liqueur
Fill with Milk or Cream.
Shake.

GREEN SNEAKERS
Fill glass with ice.
1 oz Vodka
1/2 oz Melon Liqueur
1/2 oz Triple Sec
2 oz Orange Juice
Shake.
Serve or strain into chilled glass.

GREEN SPIDER
Fill glass with ice.
2 oz Vodka
1 oz Green Creme De Menthe
Stir.
Serve or strain into chilled glass.

GREYHOUND
Fill glass with ice.
2 oz Vodka
Fill with Grapefruit Juice.
Garnish with Lime.

GROG
2 oz Amber Rum
1 tsp Sugar
Dash of Lemon Juice
3 whole cloves
1 Cinnamon Stick
Fill with boiling water.
Stir.
Garnish with Lemon.

GROUND ZERO aka MINT CONDITION
Fill glass with ice.
3/4 oz Vodka
1/2 oz Coffee Liqueur
3/4 oz Bourbon
3/4 oz Peppermint Schnapps
Shake.
Serve or strain into chilled glass.

G-SPOT
Fill glass with ice.
1 oz Vodka
1 oz Orange Liqueur
1 oz Cranberry Juice
Stir.
Strain into chilled glass.

GUANA GRABBER
Fill glass with ice.
3/4 oz Light Rum
3/4 oz Dark Rum
1 oz Coconut Rum
Dash of Grapefruit Juice
Dash of Grenadine
Fill with Pineapple Juice.
Shake.
Garnish with Cherry.

GUILLOTINE
Fill glass with ice.
3/4 oz Vodka
3/4 oz Tequila
3/4 oz Mentholated Schnapps
Shake.
Strain into chilled glass.

GUMBY
Fill glass with ice.
1 oz Vodka
1 oz Melon Liqueur
1 oz Sour Mix
Shake.
Fill with Lemon-Lime Soda.

GUMDROP
Fill glass with ice.
1 oz Amaretto
1 oz Dark Creme De Cacao
Strain into chilled glass.

G

GUN RUNNER COFFEE
1 oz Irish Whiskey
1/2 oz Irish Cream
1/2 oz Coffee Liqueur
Fill with hot Black Coffee.
Top with Whipped Cream.
Sprinkle with Brown Sugar.

GUN RUNNER ICED COFFEE
Fill glass with ice.
1 oz Irish Whiskey
1/2 oz Irish Cream
1/2 oz Coffee Liqueur
Fill with Iced Coffee.
Add sugar or sweetener to taste.

GYPSY
Fill glass with ice.
2 oz Vodka
1/2 oz Benedictine
1 tsp Lemon Juice or Sour Mix
1 tsp Orange Juice
Shake.
Serve or strain into chilled glass.
Garnish with Orange.

HAIRY APE
Fill glass with ice.
1 oz Vodka
1 oz Banana Liqueur
Fill with Orange Juice.
Shake.

HAIRY MARY
Fill glass with ice.
2 oz Grain Alcohol
Fill with Bloody Mary Mix.

HAIRY NAVEL
Fill glass with ice.
1 oz Vodka
1 oz Peach Schnapps
Fill glass with Orange Juice.
Garnish with Orange.

HALLEY'S COMFORT aka HALLEY'S COMET
Fill glass with ice.
1 1/2 oz Southern Comfort
1 1/2 oz Peach Schnapps
Fill glass with Soda Water.

HAMMER
Fill glass with ice.
2 oz Tequila
Fill with Orange Juice.

HAMMER (floater)
1 1/2 oz Sambuca (bottom)
1/2 oz Brandy (top)

HAMMERHEAD
Fill glass with ice.
1 oz Amber Rum
1 oz Amaretto
1 oz Curacao
1 or 2 dashes of Southern Comfort
Strain into chilled glass.

HAMMERHEAD 2
Fill glass with ice.
1/2 oz Vodka
1/2 oz Light Rum
1/2 oz Spiced Rum
1/2 oz Coconut Rum
Fill with equal parts Pineapple and
Orange Juice.

HAND GRENADE (floater)
1 oz Peach Schnapps (bottom)
1/2 oz Soda Water
1/2 oz 151-Proof Rum (top)
Ignite.

HAND GRENADE 2 (floater)
1/2 oz Jaegermeister (bottom)
1/2 oz Peppermint Schnapps
1/2 oz 151-Proof Rum (top)

HANGOVER RELIEVER
1 B-Complex Vitamin.
Glass filled with Soda Water,
with 5-10 dashes of Bitters in it.

HAPPY FELLER
Fill glass with ice.
1 1/2 oz Vodka
1/2 oz Black Raspberry Liqueur
1/2 oz Orange Liqueur
Dash of Lime Juice
Strain into chilled glass.

HAPPY JACK
Fill glass with ice.
1 oz Bourbon
1 oz Apple Brandy
Stir.
Strain into chilled glass.

HAPPY SUMMER
Fill glass with ice.
1 1/2 oz Amber Rum
1 1/2 oz Melon Liqueur
Fill with Orange Juice.
Michael T. Duratti

HARBOR LIGHTS (floater)
1 oz Galliano (bottom)
1 oz Brandy (top)
Ignite.

HARBOR LIGHTS 2 (floater)
3/4 oz Coffee Liqueur (bottom)
3/4 oz Tequila
or Southern Comfort
3/4 oz 151-Proof Rum (top)
Ignite.

HARD HAT
Fill glass with ice.
2 oz Rum
Dash of Lime Juice
1 tsp Sugar
Fill with Soda Water.

HARD NIPPLE (floater)
1 oz Irish Cream (bottom)
1 oz Peppermint Schnapps (top)

HARLEM COCKTAIL
Fill glass with ice.
1 1/2 oz Gin
1 tsp of Cherry Liqueur
1 oz Pineapple Juice
Shake.
Strain into chilled glass.
Garnish with Pineapple.

H. D. RIDER
1 oz Bourbon
1 oz Tequila or Yukon Jack

HARMONY
Fill glass with ice.
1 1/2 oz Ginger Liqueur
1/2 oz Peach Schnapps
Fill with Orange Juice.
Shake.
Garnish with Orange.

HARVARD
Fill glass with ice.
1 1/2 oz Brandy
3/4 oz Sweet Vermouth
1/4 oz Lemon Juice or Sour Mix
1 tsp Grenadine
Dash of Bitters
Shake.
Strain into chilled glass.

HARVEY WALLBANGER
Fill glass with ice.
1 1/2 oz Vodka
Fill with Orange Juice.
Top with Galliano.
Garnish with Orange.

HARVEY WALLBANGER (frozen)
In Blender:
1/2 cup of Ice
1 1/2 oz Vodka
Dash of Orange Juice
1/2 scoop Orange Sherbet
Blend until smooth.
Top with Galliano.

HASTA LA VISTA, BABY
Fill glass with ice.
1/2 oz Vodka
1/2 oz Tequila
1/2 oz Triple Sec
1/2 oz Peach Schnapps
1/2 oz Amaretto
1/2 oz B&B
Dash of Dry Vermouth
Dash of Lime Juice
Fill with equal parts of Orange and
Pineapple Juice.
Shake.

HAVANA
Fill glass with ice.
1 1/2 oz Amber Rum
1/2 oz Sherry
1 /1/2 oz Sour Mix
Shake.
Strain into chilled glass.
Garnish with Orange.

HAWAIIAN
Fill glass with ice.
2 oz Gin
1/2 oz Triple Sec
1/2 oz Pineapple Juice
Shake.
Strain into chilled glass.

HAWAIIAN 2
Fill glass with ice.
1 oz Amaretto
1 oz Southern Comfort
Dash of Orange Juice
Dash of Pineapple Juice
Dash of Grenadine
Shake.
Strain into chilled glass.

HAWAIIAN 3
Fill glass with ice.
1 oz Vodka
1 oz Blended Whiskey
1/2 oz Amaretto
Dash of Grenadine
Fill with equal parts Orange Juice
and Pineapple Juice.
Shake.
Garnish with Cherry and Pineapple.

HAWAIIAN COCKTAIL
Fill glass 3/4 with ice.
Fill 3/4 with desired White Wine.
Dash of Pineapple Juice
Dash of Pink Grapefruit Juice

HAWAIIAN EYE (frozen)
In Blender:
1 cup of Ice
3/4 oz Vodka
3/4 oz Coffee Liqueur
1 tsp Bourbon
1 tsp Banana Liqueur
1 Egg White
Dash of Cream
2 oz Pineapple Juice.
Blend until smooth.
If too thick add juice.
If too thin add ice.

HAWAIIAN GARDEN'S SLING
Fill glass with ice.
1 oz Rum
1 oz Sloe Gin
Dash of Grenadine
Fill with Sour Mix.
Shake.

G
H

HAWAIIAN MARGARITA (frozen)
In Blender:
1 cup of Ice
1 1/2 oz Tequila
1/2 oz Triple Sec
2 oz fresh or frozen
Strawberries
2 oz fresh or canned
Pineapple
Dash of Sour Mix
Blend until smooth.

HAWAIIAN NIGHTS
Fill glass with ice.
2 oz Rum
Fill with Pineapple Juice.
Float 1/4 oz Cherry Brandy
on top.

HAWAIIAN PUNCHED
Fill glass with ice.
3/4 oz Vodka
3/4 oz Southern Comfort
3/4 oz Amaretto
Dash of Sloe Gin or Grenadine
Fill with Pineapple Juice.
Shake.
Garnish with Pineapple.

HAWAIIAN PUNCHED 2
Fill glass with ice.
1 oz Vodka
1 oz Melon Liqueur
1 oz Amaretto
Dash of Southern Comfort
Fill with Cranberry Juice.
Shake.

HAWAIIAN PUNCHED 3
Fill glass with ice.
1/2 oz Vodka
1/2 oz Southern Comfort
1/2 oz Triple Sec
1/2 oz Amaretto
Dash of Pineapple Juice
Dash of Sour Mix
Dash of Cranberry Juice
Dash of Grenadine
Shake.
Garnish with Cherry and Orange.

HAWAIIAN SEABREEZE aka BAY BREEZE, DOWNEASTER
Fill glass with ice.
2 oz Vodka
Fill with equal parts Pineapple and
Cranberry Juice.
Garnish with Lime.

HEAD
Fill glass with ice.
1 oz Root Beer Schnapps
1 oz Cream
Shake.

HEADHUNTER
Fill glass with ice.
2 oz Rum
1 oz Vodka
1 Tbsp Cream of Coconut
Dash of Cream
1 oz Orange Juice
Fill with Pineapple Juice.
Shake.
Garnish with Pineapple.

HEADREST aka UPSIDE DOWN MARGARITA
Rest head on bar.
Have friend pour ingredients into
mouth.
1 oz Tequila
1/2 oz Triple Sec
Dash of Lime Juice
Dash of Sour Mix
Dash of Orange Juice
Slosh around mouth.
Swallow!

HEART THROB
Fill glass with ice.
2 oz Amaretto
Fill with equal parts Orange and
Cranberry Juice.
Shake.

HEARTBREAK
Fill glass with ice.
2 1/2 oz Blended Whiskey
Fill with Cranberry Juice
Top with 1/2 oz Brandy.

H. BAR (frozen)
In Blender:
1/2 cup of Ice
1 1/2 oz Vodka
1 oz Dark Creme De Cacao
1 Toffee Bar
1/2 scoop of Vanilla Ice Cream
Blend until smooth.
If too thick add milk or cream.
If too thin add ice or ice cream.

HEATHER COFFEE aka RUSTY NAIL COFFEE
1 oz Scotch
1 oz Drambuie
Fill with hot Black Coffee.
Top with Whipped Cream.
Sprinkle with Cinnamon.

HEATWAVE
Fill glass with ice.
1 oz Dark Rum
1/2 oz Peach Schnapps
Fill with Pineapple Juice.
Dash of Grenadine
Stir.
Garnish with Cherry and Pineapple.

HENRY MORGAN'S GROG
Fill glass with ice.
1 1/2 oz Whiskey
1 oz Pernod
1/2 oz Dark Rum
1 oz Cream
Shake.
Sprinkle ground Nutmeg
on top.

HIGH JAMAICAN WIND (floater)
Fill glass with ice.
1 1/2 oz Dark Rum (bottom)
1/2 oz Coffee Liqueur
1/2 oz Milk or Cream (top)

HIGH ROLLER aka
PRINCE IGOR
Fill glass with ice.
1 1/2 oz Vodka
3/4 oz Orange Liqueur
Dash of Grenadine
Fill with Orange Juice.
Shake.
Garnish with Orange and Cherry.

HIGHBALL
Fill glass with ice.
2 oz Whiskey
Fill with Water or Soda Water
or Ginger Ale.

HIGHLAND COFFEE
1 1/2 oz Scotch
1/2 oz B&B
Fill with hot Black Coffee.
Top with Whipped Cream.

HIGHLAND FLING
Fill glass with ice.
1 1/2 oz Scotch
1/2 oz Sweet Vermouth
2-3 dashes of Orange Bitters
Shake.
Strain into chilled glass.
Garnish with Olive.

HOFFMAN HOUSE
Fill glass with ice.
1 1/2 oz Gin
1/2 oz Dry Vermouth
2-3 dashes of Orange Bitters
Stir.
Strain into chilled glass.
Garnish with Olive.

HOG SNORT
Fill glass with ice.
1 oz Coconut Rum
1 oz Blue Curacao
Dash of Sour Mix
Dash of Pineapple Juice
Shake.
Strain into shot glass.

HOGBACK GROWLER
1 oz 151-Proof Rum
1 oz Brandy

HOLE IN ONE (floater)
1 oz Melon Liqueur (bottom)
1 oz Apple Brandy (top)
Add one drop of Cream into center
of drink.

HOLLYWOOD aka
RASPBERRY SMASH
Fill glass with ice.
1 1/2 oz Vodka
1/2 oz Black Raspberry Liqueur
Fill with Pineapple Juice.
Shake.
Garnish with Pineapple.

HOLLYWOOD 2
Fill glass with ice.
1 oz Vodka
1/2 oz Black Raspberry Liqueur
1/2 oz Peach Schnapps
Fill with Pineapple Juice.
Shake.

HOLY HAIL ROSEMARY
Fill glass with ice.
1 1/2 oz Peppered Vodka
5-7 dashes of Tabasco Sauce
Dash of Tomato Juice
Shake.
Strain into short glass.

HOMECOMING
Fill glass with ice.
1 oz Amaretto
1 oz Irish Cream
Shake.
Strain into chilled glass or pour
contents (with ice) into short glass.

HONEY BEE
Fill glass with ice.
2 oz Rum
1/2 oz Honey
1/2 oz Lemon Juice or Sour Mix
Shake.
Strain into chilled glass.

HONEYDEW
Fill glass with ice.
1 1/2 oz Melon Liqueur
2 oz Sour Mix
1/2 tsp Sugar
Shake.
Fill with Champagne.

HONEYMOON
Fill glass with ice.
3/4 oz Apple Brandy
3/4 oz Benedictine
1 tsp Triple Sec or Curacao
1 oz Lemon Juice or Sour Mix
Shake.
Strain into chilled glass.

H

HONOLULU
Fill glass with ice.
3/4 oz Gin
3/4 oz Benedictine
3/4 oz Cherry Liqueur
Stir.
Strain into chilled glass.

HONOLULU (frozen)
In Blender:
1 cup of Ice
1 1/2 oz Rum
Dash of Grenadine
Dash of Sour Mix
1/2 cup of fresh or canned
Pineapple
Blend for 3-6 seconds on low
speed.

HOOPLA
Fill glass with ice.
3/4 oz Brandy
3/4 oz Orange Liqueur
3/4 oz Lillet
3/4 oz Lemon Juice
or Sour Mix
Shake.
Strain into chilled glass.
Garnish with Lemon Twist.

HOOSIER ROOSTER aka RED ROOSTER
Fill 1 shot glass with Gold Tequila.
Fill 1 shot glass with Orange Juice.
Fill 1 shot glass with Bloody Mary
mix.
Drink in order given one after the
other.
No Reserve Roosters.

HOOT MAN
Fill glass with ice.
1 1/2 oz Scotch
3/4 oz Sweet Vermouth
1 tsp Benedictine
Stir.
Strain into chilled glass.
Garnish with Lemon Twist.

HOOTER
Fill glass with ice.
1 1/2 oz Vodka
1/2 oz Amaretto
Fill with Pineapple Juice.
Shake.

HOOTER 2
1 oz Amaretto
1 oz Coconut Rum
Dash of Grenadine
Fill with Pineapple Juice.
Shake.
Christine Fionda

HOOTIE
Fill glass with ice.
1 1/2 oz Vodka
1/2 oz Black Raspberry Liqueur
Fill with Cranberry Juice.
Paul Surpitski

HOP-SKIP-AND-GO-NAKED
Fill glass with ice.
1 oz Vodka
1 oz Gin
Dash of Lime Juice
Fill with Orange Juice (leaving 1/2
inch from top)
Float Beer on top.

HOP TOAD
Fill glass with ice.
1 oz Rum
1 oz Apricot Brandy
1 oz Lime Juice
Stir.
Strain into chilled glass.

HORSE'S NECK
Fill glass with ice.
2 oz Whiskey
Fill with Ginger Ale.
Garnish with Lemon Twist.
(In the original recipe, a whole
lemon should be peeled in a
continuous spiral for garnish.)

HOT APPLE PIE
2 oz Tuaca
Fill with hot Apple Cider.
Top with Whipped Cream.
Garnish with Cinnamon Stick.

HOT APPLE PIE 2
Fill glass ice.
1 oz Vodka
1 oz Apple Brandy
2 oz Apple Juice
Shake.
Strain into chilled glass.
1 oz Lemon-Lime Soda
Sprinkle with Cinnamon.

HOT APPLE TODDY
2 oz Whiskey or Apple Brandy
1 tsp Honey or Sugar
Fill with hot Apple Cider.
Stir.
Garnish with Lemon, Cinnamon
Stick, and 2-3 whole Cloves.

HOT BUTTERED RUM
2 oz Dark Rum
1/2 oz Sugar Syrup
Pinch of Nutmeg
Fill with hot Water.
Garnish with Cinnamon Stick and
Pat of Butter.

HOT DOG
Fill glass with ice.
2 oz Peppered Vodka
Fill with Grapefruit Juice.

HOT DOG 2
Rub rim of glass with Lime
and dip one side of glass in
Kosher Salt.
Fill glass with Beer.
Add 5-7 drops of Tabasco Sauce.

HOT MILK PUNCH
2 oz Bourbon
1/2 oz Sugar Syrup
or 1/2 tsp Sugar
Fill with hot Milk.
Stir.
Sprinkle with Nutmeg.

HOT NAIL
2 oz Scotch
1 oz Drambuie
Dash of Lemon Juice
Fill with boiling Water.
Garnish with Orange, Lemon, and
Cinnamon Stick.

HOT PANTS
Fill glass with ice.
1 1/2 oz Tequila
1/2 oz Peppermint Schnapps
Dash of Grenadine
1 oz Grapefruit Juice
Shake and pour contents (with ice)
into second glass rimmed with salt.

HOT PEPPERMINT PATTY
1 oz Peppermint Schnapps
1/2 oz Dark Creme De Cacao
1 tsp Creme De menthe
Fill with Hot Chocolate.
Top with Whipped Cream.
Sprinkle with Shaved Chocolate or
Sprinkles.

HOT RASPBERRY DREAM
1 oz Black Raspberry Liqueur
1 oz Dark Creme De Cacao
4-6 oz steamed Milk
Stir.

HOT SCOTCH
1 oz Scotch
1/4 oz Drambuie
1 oz Lemon Juice
1/2 tsp Sugar
2 oz hot Water
Stir.
Garnish with Lemon.

HOT SEX
1 oz Coffee Liqueur
1 oz Orange Liqueur
Microwave for 10-15 seconds.

HOT TAMALE
Fill glass with ice.
1 1/2 oz Cinnamon Schnapps
1/2 oz Grenadine
Strain into shot glass.
Garnish with Hot Candy.

HOT TODDY
2 oz Whiskey
1 tsp Honey or Sugar
Fill with boiling Water.
Stir.
Garnish with a Lemon,
Cinnamon Stick, and
2-3 whole Cloves.

HOT TUB
Fill glass with ice.
1 1/2 oz Vodka
1/2 oz Black Raspberry Liqueur
Dash of Sour Mix
Dash of Cranberry Juice
Shake.
Fill with Champagne.
Strain into chilled glass.

HOUND DOG
Fill glass with ice.
2 oz Rum
Fill with Grapefruit Juice.
Stir.

HOUNDSTOOTH
Fill glass with ice.
1 oz Vodka
1/2 oz White Creme De Cacao
1/2 oz Blackberry Brandy
Stir.
Serve or strain into chilled glass.

HUDSON BAY
Fill glass with ice.
1 oz Gin
1/2 oz Cherry Brandy
1 1/2 tsp Lime Juice
1 tsp Orange Juice
Shake.
Strain into chilled glass.

HUETCHEN
Fill glass with ice.
2 oz Brandy
Fill with Cola.

HUMMER (frozen)
In Blender:
1/2 cup of Ice
1 oz Dark Rum
1 oz Coffee Liqueur
Scoop of Vanilla Ice Cream
Blend until smooth.
If too thick add milk or cream.
If too thin add ice or ice cream.

H

HUNTER'S COCKTAIL
Fill glass with ice.
1 1/2 oz Whiskey
1/2 oz Cherry Brandy
Stir.
Garnish with Cherry.

HUNTRESS COCKTAIL
Fill glass with ice.
1 oz Bourbon
1 oz Cherry Liqueur
1 oz Cream or Milk
Dash of Triple Sec
Shake.
Strain into chilled glass.

HURRICANE
Fill glass with ice.
1 oz Light Rum
1 oz Amber Rum
1/2 oz Passion Fruit Syrup
1/2 oz Lime Juice
Shake.
Strain into chilled glass.
Garnish with Lime.

HURRICANE 2
Fill glass with ice.
1/2 oz Gin
1/2 oz Light Rum
1/2 oz Dark Rum
1/2 oz Amaretto
Dash of Grenadine
Fill with equal parts Pineapple,
Orange and Grapefruit Juice.
Shake.
Garnish with Orange, Lemon, Lime
and Cherry.

I FOR AN I aka
IRISH BROUGUE
Fill glass with ice.
1 1/2 oz Irish Whiskey
1/2 oz Irish Mist
Stir.
Serve or strain into chilled glass.
Garnish with Lemon Twist.

ICE BOAT
Fill glass with ice.
1 1/2 oz Vodka
1 1/2 oz Peppermint Schnapps
Stir.
Strain into chilled glass.

ICE PICK
Fill glass with ice.
2 oz Vodka or Tequila
Fill with Iced Tea.
Flavor with sugar and/or lemon as
desired.
Garnish with Lemon.

ICEBERG
Fill glass with ice.
2 oz Vodka
1 tsp Pernod or Peppermint
Schnapps
Shake.
Strain into chilled glass.

ICHBIEN
Fill glass with ice.
2 oz Apple Brandy
1/2 oz Curacao
1 Egg Yolk
2 oz Milk or Cream
Shake.
Strain into chilled glass.
Garnish with Nutmeg.

IDEAL
Fill glass with ice.
1 1/2 oz Gin
1/2 oz Dry or Sweet Vermouth
1 Tbsp Grapefruit Juice
1 tsp Cherry Liqueur
Shake.
Strain into chilled glass.
Garnish with Cherry.

IGUANA
Fill glass with ice.
1/2 oz Vodka
1/2 oz Tequila
1/4 oz Coffee Liqueur
1 1/2 oz Sour Mix (optional)
Shake.
Strain into chilled glass.
Garnish with Lime.

IL MAGNIFICO aka
IL PARADISO (frozen)
In Blender:
1 cup of Ice
1 oz Tuaca
1 oz Curacao
1 oz Cream
Blend for 3 or 4 seconds on low
speed.

INCOME TAX
Fill glass with ice.
1 oz Gin
Dash of Sweet Vermouth
Dash of Dry Vermouth
Dash of Orange Juice
Dash of Bitters
Shake.
Serve or strain into chilled glass.

INDIAN SUMMER
2 oz Apple Brandy
Pinch of Sugar
Pinch of Cinnamon
Fill with hot Apple Cider.
Stir.
Garnish with Cinnamon Stick.

INDIAN SUMMER 2
Fill glass with ice.
1 oz Vodka
1 oz Coffee Brandy
2 oz Pineapple Juice
Shake.
Strain into shot glass.

INDIAN SUMMER HUMMER
Fill glass with ice.
1 oz Dark Rum
1/2 oz Apricot Brandy
1/2 oz Black Raspberry Liqueur
Fill with Pineapple Juice.
Shake.

INK STREET
Fill glass with ice.
2 oz Whiskey
Fill with equal parts Orange Juice
and Sour Mix.
Shake.
Strain into chilled glass.
Garnish with Orange.

INTERNATIONAL STINGER
Fill glass with ice.
1 1/2 oz Metaxa
1/2 oz Galliano
Stir.
Serve or strain into chilled glass.

INVERTED NAIL (floater)
1 oz Drambuie (bottom)
1 oz Single Malt Scotch (top)

IRA COCKTAIL
1 1/2 oz Irish Whiskey
1 oz Irish Cream
Stir.

IRISH ANGEL
Fill glass with ice.
1 oz Irish Whiskey
1/2 oz Dark Creme De Cacao
1/2 oz White Creme De Menthe
Fill with Cream.
Shake.

IRISH BROGUE aka
I FOR AN I
Fill glass with ice.
1 1/2 oz Irish Whiskey
1/2 oz Irish Mist
Stir.
Serve or strain into chilled glass.
Garnish with Lemon Twist.

IRISH BUCK
Fill glass with ice.
2 oz Irish Whiskey
Fill with Ginger Ale.
Garnish with Lemon Twist.

IRISH COFFEE
2 oz Irish Whiskey
Fill with hot Black Coffee.
Top with Whipped Cream.
Dribble 5-6 drops of Green
Creme De Menthe on top.

IRISH COFFEE ROYALE
1 oz Irish Whiskey
1 oz Coffee Liqueur
1/2 tsp Sugar
Fill with hot Black Coffee.
Top with Whipped Cream.
Dribble 5-6 drops of Green Creme
De Menthe on top.

IRISH COW
In a saucepan:
4 oz Irish Cream
4 oz Milk
Warm on low heat
Pour into tempered glass.
Garnish with Nutmeg.

IRISH CREAM SODA
Fill glass with ice.
2 oz Irish Cream
Fill with Soda Water.

IRISH FIX
Fill glass with ice.
2 oz Irish Whiskey
1/2 oz Irish Mist
1 oz Pineapple Juice
1/2 oz Lemon Juice
or Sour Mix
1/2 tsp Sugar Syrup
Shake.
Garnish with Lemon.

IRISH GENTLEMAN
1 oz Irish Whiskey
1 oz Irish Cream
Fill with hot Black Coffee.
Top with Whipped Cream.
Drizzle Green Creme De Menthe
on top.

IRISH HEADLOCK
1/2 oz Irish Whiskey
1/2 oz Irish Cream
1/2 oz Brandy
1/2 oz Amaretto
Shake.
Strain into chilled glass.

IRISH ICED COFFEE
Fill glass with ice.
2 oz Irish Whiskey
Fill with Iced Coffee.
Add cream or milk and sugar or
sweetener to taste.

IRISH MAIDEN COFFEE
1 oz Irish Whiskey
1 oz Irish Cream
Fill with hot Black Coffee.
Top with Whipped Cream.
Dribble 1/2 oz Green Creme De
Menthe on top.

IRISH MAIDEN ICED COFFEE
Fill glass with ice.
1 oz Irish Whiskey
1 oz Irish Cream
Fill with Iced Coffee.
Sugar to taste.

IRISH MANHATTAN
(Caution: Sweet means use more
Sweet Vermouth than usual.
Dry can either mean make drink
with Dry Vermouth instead of Sweet
Vermouth or less Sweet Vermouth
than usual.
Perfect means use Sweet and Dry
Vermouth.)
Fill glass with ice.
2 oz Irish Whiskey
1/2 oz Sweet Vermouth
Stir.
Strain into chilled glass
or pour contents (with ice) into
short glass.
Garnish with Cherry or Lemon
Twist.

IRISH MARIA (floater)
1 oz Tia Maria (bottom)
1 oz Irish Cream (top)

IRISH MOCHA COOLER
Fill glass with ice.
2 oz Irish Whiskey
1 oz Dark Creme De Cacao
Fill with Iced Coffee.

IRISH MONEY COFFEE
1 oz Irish Whiskey
1/2 oz Dark Creme De Cacao
Fill with hot Black Coffee.
Top with Whipped Cream.

IRISH MONK
Fill glass with ice.
1 oz Irish Cream or Irish Whiskey
1 oz Hazelnut Liqueur
Stir.

IRISH MONK COFFEE
1 oz Irish Whiskey or Irish Cream
1 oz Hazelnut Liqueur
Fill with hot Black Coffee.
Top with Whipped Cream.

IRISH ROVER
Fill glass with ice.
1 oz Irish Whiskey
1 oz Irish Cream
1 oz Coffee Liqueur
Shake.

IRISH SKIPPER COFFEE
3/4 oz Irish Mist
3/4 oz Irish Cream
3/4 oz White Creme De Cacao
Fill with hot Black Coffee.
Top with Whipped Cream.

IRISH SPRING
Fill glass with ice.
1 oz Irish Whiskey
1/2 oz Peach Schnapps
1 oz Orange Juice
1 oz Sour Mix
Shake.
Garnish with Orange and Cherry.

IRISH STINGER aka
GREEN HORNET
Fill glass with ice.
1 1/2 oz Brandy
1/2 oz Green Creme De Menthe
Stir.
Serve or strain into chilled glass.

IRISH TEA
Fill glass with ice.
1/2 oz Vodka
1/2 oz Gin
1/2 oz Rum
1/2 oz Triple Sec
1/2 oz Melon Liqueur
Fill with Lemon-Lime Soda.

ISRAELI COFFEE
2 oz Sabra Liqueur
Fill with hot Black Coffee.
Top with Whipped Cream.

ITALIAN COFFEE
2 oz Amaretto
Fill with hot Black Coffee.
Top with Whipped Cream.
Sprinkle with Shaved Almonds.

ITALIAN COFFEE 2
2 oz Galliano
Fill with hot Black Coffee.
Top with Whipped Cream.
Sprinkle with Cinnamon.

ITALIAN DELIGHT
Fill glass with ice.
1 oz Amaretto
1/2 oz Orange Juice
1 1/2 oz Cream
Shake.
Strain into chilled glass.
Garnish with Cherry.

ITALIAN ICED COFFEE
Fill glass with ice.
2 oz Amaretto or Galliano
Fill with Iced Coffee.
Add cream or milk and
sugar or sweetener to taste.

ITALIAN SCREW aka GOLDEN SCREW
Fill glass with ice.
2 oz Galliano
Fill with Orange Juice.
Shake.

ITALIAN STALLION
Fill glass with ice.
1 1/2 oz Scotch
1/2 oz Galliano
Stir.

ITALIAN STALLION 2
Fill glass with ice.
1 1/2 oz Bourbon
1/2 oz Sweet Vermouth
1/2 oz Campari
Dash of Bitters
Stir.
Strain into chilled glass.
Garnish with Lemon Twist.

ITALIAN STINGER
Fill glass with ice.
1 1/2 oz Brandy
1/2 oz Galliano
Stir.
Serve or strain into chilled glass.

ITCHY BITCHY SMELLY NELLY
Fill glass with ice.
1 oz Coconut Rum
1 oz Melon Liqueur
Fill (leaving 1/2 inch from top) with equal parts Sour Mix and Orange Juice.
Shake.
Top with Lemon-Lime Soda.
The Hogettes, Hog's Breath Saloon, Key West

IXTAPA
Fill glass with ice.
1 1/2 oz Coffee Liqueur
1/2 oz Tequila
Stir.
Strain into chilled glass.

J. OFF (floater)
1 1/2 oz Bourbon (bottom)
1/2 oz Irish Cream (top)

JACK ROSE
Fill glass with ice.
2 oz Apple Brandy
Dash of Grenadine
Fill with Sour Mix.
Shake.
Garnish with Lemon.

JACKALOPE
Fill glass with ice.
3/4 oz Dark Rum
3/4 oz Coffee Liqueur
3/4 oz Amaretto
3 oz Pineapple Juice
Shake.
Strain into chilled glass.
Top with 1/2 oz Dark Creme De Cacao.

JACKARITA
Fill glass with ice.
1 1/2 oz Bourbon
1/2 oz Triple Sec
Dash of Lime Juice
3 oz Sour Mix
Dash of Orange Juice (optional)
Shake.
Serve or strain into chilled glass.

JACKHAMMER
Fill glass with ice.
1 1/2 oz Bourbon
1/2 oz Triple Sec
Fill with Sour Mix.
Shake.

JACK-IN-THE-BOX
Fill glass with ice.
1 1/2 oz Apple Brandy
1 oz Pineapple Juice
Dash of Lemon Juice
2-3 dashes of Bitters
Shake.
Strain into chilled glass.

JADE
Fill glass with ice.
1 1/2 oz Dark Rum
1/2 tsp Triple Sec or Curacao
1/2 tsp Green Creme De Menthe
Dash of Lime Juice
1 tsp of Powdered Sugar
or Sugar Syrup.
Shake.
Serve or strain into chilled glass.
Garnish with Lime.

JAEGER MONSTER
Fill glass with ice.
1 oz Jaegermeister
1/2 oz Amaretto
Dash of Grenadine
Fill with Orange Juice.
Shake.
Garnish with Orange.

JAEGER SALSA
Fill glass with ice.
2 oz Jaegermeister
2 tsp Salsa
Fill with Bloody Mary Mix.
Shake.
Pour into glass with salted rim (optional).
Garnish with Lemon and/or Lime and Celery.

I
J

JAEGERITA
Fill glass with ice.
1/2 oz Jaegermeister
1/2 oz Gold Tequila
1/2 oz Orange Liqueur
Dash of Lime Juice
Dash of Sour Mix
Shake.
Strain into chilled glass.

JAMAICA COOLER
Fill glass with ice.
2 oz Dark Rum
1/2 oz Lemon Juice or Sour Mix
2 dashes of Orange Bitters
1 tsp Sugar
Shake until sugar dissolves.
Fill with Lemon-Lime Soda.

JAMAICA ME CRAZY
Fill glass with ice.
1 1/2 oz Dark Rum
1/2 oz Coffee Liqueur
Fill with Pineapple Juice.
Shake.

JAMAICAN
Fill glass with ice.
1 oz Dark Rum
1 oz Coffee Liqueur
1 oz Lime Juice
Dash of Bitters
Fill with Lemon-Lime Soda.

JAMAICAN COFFEE
1 oz Tia Maria or 2 oz Tia Maria
and no second liqueur.
1 oz Rum or Brandy
Fill with hot Black Coffee.
Top with Whipped Cream.
Sprinkle with Cinnamon.

JAMAICAN DELIGHT
Fill glass with ice.
1 oz Amber Rum
3/4 oz Apricot Brandy
3 oz Pineapple Juice
1/2 oz Lime Juice
1/2 oz Sugar Syrup
Shake.

JAMAICAN DUST
Fill glass with ice.
1 oz Dark Rum
1 oz Tia Maria
Fill with Pineapple Juice.
Shake.
Garnish with Lime.

JAMAICAN KISS
Fill glass with ice.
1 oz Amber Rum
1/2 oz Tia Maria
2 oz Milk
1/2 oz Sugar Syrup
Shake.

JAMAICAN MILK SHAKE (frozen)
In Blender:
1/2 cup of Ice
2 oz Bourbon
1 1/2 oz Dark Rum
Scoop of Vanilla Ice Cream
Dash of vanilla extract
Blend until smooth.
If too thick add Milk.
If too thin add ice or ice cream.

JAMAICAN PINE
Fill glass with ice.
2 oz Dark Rum
Fill with Pineapple Juice.
Garnish with Lime.

JAMAICAN WIND
Fill glass with ice.
1 1/2 oz Dark Rum
1/2 oz Coffee Liqueur
Stir.

JAPANESE FIZZ
Fill glass with ice.
2 oz Whiskey
3/4 oz Port
1/2 oz Lemon Juice
1 tsp Sugar Syrup
1 Egg White (optional)
Shake.
Fill glass with Soda Water.
Garnish with Pineapple and/or
Orange.

JELLY BEAN
Fill glass with ice.
1 oz Anisette
1 oz Blackberry Brandy
Stir.

JELLY BEAN (floater)
1/2 oz Blackberry Brandy or
Grenadine (bottom)
1/2 oz Anisette
1/2 oz Southern Comfort (top)

JELLY FISH (floater)
1 1/2 oz White Creme De Cacao
(bottom)
1/2 oz Irish Cream (top)
Place 2-3 drops of Grenadine in
center of glass.

JEWEL
Fill glass with ice.
3/4 oz Gin
3/4 oz Sweet Vermouth
3/4 oz Green Chartreuse
1-3 dashes of Orange Bitters
Shake.
Serve or strain into chilled glass.
Garnish with a Lemon Twist.

JOCKEY CLUB
Fill glass with ice.
1 1/2 oz Gin
1/4 oz White Creme De Cacao
1/2 oz Lemon Juice
Dash of Bitters
Shake.
Strain into chilled glass.

JOE COLLINS aka
MIKE COLLINS
Fill glass with ice.
2 oz Scotch
Fill with Sour Mix.
Shake.
Dash of Soda Water
Garnish with Cherry and Orange.

JOHN COLLINS
Fill glass with ice.
2 oz Whiskey
Fill with Sour Mix.
Shake.
Dash of Soda Water
Garnish with Cherry and Orange.

JOHNNIE
Fill glass with ice.
1 1/2 oz Sloe Gin
3/4 oz Orange Liqueur or Triple Sec
or Curacao
1 tsp Anisette
Shake.
Strain into chilled glass.

JOLL-E RANCHER
Fill glass with ice.
1 oz Peach Schnapps
1 oz Apple Brandy
Fill with Cranberry Juice.

JOLLY ROGER
Fill glass with ice.
1 oz Rum
1 oz Drambuie
1/2 oz Lime Juice
Dash of Scotch
Shake.
Fill with Soda Water.

JOLLY ROGER 2
Fill glass with ice.
1 oz Dark Rum
1 oz Banana Liqueur
2 oz Lemon Juice
Shake.

JUDGE, Jr.
Fill glass with ice.
1 oz Gin
1 oz Rum
Dash of Grenadine
1/2 oz Lemon Juice
Shake.
Strain into chilled glass.

JUMP UP AND KISS ME
Fill glass with ice.
1 1/2 oz Light Rum
1/2 oz Galliano
1/2 oz Apricot Brandy
1/2 Egg White
Dash of Sour Mix
Fill with equal parts Orange and
Pineapple Juice.
Shake.

JUMP UP AND KISS ME 2
Fill glass with ice.
1 1/2 oz Dark Rum
Dash of Bitters
1/2 oz Lime Juice
Fill with Pineapple Juice.
Shake.
Garnish with Pineapple and Lime.

JUNGLE JIM aka
YELLOW RUSSIAN
Fill glass with ice.
1 oz Vodka
1 oz Banana Liqueur
Fill with Milk or Cream.
Shake.

JUPITER COCKTAIL
Fill glass with ice.
1 1/2 oz Gin
1/2 oz Dry Vermouth
1 tsp Parfait Amour
or Creme De Violette
1 tsp Orange Juice
Shake.
Strain into chilled glass.

KAHLUA CLUB aka COBRA
Fill glass with ice.
2 oz Coffee Liqueur
Fill with Soda Water.
Garnish with Lime.

KAHLUA COFFEE
aka MEXICAN COFFEE
2 oz Coffee Liqueur
Fill with hot Black Coffee
Top with Whipped Cream.
Sprinkle with Shaved
Chocolate or Sprinkles.

KAHLUA SOUR
Fill glass with ice.
2 oz Coffee Liqueur
Fill with Sour Mix.
Shake.
Garnish with Cherry and Orange.

KAMIKAZE aka BULLFROG
Fill glass with ice.
2 oz Vodka
1/2 oz Triple Sec
1 oz Lime Juice
Shake.
Serve or strain into chilled glass.
Garnish with Lime.

J

K

KAPPA COLADA (frozen)
In Blender:
1/2 cup of Ice
2 oz Brandy
2 Tbsp Cream of Coconut
1/2 cup of fresh or canned Pineapple
1 Tbsp Vanilla Ice Cream
Blend until smooth.
If too thick add fruit or juice.
If too thin add ice or ice cream.
Garnish with Pineapple and Cherry.

KATINKA
Fill glass with ice.
1 1/2 oz Vodka
1/2 oz Apricot Brandy
1/2 oz Lime Juice
Stir.
Strain into chilled glass.
Garnish with mint sprig.

KENTUCKY COCKTAIL
Fill glass with ice.
2 oz Bourbon
1 oz Pineapple Juice
Shake.
Strain into chilled glass.

KENTUCKY COFFEE
2 oz Bourbon
1/2 tsp Sugar
Fill with hot Black Coffee.
Top with Whipped Cream
or float high-Proof Bourbon
on top and ignite.

KENTUCKY COLONEL
Fill glass with ice.
1 1/2 oz Bourbon
1/2 oz Benedictine
Stir.
Serve or strain into chilled glass.
Garnish with Lemon Twist.

KENTUCKY COOLER
Fill glass with ice.
1 1/2 oz Bourbon
1/2 oz Brandy
1 oz Sour Mix
2 tsp of Sugar Syrup
Shake.
Fill with Soda Water.
Float 1/4 oz Dark Rum on top.

KENTUCKY ORANGE BLOSSOM
Fill glass with ice.
1 1/2 oz Bourbon
1/2 oz Triple Sec
1 oz Orange Juice
Shake.
Garnish with Lemon.

KENTUCKY SCREWDRIVER aka BLACK-EYED SUSAN, YELLOW JACKET
Fill glass with ice.
2 oz Bourbon
Fill with Orange Juice.

KENTUCKY SWAMPWATER
Fill glass with ice.
2 oz Bourbon
1/2 oz Blue Curacao
Dash of Sour Mix
Fill with Orange Juice.

KEOKE CAPPUCCINO
1/2 oz Coffee Liqueur
1/2 oz Cognac or Brandy
1/2 oz Dark Creme De Cacao
Fill with Espresso.
Top with Steamed Milk.
Sprinkle with Powdered Cacao.

KEOKE COFFEE
3/4 oz Coffee Liqueur
3/4 oz Cognac or Brandy
3/4 oz Dark Creme De Cacao
Fill with hot Black Coffee.
Top with Whipped Cream.
Sprinkle with Cinnamon.

KERRY COOLER
Fill glass with ice.
2 oz Irish Whiskey
1 1/2 oz Sherry
1 oz Orgeat Syrup
1 oz Lemon Juice or Sour Mix
Shake.
Fill with Soda Water.

KEY LARGO (frozen)
In Blender:
1/2 cup of Ice
2 oz Dark Rum
1 oz Cream of Coconut
Scoop of Orange Sherbet
Blend until smooth.
Garnish with Orange.

KEY LIME PIE (frozen)
In Blender:
1 cup of Ice
2 oz Light Rum
3 Tbsp frozen concentrated Limeade
Dash of Lime Juice
Blend until smooth.
Garnish with Lime and a Graham Cracker.

KEY LIME SHOOTER
Fill glass with ice.
1 oz Rum or Vodka
1 oz Licor 43
Dash of Sour Mix
Dash of Cream
Dash of Orange Juice
Dash of Lime Juice
Shake.
Strain into chilled glass.

KEY WEST
Fill glass with ice.
1 oz Dark Rum
1/2 oz Banana Liqueur
1/2 oz Black Raspberry Liqueur
Fill with equal parts Sour Mix and
Orange Juice.
Shake.
Top with Soda Water.
Garnish with Cherry and Orange.

KGB
Fill glass with ice.
1 1/2 oz Gin
1/4 oz Kirschwasser
Dash of Apricot Brandy
Dash of Lemon Juice
Shake.
Strain into chilled glass.
Garnish with Lemon Twist.

KILLER BEE (floater)
1 oz Bearenjaeger (bottom)
1 oz Jaegermeister (top)

KILLER COOL AID
Fill glass with ice.
1/4 oz Vodka
1/4 oz Gin
1/4 oz Rum
1/4 oz Black Raspberry Liqueur
Dash of Sour Mix
Fill with Cranberry Juice.

KILLER COOL AID (floater)
2 oz Cranberry Juice (bottom)
1/2 oz Amaretto
1/2 oz Peach Schnapps
1 oz Vodka (top)

KING ALPHONSE (floater)
2 oz Coffee Liqueur (bottom)
1 oz Cream (top)

KING COBRA
Fill glass with ice.
1 oz Rum
1 oz Coffee Liqueur
Fill with Soda Water.
Garnish with Lime.

KING KONG COFFEE
3/4 oz Cognac or Brandy
3/4 oz Coffee Liqueur
3/4 oz Orange Liqueur
Fill with hot Black Coffee.
Top with Whipped Cream.
Garnish with Orange and
Cinnamon.

KING'S CUP
Fill glass with ice.
1 oz Galliano
1 oz Amaretto
Fill with Milk.
Shake.

KING'S PEG
Fill glass half full with ice.
2 oz Cognac or Brandy
Fill with Champagne.

KINGSTON COFFEE
1/2 oz Dark Rum
1/2 oz Coffee Liqueur
1/2 oz Irish Cream
1/2 oz Chocolate Syrup
Fill with hot Black Coffee.
Top with Whipped Cream.
Drizzle with Chocolate Syrup.

KIOLOA
Fill glass with ice.
1 oz Coffee Liqueur
1/2 oz Amber Rum
1 oz Cream
Shake.

KIR
1/2 oz Creme De Cassis
Fill with White Wine.
Garnish with Lemon Twist.

KIR ROYALE
1/2 oz Black Raspberry Liqueur
Fill with Champagne.
Garnish with Lemon Twist.

KISS
Fill glass with ice.
1 1/2 oz Vodka
1/2 oz Chocolate Liqueur
1/4 oz Cherry Liqueur
3/4 oz Cream or Milk
Shake.
Strain into chilled glass.

KISS IN THE DARK
Fill glass with ice.
3/4 oz Gin
3/4 oz Cherry Brandy
1/2 oz Dry Vermouth
Shake.
Strain into chilled glass.

KISS ME QUICK
Fill glass with ice.
2 oz Pernod
1/2 oz Curacao
3 dashes of Bitters
Stir.
Fill with Soda Water.

KISS THE BOYS GOODBYE
Fill glass with ice.
1 oz Sloe Gin
1 oz Brandy
1/4 oz Lemon Juice
1/2 Egg White
Shake.
Strain into chilled glass.

K

KIWI
Fill glass with ice.
1 oz Banana Liqueur
1 oz Strawberry Liqueur
Fill with Orange Juice.
Shake.

KLONDIKE COOLER
Fill glass with ice.
2 oz Whiskey
Dash of Orange Juice
Fill with Ginger Ale
or Soda Water.
Garnish with Lemon Twist or
Orange Twist.

KNICKERBOCKER
Fill glass with ice.
1 1/2 oz Gin
1/2 oz Dry Vermouth
1 tsp Sweet Vermouth
Stir.
Strain into chilled glass.

KOMANIWANALAYA
Fill glass with ice.
1/2 oz 151-Proof Rum
1/2 oz Amaretto
1 oz Pineapple Juice
1 oz Cranberry Juice
Shake.
Strain into chilled glass.
Top with 1/2 oz Dark Rum.

KOWLOON
Fill glass with ice.
1 oz Orange Liqueur
1 oz Coffee Liqueur
Fill with Orange Juice.
Shake.
Garnish with Orange.

KREMLIN COCKTAIL
Fill glass with ice.
1 oz Vodka
1 oz White Creme De Cacao
1 oz Cream
Shake.
Strain into chilled glass.

KRETCHMA
Fill glass with ice.
1 oz Vodka
1 oz White Creme De Cacao
Dash of Grenadine
1 Tbsp Lemon Juice
Shake.
Strain into chilled glass.

KUWAITI COOLER
Fill glass with ice.
1 oz Melon Liqueur
1 oz Key Largo Schnapps
Dash of Sour Mix
Shake.
Strain into chilled glass.
Fill with Soda Water.

KYOTO
Fill glass with ice.
1 1/2 oz Gin
1/2 oz Dry Vermouth
1/2 oz Melon Liqueur
or Apricot Brandy
1/2 oz Triple Sec
Dash of Lemon Juice (optional)
Shake.
Strain into chilled glass.

LA BAMBA
Fill glass with ice.
1 1/2 oz Tequila
1/2 oz Orange Liqueur
Fill with equal parts Pineapple and
Orange Juice.
Shake.
Strain into chilled glass.
Top with Grenadine.

LA JOLLA
Fill glass with ice.
1 1/2 oz Brandy
1/2 oz Banana Liqueur
1 tsp Orange Juice
2 tsp Lemon Juice or Sour Mix
Shake.
Strain into chilled glass.

LA MOSCA
Either fill pony glass with Sambuca or
3 oz Sambuca in Brandy snifter.
Add 3 Coffee Beans, for health wealth
and happiness.

LADIES
Fill glass with ice.
1 1/2 oz Whiskey
1 tsp Anisette
1/2 tsp Pernod
2 dashes of Bitters
Shake.
Strain into chilled glass.
Garnish with Pineapple.

LADY BE GOOD
Fill glass with ice.
1 1/2 oz Brandy
1/2 oz White Creme De Menthe
1/2 oz Sweet Vermouth
Shake.
Strain into chilled glass.

LADYFINGER
Fill glass with ice.
1 oz Gin
1/2 oz Kirschwasser
1/2 oz Cherry Brandy
Shake.
Strain into chilled glass.

LAKE STREET LEMONADE
Fill glass with ice.
1 1/2 oz Vodka
1/2 oz Amaretto
Fill with Lemonade.
Stir.
Garnish with Lemon.

LALLAH ROOKH
Fill glass with ice.
1 1/2 oz Rum
3/4 oz Cognac or Brandy
1/2 oz Creme De Vanilla or Vanilla Extract
1 tsp Sugar Syrup
Shake.
Top with Whipped Cream.

L.A.P.D.
Fill glass with ice.
1 oz Gold Tequila
1/2 oz Blue Curacao
1/4 oz Grenadine
Stir.
Strain into chilled glass.

LAS BRISAS (frozen)
In Blender:
1/2 cup of Ice
1 oz Vodka
1 oz Coconut Rum
1/2 cup fresh or canned Pineapple
1/2 scoop Vanilla Ice Cream
Blend until smooth.

LASKY
Fill glass with ice.
3/4 oz Gin
3/4 oz Swedish Punch
3/4 oz Grape Juice
Shake.
Serve or strain into chilled glass.

LATIN LOVER
Fill glass with ice.
1 1/2 oz Tequila
1/2 oz Amaretto
Stir.

LAWHILL
Fill glass with ice.
1 1/2 oz Whiskey
1/2 oz Dry Vermouth
1/4 oz Pernod
1/4 oz Cherry Liqueur
1/2 oz Orange Juice
Dash of Bitters
Shake.
Strain into chilled glass.

LAYER CAKE aka
FIFTH AVENUE (floater)
3/4 oz Dark Creme De Cacao (bottom)
3/4 oz Apricot Brandy
1/2 oz Milk (top)

LAZER BEAM
Fill glass with ice.
1 oz Bourbon
1 oz Southern Comfort
Fill with Cranberry Juice.
Stir.

LAZER BEAM 2
Fill glass with ice.
1/2 oz Bourbon
1/2 oz Tequila
1/2 oz Amaretto
1/2 oz Triple Sec
Fill with Sour Mix.
Shake
Garnish with Lemon and Cherry.

LEAF
Fill glass with ice.
1 oz Light Rum
1 oz Melon Liqueur
1 oz Cream
Shake.
Strain into chilled glass.

LEAP FROG
Fill glass with ice.
2 oz Gin
1/2 oz Lemon Juice
Fill with Ginger Ale.
Garnish with Lemon.

LEAP YEAR
Fill glass with ice.
1 1/2 oz Gin
1/2 oz Orange Liqueur or Triple Sec
1/2 oz Sweet Vermouth
1 tsp Lemon Juice
Stir.
Strain into chilled glass.

LEAVE IT TO ME
Fill glass with ice.
1 oz Gin
1/2 oz Apricot Brandy
1/2 oz Dry Vermouth
1/4 oz Lemon Juice
1/4 oz Grenadine
Shake.
Strain into chilled glass.

LEBANESE COFFEE
1 oz Apricot Brandy
1 oz Coffee Liqueur
Fill with hot Black Coffee.
Top with Whipped Cream.

'LECTRIC LEMONADE
Fill glass with ice.
1/2 oz Vodka
1/2 oz Gin
1/2 oz Light Rum
1/2 oz Tequila
1/2 oz Triple Sec
2 oz Sour Mix
Shake.
Fill with Lemon-Lime Soda.

LEFT BANK
Fill glass with ice.
1 oz Irish Cream
1 oz Black Raspberry Liqueur
Stir.

LEFT-HANDED SCREWDRIVER
Fill glass with ice.
2 oz Gin
Fill with Orange Juice.
Stir.
Garnish with Orange or Lime.

LEG SPREADER
Fill glass with ice.
1 oz Galliano
1 oz Coffee Liqueur
Strain into chilled glass.

LEISURE SUIT
Fill glass with ice.
1 oz Banana Liqueur
1 oz Galliano
Fill with equal parts Orange,
Cranberry and Pineapple Juice.

LEMON DROP
Moisten inside of shot glass with
Lemon Juice.
Coat inside of glass with Sugar.
Fill shot glass with chilled Vodka.

LEMON DROP 2
Fill shot glass with Citrus Vodka.
Coat Lemon wedge with Sugar.

LEMON FRAPPE
Fill large stemmed glass (Red Wine
glass, Champagne saucer) with
crushed ice.
1 oz Tuaca
1 oz Sour Mix

LEMON SLUSH (frozen)
In Blender:
1 cup of Ice
2 oz Vodka
3 Tbsp Lemonade concentrate
Blend until smooth.

LEMONADE (modern)
Fill glass with ice.
1 1/2 oz Sloe Gin
1 1/2 oz Sherry
1 oz Sugar Syrup
or 1 tsp Powdered Sugar
2 oz Lemon Juice
Shake.
Top with Soda Water.

LEPRECHAUN
Fill glass with ice.
2 oz Irish Whiskey
Fill with Tonic Water.
Garnish with a Lemon Twist.

LEPRECHAUN 2
Fill glass with ice.
1 oz Vodka
1/2 oz Peach Schnapps
1/2 oz Blue Curacao
Fill with Orange Juice.

LESLIE
3 oz White Wine
3 oz Cranberry juice
3 oz Lemon-Lime Soda
Garnish with Lemon and Lime.

LETHAL INJECTION
Fill glass with ice.
1/2 oz Dark Rum
1/2 oz Spiced Rum
1/2 oz Coconut Rum
1/2 oz Amaretto
or Creme De Nouyax
1 oz Orange Juice
1 oz Pineapple Juice
Shake.
Strain into chilled glass.

LIBERTY COCKTAIL
Fill glass with ice.
1 1/2 oz Apple Brandy
3/4 oz Rum
1/4 tsp Sugar Syrup
Stir.
Strain into chilled glass.
Garnish with Cherry.

LICORICE STICK
Fill glass with ice.
1 1/2 oz Anisette
Fill with Milk or Cream.
Top with 1/2 oz Galliano.
Stir with Licorice Stick.

LICORICE WHIP (floater)
3/4 oz Coffee Liqueur (bottom)
3/4 oz Irish Cream
3/4 oz Ouzo (top)

LIEBFRAUMILCH
Fill glass with ice.
1 1/2 oz White Creme De Cacao
1 1/2 oz Cream or Milk
1/2 oz Lime Juice
Shake.
Strain into chilled glass.

LIFE-SAVER (floater)
1 oz Banana Liqueur (bottom)
1 oz Blackberry Brandy (top)

LIFE-SAVOR
Fill glass with ice.
1/2 oz Triple Sec
1/2 oz Melon Liqueur
1/2 oz Coconut Rum
Fill with Orange Juice.
Shake.

LIGHTHOUSE
Fill glass with ice.
1/2 oz Tequila
1/2 oz Coffee Liqueur
1/2 oz Peppermint Schnapps
Stir.
Strain into chilled glass.
Top with 1/2 oz 151-Proof Rum.

LILLET NOUYAX
Fill glass with ice.
1 1/2 oz Lillet Blanc
1/2 oz Gin
1 tsp Creme De Nouyax
Shake.
Strain into chilled glass.
Garnish with Orange Twist.

LIMBO
Fill glass with ice.
2 oz Rum
1/2 oz Banana Liqueur
1 oz Orange Juice
Shake.
Strain into chilled glass.

LIME RICKEY
Fill glass with ice.
1 1/2 oz Gin
1/2 oz Lime Juice
Fill with Soda Water.
Stir.
Garnish with Lime.

LINSTEAD
Fill glass with ice.
1 1/2 oz Whiskey
Dash of Pernod
1 oz Pineapple Juice
Dash of Lemon Juice
3 dashes of Bitters (optional)
Shake.
Strain into chilled glass.

LION TAMER
Fill glass with ice.
3/4 oz Southern Comfort
1/4 oz Lime Juice
Stir.
Strain into chilled glass.

LIQUID COCA
Fill glass with ice.
3/4 oz 151-Proof Rum
3/4 oz 100-Proof Peppermint
Schnapps
3/4 oz Jaegermeister
Stir.
Strain into chilled glass.

LIQUID VALIUM
Fill glass with ice.
1 oz Vodka
1/2 oz Peppermint Schnapps
Stir.

LITTLE DEVIL
Fill glass with ice.
1 oz Gin
1 oz Rum
1/2 oz Triple Sec
1/2 oz Lemon Juice
or Sour Mix
Shake.
Strain into chilled glass.

LITTLE GREEN MEN
1 oz Sambuca
1 oz Melon Liqueur

LITTLE PRINCESS
Fill glass with ice.
1 1/2 oz Rum
1 1/2 oz Sweet Vermouth
Shake.
Strain into chilled glass.

LITTLE PURPLE MEN
1 oz Sambuca
1 oz Black Raspberry Liqueur

LOBOTOMY
Fill glass with ice.
1 oz Amaretto
1 oz Black Raspberry Liqueur
1 oz Pineapple Juice
Shake.
Strain into chilled glass.
Fill with Champagne.

LOLITA
Fill glass with ice.
1 1/2 oz Tequila
1/4 oz Lime Juice
1 tsp Honey
3-4 dashes of Bitters
Stir.

LOLLIPOP
Fill glass with ice.
3/4 oz Orange Liqueur
3/4 oz Kirschwasser
3/4 oz Green Chartreuse
Dash of Maraschino Liqueur
Shake.

LONDON SOUR
Fill glass with ice.
2 oz Scotch
Dash of Orange Curacao
or Triple Sec
Dash of Orange Juice
Fill with Sour Mix.
Shake.

LONDON SPECIAL aka
CHAMPAGNE COCKTAIL
In a Champagne glass:
1 Sugar Cube
2 dashes of Bitters
Fill with Champagne.
Garnish with Orange Twist.

LONDON STINGER
Fill glass with ice.
1 1/2 oz Gin
1/2 oz White Creme De Menthe
Stir.
Serve or strain into chilled glass.

L

LONE TREE
Fill glass with ice.
3/4 oz Gin
3/4 oz Dry Vermouth
3/4 oz Sweet Vermouth
3 dashes of Orange Bitters
Stir.
Strain into chilled glass.
Garnish with Olive.

LONG BEACH ICED TEA
Fill glass with ice.
1/2 oz Vodka
1/2 oz Gin
1/2 oz Rum
1/2 oz Tequila
1/2 oz Triple Sec
1 oz Orange Juice
Fill with equal parts Sour Mix and
Cranberry Juice.
Top with Cola (optional).
Garnish with Lemon.

LONG HOT NIGHT
Fill glass with ice.
2 oz Bourbon
Fill with equal parts Pineapple and
Cranberry Juice.

LONG ISLAND ICED TEA
Fill glass with ice.
1/2 oz Vodka
1/2 oz Gin
1/2 oz Rum
1/2 oz Tequila
1/2 oz Triple Sec
1 oz Sour Mix
Top with Cola.
Garnish with Lemon.

LONG ISLAND LEMONADE
Fill glass with ice.
1/2 oz Vodka
1/2 oz Gin
1/2 oz Rum
1/2 oz Tequila
1/2 oz Triple Sec
1 oz Sour Mix
Top with Lemon-Lime Soda.
Garnish with Lemon.

LOOK OUT BELOW
Fill glass with ice.
1 1/2 oz 151-Proof Rum
2 tsp Lime Juice
1 tsp Grenadine
Shake.

LOS ANGELES COCKTAIL
Fill glass with ice.
2 oz Whiskey
2-3 dashes of Sweet Vermouth
1/2 oz Lemon Juice
1 oz Sugar Syrup
1/2 raw Egg
Shake.

LOS ANGELES ICED TEA
Fill glass with ice.
1/2 oz Vodka
1/2 oz Gin
1/2 oz Rum
1/2 oz Tequila
1/2 oz Melon Liqueur
2 oz Sour Mix
Fill with Lemon-Lime Soda.
Garnish with Lemon.

LOUDSPEAKER
Fill glass with ice.
1 oz Gin
1 oz Brandy
1/4 oz Orange Liqueur
1/2 oz Lemon Juice
Stir.
Strain into chilled glass.

LOUISIANA SHOOTER aka
OYSTER SHOT
In shot glass:
1 raw Oyster
1-3 dashes of Hot Sauce
1/4 tsp Horseradish
Fill with Vodka or Peppermint
Vodka.

LOVE
Fill glass with ice.
4 oz Sloe Gin
1 Egg White
1 oz Lemon Juice
1/2 oz Raspberry Syrup or
Grenadine
Shake.
Strain into two chilled glass.

LOVE POTION (frozen)
In Blender:
1 cup of Ice
1 oz Rum
1 oz Banana Liqueur
1/2 oz Triple Sec
1 oz Orange Juice
1 oz Pineapple Juice
1/2 peeled ripe Banana
Blend 2-5 seconds on low
speed.
Garnish with Orange,
Pineapple and Banana.

LOVE POTION #9 (frozen)
In Blender:
1/2 cup of Ice
1 oz Vodka
1/2 oz White Creme De Cacao
1/2 cup fresh or frozen
Strawberries
Scoop of Vanilla Ice Cream
Blend until smooth.
If too thick add berries or milk.
If too thin add ice or ice cream.
Garnish with strawberry.

LOW TIDE
Fill glass with ice.
1 1/2 oz Vodka
1/2 oz Maui Schnapps
Fill with equal parts of Orange and
Cranberry Juice.
Mark Ellison

L. S. D.
Fill glass with ice.
1 oz Scotch
1 oz Drambuie
1 oz Lemonade
Shake.
Strain into chilled glass.

LUAU
Fill glass with ice.
1 oz Coconut Rum
1 oz Maui Schnapps
Fill with Pineapple Juice.
Shake.
Garnish with Pineapple and Cherry.

LUBE JOB
Fill glass with ice.
1 oz Vodka
1 oz Irish Cream
Stir.

LUGER
Fill glass with ice.
1 oz Brandy
1 oz Apple Brandy
Shake.
Strain into chilled glass.

LYNCHBURG LEMONADE
Fill glass with ice.
2 oz Bourbon
1/2 oz Triple Sec
Fill with Lemon-Lime Soda.

M-16 (floater)
1/2 oz Tia Maria (bottom)
1/2 oz Irish Cream
1/2 oz Orange Liqueur (top)

MACAROON
Fill glass with ice.
1 oz Black Raspberry Liqueur
1 oz Cookies and Cream Liqueur
Stir.

MACKENZIE GOLD
Fill glass with ice.
2 oz Yukon Jack
Fill with Grapefruit Juice.

MAD MAX
Fill glass with ice.
3 oz Champagne
Dash of Black Raspberry Liqueur
Fill with equal parts Cranberry and
Orange Juice.
Garnish with Orange.

MAD MONK
1 oz Hazelnut Liqueur
1 oz Peppermint Schnapps
Fill with equal parts Hot Chocolate
and hot Coffee.
Top with Whipped Cream.
Sprinkle with Shaved
Chocolate or Sprinkles.

MADEIRA COCKTAIL
Fill glass with ice.
1 1/2 oz Whiskey
1 1/2 oz Madeira
1 tsp Grenadine
Dash of Lemon Juice
Shake.
Garnish with Lemon.

MADRAS
Fill glass with ice.
2 oz Vodka
Fill with equal parts Cranberry and
Orange Juice.

MADTOWN MILKSHAKE
In Blender:
1/2 cup of Ice
3/4 oz Irish Cream
3/4 oz Black Raspberry Liqueur
3/4 oz Hazelnut Liqueur
1/2 scoop Vanilla Ice Cream
Blend until smooth.
If too thick add Milk.
If too thin add ice or ice cream.

MAGGOT
Pour both liqueurs at the same time
on opposite sides of shot glass.
1 oz Irish Cream
1 oz Green Creme De Menthe

MAI TAI (frozen)
In Blender:
1 cup of Ice
1 oz Light Rum
1/2 oz Dark Rum
1/2 oz Apricot Brandy
1/2 cup of fresh or canned
Pineapple
Splash of Sour Mix
Splash Orange Juice
Blend for 3-4 seconds on low
speed.
Top with Dark Rum.
Garnish with Lime and Orange.

MAIDEN'S BLUSH
Fill glass with ice.
1 1/2 oz Gin
1 tsp Triple Sec or Curacao
1/2 tsp Lemon Juice
1/2 tsp Grenadine
Shake.
Strain into chilled glass.

L
M

MAIDEN'S PRAYER
Fill glass with ice.
1 1/2 oz Gin
3/4 oz Triple Sec
1/2 oz Lemon Juice
Dash of Orange Juice
Shake.
Strain into chilled glass.

MAINBRACE
Fill glass with ice.
1 1/2 oz Gin
3/4 oz Triple Sec
1 oz Grape Juice
Shake.
Strain into chilled glass.

MALIBU DRIVER
Fill glass with ice.
3 oz Coconut Rum
Fill with Orange Juice.
Stir.
Garnish with Orange.

MALIBU MONSOON
Fill glass with ice.
1 1/2 oz Rum
3/4 oz Malibu Liqueur
Dash of Orange Liqueur
1 oz Pineapple Juice
Dash of Cranberry Juice
Shake.
Add 3 drops of Grenadine.
Garnish with Cherry and Orange.

MALIBU SUNSET
Fill glass with ice.
2 oz Coconut Rum
Fill with Pineapple Juice.
Pour 1/2 oz Creme De Nouyax
down spoon to bottom of glass.
Garnish with Pineapple.

MALIBU WAVE
Fill glass with ice.
1 oz Tequila
1/2 oz Triple Sec
1 tsp Blue Curacao
1 1/2 oz Sour Mix
Shake.
Garnish with Lime.

MAMIE TAYLOR
Fill glass with ice.
3 oz Scotch
1/2 oz Lime Juice
Fill with Ginger Ale.
Stir.
Garnish with Lemon.

MAN O'WAR
Fill glass with ice.
2 oz Bourbon
1 oz Orange Curacao
1/2 oz Sweet Vermouth
Dash of Lime Juice
Shake.
Strain into chilled glass.

MANHASSET
Fill glass with ice.
1 1/2 oz Whiskey
1/4 oz Sweet Vermouth
1/4 oz Dry Vermouth
1 oz Lemon Juice
Shake.
Strain into chilled glass.
Garnish with Lemon Twist.

MANHATTAN
(*CAUTION:* DRY can mean either
make drink with Dry Vermouth or
less Sweet Vermouth than usual.
PERFECT means use equal
amounts of Sweet and Dry
Vermouth.
SWEET means use more Sweet
Vermouth than usual. NAKED
means no Vermouth
at all.)
Fill glass with ice.
2 oz Whiskey
1/2 oz Sweet Vermouth
Stir.
Strain into chilled glass or pour
contents (with ice) into short glass.
Garnish with Cherry or Lemon
Twist.

MAPLE LEAF
Fill glass with ice.
1 oz Canadian Whiskey
1/4 oz Lemon Juice
1 tsp Maple Syrup
Shake.
Strain into chilled glass.

MARCONI WIRELESS
Fill glass with ice.
1 1/2 oz Apple Brandy
1/2 oz Sweet Vermouth
2-3 dashes of Orange Bitters
Shake.
Strain into chilled glass.

MARGARITA
Fill glass with ice.
1 1/2 oz Tequila
1/2 oz Triple Sec
Dash of Lime Juice
3 oz Sour Mix
Dash of Orange Juice (optional)
Shake.
Rub rim of second glass with Lime
and dip into kosher salt.
Pour contents (with ice)
or strain into salted glass.
Garnish with Lime.

MARGARITA (frozen)

In Blender:
1 cup of Ice
1 1/2 oz Tequila
1/2 oz Triple Sec
1/2 oz Lime Juice
3 oz Sour Mix
Blend until smooth.
If too thick add juice.
If too thin add ice.
Rub rim of glass with Lime and dip
into Kosher Salt.
Pour contents into salted glass.

MARLON BRANDO (floater)

Fill glass with ice.
1 1/2 oz Scotch (bottom)
1/2 oz Amaretto
1/4 oz of Cream (top)

MARMALADE

Fill glass with ice.
1 oz Benedictine
3/4 oz Curacao
Dash of Orange Juice
Fill with Tonic Water.
Stir.
Garnish with Orange.

MARTINEZ

Fill glass with ice.
1 1/2 oz Gin
2 oz Dry Vermouth
2 dashes of Maraschino Liqueur or
Triple Sec
2 dashes of Bitters
Shake.
Serve or strain into chilled glass.
Garnish with Cherry.

MARTINI

(*CAUTION:* DRY usually means
less Vermouth than usual.
EXTRA DRY can mean even less
Vermouth than usual or
no Vermouth at all.)
Fill glass with ice.
2 oz Gin or Vodka
1/2 oz Dry Vermouth
Stir.
Strain into chilled glass
or pour contents (with ice)
into short glass.
Garnish with Lemon Twist or Olives
or cocktail onions.

MARY GARDEN

Fill glass with ice.
1 1/2 oz Dubonnet
3/4 oz Dry Vermouth
Shake.
Strain into chilled glass.

MARY PICKFORD

Fill glass with ice.
1 1/2 oz Rum
3/4 oz Pineapple Juice
Dash of Grenadine
Shake.
Strain into chilled glass.

MATADOR

Fill glass with ice.
1 1/2 oz Tequila
1 1/2 oz Pineapple Juice
1/2 oz Lime Juice
1/2 tsp Sugar Syrup
Shake.
Strain into chilled glass.

MAURICE

Fill glass with ice.
1 oz Gin
1/2 oz Dry Vermouth
1/2 oz Sweet Vermouth
1/2 oz Orange Juice
Dash of Bitters
Shake.
Strain into chilled glass.

MAXIM

Fill glass with ice.
1 1/2 oz Gin
1 oz Dry Vermouth
Dash of White Creme De Cacao
Shake.
Strain into chilled glass.

MAXIM'S A LONDRES

Fill glass with ice.
1 1/2 oz Brandy
Dash of Orange Liqueur
Dash of Orange Juice
Shake.
Strain into chilled glass.
Fill with Champagne.
Garnish with Orange Twist.

MAY BLOSSOM FIZZ

Fill glass with ice.
2 oz Swedish Punch
2 oz Lemon Juice
Dash of Grenadine
Shake.
Fill with Soda Water.

McCLELLAND

Fill glass with ice.
1 1/2 oz Sloe Gin
3/4 oz Triple Sec or Curacao
2 dashes of Orange Bitters
Shake.
Strain into chilled glass.

MEADOWLARK LEMON

Fill glass with ice.
1 1/2 oz Vodka
1/2 oz Orange Liqueur
1/2 oz Lemon Juice or Sour Mix
Stir.
Strain into chilled glass.
Garnish with Lemon.

M

MEDITERRANEAN COFFEE
1 1/2 oz Greek Brandy
1/2 oz Galliano
Fill with hot Black Coffee
Top with Whipped Cream.

MEISTER-BATION (frozen)
In Blender:
1 cup of Ice
1 1/2 oz Jaegermeister
1/2 oz Banana Llqueur
1 Tbsp Cream of Coconut
2 Tbsp Vanilla Ice Cream
1/2 cup fresh or canned Pineapple
Blend until smooth.
Garnish with packaged condom.

MELON BALL
Fill glass with ice.
1 oz Vodka
1 oz Melon Liqueur
Fill with Orange Juice.
Shake.
Garnish with Orange.

MELON BREEZE
Fill glass with ice.
1 oz Vodka
1 oz Melon Liqueur
Fill with equal parts Cranberry and
Pineapple Juice.
Shake.
Garnish with Pineapple and Cherry.

MELON COCKTAIL
Fill glass with ice.
2 oz Gin
1/2 oz Maraschino Liqueur
1/2 oz Lemon Juice
Shake.
Strain into chilled glass.
Garnish with Cherry.

MELON COLADA (frozen)
In Blender:
1 cup of Ice
1 oz Rum
1 oz Melon Liqueur
2 Tbsp Cream of Coconut
1/2 cup fresh Honeydew melon or
fresh or canned Pineapple
1 Tbsp Vanilla Ice Cream
Blend until smooth.
If too thick add juice or fruit.
If too thin add ice or ice cream.
Garnish with melon
or Pineapple and Cherry.

MELON GRIND
Fill glass with ice.
3/4 oz Vodka
3/4 oz Rum
3/4 oz Melon Liqueur
Fill with Pineapple Juice.
Shake.

MELON ROYALE
1/2 oz Melon Liqueur
Fill with Champagne.

MELON SOMBRERO
Fill glass with ice.
2 oz Melon Liqueur
Fill with Milk or Cream.
Shake.

MELON SOUR
Fill glass with ice.
2 oz Melon Liqueur
Fill with Sour Mix.
Shake.
Garnish with Orange and Cherry.

MELTDOWN
1 oz Vodka
1/2 oz Peach Schnapps
Stir.

MEMPHIS BELLE
Fill glass with ice.
1 1/2 oz Brandy
3/4 oz Southern Comfort
1/2 oz Lemon Juice
3 dashes of Bitters
Shake.
Strain into chilled glass.

MENAGE a TROIS
Fill glass with ice.
3/4 oz Irish Cream
3/4 oz Black Raspberry Liqueur
3/4 oz Hazelnut Liqueur
Fill with Milk or Cream.
Shake.

MERRY WIDOW
Fill glass with ice.
1 1/4 oz Cherry Brandy
1 1/4 oz Maraschino Liqueur
Shake.
Strain into chilled glass.

METAL HELMET
Fill glass with ice.
1 1/4 oz Banana Liqueur
3/4 oz Vodka
Fill with Milk.
Shake.

MEXICAN BLACKJACK
Fill glass with ice.
1/2 oz Tequila
1/2 oz Blended Whiskey
1/2 oz Bourbon
1/2 oz Triple Sec or Curacao
Shake.
Strain into chilled glass.

MEXICAN CAPPUCCINO
1 1/2 oz Coffee Liqueur
Fill with espresso.
Top with steamed Milk.
Sprinkle with Powdered Sugar.

MEXICAN COFFEE
2 oz Coffee Liqueur
or 2 oz Tequila
Fill with hot Black Coffee.
Top with Whipped Cream.
Sprinkle with Shaved
Chocolate or Sprinkles.

MEXICAN COFFEE 2
1 oz Tequila
1 oz Coffee Liqueur
Fill with hot Black Coffee.
Top with Whipped Cream.
Sprinkle with Shaved
Chocolate or Sprinkles.

MEXICAN FLAG (floater)
1/2 oz Sloe Gin (bottom)
1/2 oz Vodka
1/2 oz Melon Liqueur (top)

MEXICAN MISSILE
3/4 oz Tequila
3/4 oz Green Chartreuse
Dash of Tabasco Sauce

MEXICAN SCREW
Fill glass with ice.
2 oz Tequila
Fill with Orange Juice.
Garnish with Orange.

MEXICAN SEABREEZE
Fill glass with ice.
2 oz Tequila
Fill with equal parts Cranberry and
Pineapple Juice.
Garnish with Lime.

MEXICANO
Fill glass with ice.
2 oz Rum
1/2 oz Kummel
1 oz Orange Juice
3 dashes of Bitters
Shake.

MIAMI BEACH
Fill glass with ice.
2 oz Scotch
1 oz Dry Vermouth
1 oz Grapefruit Juice
Shake.
Strain into chilled glass.

MIAMI ICE
Fill glass with ice.
1/2 oz Vodka
1/2 oz Gin
1/2 oz Rum
1/2 oz Peach Schnapps
Dash of Cranberry Juice
Fill with Lemon-Lime Soda.

MIAMI MELON
Fill glass with ice.
1 oz Vodka
1 oz Melon Liqueur
Fill with Milk or Cream.
Shake.

MIAMI VICE
Fill glass with ice.
1 oz Rum
1/2 oz Blackberry Brandy
1/2 oz Banana Liqueur
Dash of Lime Juice
Dash of Grenadine
1 Tbsp Cream De Coconut
Fill with Pineapple Juice.
Shake.
Garnish with Pineapple.

MICH
Fill glass with ice.
1 1/2 oz Gin
1/2 oz Sloe Gin
Dash of Lime Juice
Fill with equal parts Sour Mix and
Grapefruit Juice.
Shake.

MIDNIGHT DREAM
Fill glass with ice.
1 1/2 oz Vodka
1/2 oz Black Raspberry Liqueur
Dash of Cream
Fill with Cranberry Juice.
Shake.

MIDNIGHT MARTINI
Fill glass with ice.
2 oz Vodka
1/4 oz Coffee Liqueur
or Coffee Brandy
Stir.
Strain into chilled glass or pour
contents (with ice) into shot glass.
Garnish with Lemon Twist.

MIDNIGHT SNOWSTORM
2 oz White Creme De Menthe
Fill with Hot Chocolate.
Stir.
Top with Whipped Cream.
Dribble 1/2 oz Green Creme De
Menthe on top.

MIDNIGHT SUN
Fill glass with ice.
2 1/2 oz Vodka
1/2 oz Grenadine
Stir.
Strain into chilled glass.

M

MIDWAY RAT
Fill glass with ice.
1 oz Rum
1/2 oz Amaretto
1/2 oz Coffee Liqueur
Fill glass with Pineapple Juice.
Shake.
Garnish with Orange, Cherry and a
Black Licorice Whip.

MIKE COLLINS aka
JOE COLLINS
Fill glass with ice.
2 oz Scotch
Fill with Sour Mix.
Shake.
Dash of Soda Water
Garnish with Orange and Cherry.

MILANO COFFEE
1 oz Rum
1 oz Amaretto
Fill with hot Black Coffee.
Top with Whipped Cream.
Garnish with Shaved Almonds.

MILLIONAIRE
Fill glass with ice.
1 1/2 oz Bourbon
1/2 oz Pernod
1 tsp Curacao or Triple Sec
1 tsp Grenadine
1/2 Egg White
Shake.
Strain into chilled glass.

MILLIONAIRE'S COFFEE
1/2 oz Coffee Liqueur
1/2 oz Irish Cream
1/2 oz Orange Liqueur
1/2 oz Hazelnut Liqueur
Fill with hot Black Coffee.
Top with Whipped Cream.
Sprinkle with Shaved
Chocolate or Sprinkles.

MIMOSA
Fill glass 3/4 with ice.
Fill 3/4 with Champagne.
Dash of Orange Liqueur
or Triple Sec (optional)
Fill with Orange Juice.
Garnish with Orange.

MIND ERASER
Fill glass with ice.
1 oz Vodka
1 oz Coffee Liqueur
Fill with Soda Water.
Garnish with a Lime.

MIND OBLITERATOR
Fill glass with ice.
1 oz Vodka
1 oz Coffee Liqueur
Fill with Champagne.

MINSTREL FRAPPE
Fill large stemmed glass (Red Wine
glass, Champagne saucer) with
crushed ice.
1/2 oz Vodka
1/2 oz Coffee Liqueur
1/2 oz Brandy
1/2 oz White Creme De Menthe

MINT CONDITION aka
GROUND ZERO
Fill glass with ice.
3/4 oz Vodka
1/2 oz Coffee Liqueur
3/4 oz Bourbon
3/4 oz Peppermint Schnapps
Shake.
Serve or strain into chilled glass.

MINT JULEP
Muddle together in a glass:
10-20 Fresh Mint Leaves
1 tsp Sugar
2 Tbsp Water
Fill with crushed Ice.
Fill 7/8 with Bourbon.
Float 1/2 oz Rum on top.
Garnish with 3 or 4 leaves.

MISSISSIPPI MUD
1/2 oz Coffee Liqueur
1/2 oz Hazelnut Liqueur
1/2 oz Triple Sec
1/2 oz Rum
Fill with hot Black Coffee.
Top with Whipped Cream.
Sprinkle with Shaved
Chocolate or Sprinkles.

MISSISSIPPI MULE
Fill glass with ice.
1 1/2 oz Gin
1 tsp Creme De Cassis
1 tsp Lemon Juice
Shake.
Garnish with Lemon.

MISSOURI MULE
Fill glass with ice.
2 oz Southern Comfort
Fill with Ginger Beer.
Stir.
Garnish with Lime.

MIST
Is another way to say "On the
rocks," but preferably with Shaved
or crushed ice.

MOCHA BERRY FRAPPE (frozen)
In Blender:
1/2 cup of Ice
1 oz Coffee Liqueur
1 oz Black Raspberry Liqueur
1 oz Dark Creme De Cacao
Scoop of Vanilla Ice Cream
Blend until smooth.
If too thick add milk or cream.
If too thin add ice or ice cream.
Sprinkle with Shaved Chocolate or
Sprinkles.

MOCHA MINT
Fill glass with ice.
3/4 oz Coffee Liqueur
or Coffee Brandy
3/4 oz White Creme De Menthe
3/4 oz White Creme De Cacao
Shake.
Strain into chilled glass.

MOCKINGBIRD
Fill glass with ice.
1 1/2 oz Tequila
1/2 oz White Creme De Menthe
1 oz Lime Juice
Shake.
Strain into chilled glass.

MODERN
Fill glass with ice.
1 1/2 oz Sloe Gin
3/4 oz Scotch
Dash of Pernod
Dash of Grenadine
Dash of Orange Bitters
Shake.

MODERN 2
Fill glass with ice.
3 oz Scotch
Dash of Dark Rum
Dash of Pernod
Dash of Lemon Juice
Dash of Orange Bitters
Shake.
Garnish with Cherry.

MOJITO
Fill glass with ice.
2 oz Light Rum
1 tsp Sugar
Dash of Lime Juice
Fill with Soda Water.
Garnish with Lime and Mint Sprigs.

MOJO
Fill glass with ice.
1 oz Rum
1 oz Cherry Brandy
3 oz Amber Beer or Ale
Fill with equal parts of Orange
Juice, Pineapple Juice,
Cola and Lemon-Lime Soda.

MOLL
Fill glass with ice.
1 oz Gin
1 oz Sloe Gin
1 oz Dry Vermouth
Dash of Orange Bitters
1/2 tsp Sugar (optional)
Shake.
Strain into chilled glass.

MON CHERIE
Fill glass with ice.
1 oz Cherry Brandy
1 oz White Creme De Cacao
1 oz of Milk or Cream.
Shake.

MONGA MONGA (frozen)
In Blender:
1 cup of Ice
1 1/2 oz Brandy
1 oz Dark Rum
1 oz Strawberry Liqueur
1 oz Lime Juice
1/2 cup fresh or frozen
Strawberries
Blend until smooth.
If too thick add fruit.
If too thin add ice.
Garnish with Lime.

MONGOLIAN MOTHER
Fill glass with ice.
Dash of Vodka
Dash of Gin
Dash of Rum
Dash of Tequila
Dash of Triple Sec
Dash of Peach Schnapps
Dash of Amaretto
Dash of Sloe Gin
Dash of Southern Comfort
Dash of 151-Proof Rum
Dash of Grenadine
Fill with equal parts Cranberry and
Orange Juice.
Shake.
Garnish with Orange, Lime, Lemon
and Cherry.

MONK JUICE
Fill glass with ice.
2 oz Hazelnut Liqueur
Fill with Milk or Cream.
Shake.
Michele Cooke

MONK SLIDE (floater)
1/2 oz Coffee Liqueur (top)
1/2 oz Irish Cream
1/2 oz Hazelnut Liqueur
(bottom)

MONK'S COFFEE
1 oz Benedictine
1 oz Orange Liqueur
Fill with hot Black Coffee.
Top with Whipped Cream.
Garnish with Orange.

M

MONKEY JUICE
Fill glass with ice.
1 1/2 oz Dark Rum
1/2 oz Irish Cream
1/2 oz Banana Liqueur
Stir.

MONKEY SPECIAL (frozen)
In Blender:
1 cup of Ice
1 oz Dark Rum
1 oz Light Rum
1/2 ripe peeled Banana
1/2 scoop Vanilla Ice Cream
Blend until smooth.
If too thick add milk or cream. If too
thin add ice or ice cream.
Sprinkle with Shaved Chocolate.

MONKEY WRENCH
Fill glass with ice.
2 oz Rum
Fill with Grapefruit Juice.

MONKEY WRENCH 2
Fill glass with ice.
1 oz Vodka
1 oz Amaretto
1 oz Orange Juice
Strain into shot glass.

MONTANA
Fill glass with ice.
1 1/2 oz Brandy
1 oz Port
1/2 oz Dry Vermouth
Stir.

MONTE CARLO
Fill glass with ice.
1 1/2 oz Whiskey
1/2 oz Benedictine
3 dashes of Bitters
Shake.

MONTE CRISTO COFFEE
1 oz Coffee Liqueur
1 oz Orange Liqueur
Fill with hot Black Coffee.
Top with Whipped Cream.
Garnish with Orange.

MONTEGO BAY COFFEE
1/2 oz Dark Rum
1/2 oz Coffee Liqueur
Fill with hot Black Coffee.
Top with Whipped Cream.
Garnish with Banana.

MONTMARTE
Fill glass with ice.
1 1/2 oz Gin
1/2 oz Sweet Vermouth
1/2 oz Triple Sec
Stir.
Strain into chilled glass.

MONTREAL CLUB BOUNCER
Fill glass with ice.
1 1/2 oz Gin
1 oz Pernod

MOODY BLUE
Fill glass with ice.
3/4 oz Vodka
3/4 oz Peach Schnapps
3/4 oz Blue Curacao
Fill with Pineapple Juice.
Shake.
H.R.C.

MOONBEAM
Fill glass with ice.
1 oz Amaretto
1 oz White Creme De Cacao
Fill with Milk or Cream.

MOONLIGHT
Fill glass with ice.
2 oz Apple Brandy
1 oz Lemon Juice
1 tsp Powdered Sugar
or Sugar Syrup
Shake.
Splash of Soda Water (optional)
Garnish with Lemon Twist.

MOONPIE (frozen)
In Blender:
1 cup of Ice
1 oz Amber Rum
Dash of Peach Schnapps
Dash of Banana Liqueur
1/2 a ripe Banana
1/2 ripe peeled Peach
Dash of Orange Juice
Blend until smooth.
Garnish with Banana.

MOOSE MILK
In a large mixing bowl:
20 oz Dark Rum
10 oz Tia Maria
40 oz Milk
1/2 gallon Vanilla Ice Cream
Stir until smooth.
Serves 20 people.

MOOSEBERRY
Fill glass with ice.
1 oz Vodka
1 oz Amaretto
2 oz Cranberry Juice
2 oz Sour Mix
Shake.
Strain into chilled glass.
Top with 1/2 oz Orange Liqueur.

MORNING
Fill glass with ice.
1 oz Brandy
1 oz Dry Vermouth
Dash of Triple Sec or Curacao
Dash of Maraschino Liqueur
Dash of Pernod
2 dashes of Orange Bitters
Stir.

MORNING GLORY
Fill glass with ice.
1 oz Scotch
1 oz Brandy
Dash of Pernod
2 dashes of Curacao
2 dashes of Bitters
Shake.
Top with Soda Water.
Stir with a spoon dipped in water
and coated with sugar.

MOSCOW MIMOSA
Fill glass with ice.
1/2 oz Vodka
Fill with equal parts Champagne
and Orange Juice.

MOSCOW MULE
Fill glass with ice.
2 oz Vodka
Fill with Ginger Beer.
Stir.
Garnish with Lime.

MOTHER LOVE
Fill glass with ice.
1 1/2 oz Canadian Whiskey
1/2 oz Peppermint Schnapps
Stir.

MOTHER SHERMAN
Fill glass with ice.
1 1/2 oz Apricot Brandy
1 oz Orange Juice
3-4 dashes of Orange Bitters
Shake.
Garnish with Orange.

MOULIN ROUGE
Fill glass with ice.
1 1/2 oz Sloe Gin
1/2 oz Sweet Vermouth
3 dashes of Bitters
Shake.
Strain into chilled glass.

MOUND BAR
2 oz Coconut Rum
Fill with Hot Chocolate.
Top with Whipped Cream.
Sprinkle with Shaved Chocolate.

MOUND BAR 2
Fill glass with ice.
3/4 oz Coconut Rum
3/4 oz Dark Creme De Cacao
3/4 oz Irish Cream
3/4 oz Milk or Cream
Shake.
Strain into chilled glass.

MOUNT FUJI
Fill glass with ice.
1 1/2 oz Gin
1/2 oz Lemon Juice
1/2 oz Heavy Cream
1 tsp Pineapple Juice
1 Egg White
3 dashes of Maraschino Liqueur
Shake.

MOUNT VESUVIUS
Fill glass with ice.
1 oz Coconut Rum
1 oz Triple Sec
Dash of Grenadine
Fill with Orange Juice.
Shake.
Top with 151-Proof Rum.

MOUNTAIN RED PUNCH
Fill glass with ice.
1/2 oz Amaretto
1/2 oz Brandy
1/2 oz Cherry Brandy
2 oz Ginger Ale
Fill with Red Wine.

MUDSLIDE
Fill glass with ice.
1 oz Coffee Liqueur
1 oz Irish Cream
1 oz Vodka
Shake.

MUDSLIDE 2
Fill glass with ice.
1 oz Vodka
1 oz Coffee Liqueur
1 oz Irish Cream
Fill with Milk or Cream.

MUDSLIDE 3
Fill glass with ice.
1 oz Dark Creme De Cacao
1 oz Irish Cream
Shake.

MUDSLIDE (floater)
1/2 oz Coffee Liqueur (bottom)
1/2 oz Irish Cream
1/2 oz Vodka (top)

M

MUDSLIDE (frozen)
In Blender:
1/2 cup of Ice
1 oz Coffee Liqueur
1 oz Irish Cream
1 oz Vodka
Scoop of Vanilla Ice Cream
Blend until smooth.
If too thick add milk or cream.
If too thin add ice or ice cream.
Sprinkle with Shaved Chocolate or
Sprinkles.

MUDSLING
1/2 oz Coffee Liqueur
1/2 oz Irish Cream
1/2 oz Vodka
Fill with Hot Chocolate.
Top with Whipped Cream.
Sprinkle with Shaved Chocolate.

MULE SKINNER
1 1/2 oz Bourbon
1/2 oz Blackberry Brandy

MULE'S HIND LEG
Fill glass with ice.
3/4 oz Gin
3/4 oz Apple Brandy
3/4 oz Benedictine
3/4 oz Apricot Brandy
3/4 oz Maple Syrup
Shake.

MULLED CIDER
Place 2 smashed Cinnamon Sticks,
10 whole Cloves,
and 1 tsp Allspice Berries into
cheese cloth bag.
In saucepan on low heat, stir
together 1/2 gallon of Apple Cider,
and 1/2 cup Brown Sugar.
After sugar dissolves, place bag
containing spices in and keep
heating for 5 minutes, then serve.
Garnish with Cinnamon Stick and
Dried Apple Ring.
(serves 10-15 people)

NAKED LADY
Fill glass with ice.
1 oz Rum
1 oz Apricot Brandy
Dash of Grenadine
1 oz Sour Mix
Shake.
Strain into chilled glass.

NANTUCKET BREEZE
Fill glass with ice.
1 oz Vodka
1 oz Cranberry Liqueur
Fill with Grapefruit Juice.
Garnish with Lime.

NANTUCKET RED aka POINSETTIA
Fill glass 3/4 with ice.
Fill 3/4 with Champagne.
Fill with Cranberry Juice.
Garnish with Lime.

NAPOLEON
Fill glass with ice.
1 oz Gin
1 oz Orange Liqueur
1 oz Dubonnet Rouge
Stir.
Strain into chilled glass.
Garnish with Orange Twist.

NARRAGANSETT
Fill glass with ice.
1 1/2 oz Bourbon
1 oz Sweet Vermouth
Dash of Anisette
Stir.
Garnish with Lemon Twist.

NASTY NETTY
Fill glass with ice.
2 oz Citrus Rum
Dash of Grenadine
2 oz Sour Mix
Shake.
Fill with Lemon-Lime Soda.
Annette and Scot

NAVY GROG
Fill glass with ice.
1 oz Light Rum
1 oz Dark Rum
1/2 oz Orange Juice
1/2 oz Guava Nectar
1/2 oz Pineapple Juice
1/2 oz Lime Juice
1/2 oz Orgeat Syrup
Shake.
Garnish with Lime and Mint Sprig.

NEGRONI
Fill glass with ice.
1 oz Gin
1 oz Campari
1 oz Dry or Sweet Vermouth
Stir.
Strain into chilled glass.
Garnish with Lemon Twist.

NELSON'S BLOOD
Fill glass with ice.
2 oz Pusser's Rum
Dash of Lime Juice.
Fill with Ginger Beer.

NELSON'S BLOOD 2
1 oz Tawny Port
Fill with Champagne.

NEON
Fill glass with ice.
1 oz Citrus Vodka
1/2 oz Melon Liqueur
1/2 oz Blue Curacao
Dash of Lime Juice.
Fill with Sour Mix.
Shake.

NERVOUS BREAKDOWN
Fill glass with ice.
1 1/2 oz Vodka
1/2 oz Black Raspberry Liqueur
Fill with Soda Water.
Top with splash of Cranberry Juice.
Garnish with Lime.

NESI (floater)
1/2 oz Melon Liqueur (bottom)
1/2 oz Irish Cream
1/2 oz Jaegermeister (top)

NETHERLAND
Fill glass with ice.
1 oz Brandy
1 oz Triple Sec
Dash of Orange Juice
Shake.
Serve or strain into chilled glass.

NEUTRON BOMB (floater)
1/2 oz Coffee Liqueur (bottom)
1/2 oz Irish Cream
1/2 oz Butterscotch Schnapps (top)

NEVINS
Fill glass with ice.
1 1/2 oz Bourbon
1 oz Apricot Brandy
1 oz Grapefruit Juice
1 tsp Lemon Juice
3 dashes of Bitters
Shake.

NEW WORLD
Fill glass with ice.
1 1/2 oz Whiskey
1/2 oz Lime Juice
1 tsp Grenadine
Shake.
Serve or strain into chilled glass.
Garnish with Lime.

NEW YORK COCKTAIL
Fill glass with ice.
1 1/2 oz Whiskey
1/2 oz Lime Juice
1 tsp Sugar Syrup
or Powdered Sugar
Dash of Grenadine
Shake.
Garnish with Orange Twist.

NEW YORK SLAMMER
Fill glass with ice.
1 oz Blended Whiskey
1/2 oz Banana Liqueur
1/2 oz Sloe Gin
Fill with Orange Juice.
Shake.

NEWBURY
Fill glass with ice.
1 oz Gin
1 oz Sweet Vermouth
3 dashes of Curacao
Stir.
Strain into chilled glass.
Garnish with Orange and Lemon
Twist.

NIAGARA FALLS
Fill glass with ice.
1 1/2 oz Whiskey
1/2 oz Irish Mist
1/2 oz Heavy Cream
Shake.
Strain into chilled glass.

NIGHTINGALE
Fill glass with ice.
1 oz Banana Liqueur
1/2 oz Curacao
1 oz Cream
1/2 Egg White
Shake.
Strain into chilled glass.
Garnish with Cherry.

NIGHT TRAIN (frozen)
In Blender:
1/2 cup of Ice
1 oz Rum
1/2 oz Cherry Brandy
1/2 oz White Creme De Cacao
1 oz Cream of Coconut
Dash of Pineapple Juice
Scoop of Vanilla Ice Cream
Blend until smooth.
Garnish with Cherry.

NINETEEN
Fill glass with ice.
2 oz Dry Vermouth
1/2 oz Gin
1/2 oz Kirschwasser
Dash of Pernod
1 tsp Sugar Syrup
Shake.
Strain into chilled glass.

NINETEEN PICK-ME-UP
Fill glass with ice.
1 1/2 oz Pernod
3/4 oz Gin
3 dashes of Sugar Syrup
3 dashes of Bitters
3 dashes of Orange Bitters
Shake.
Top with Soda Water.

M
N

NINE-ONE-ONE or 911 aka
24 KARAT NIGHTMARE
1 oz 100-Proof Cinnamon
Schnapps
1 oz 100-Proof Peppermint
Schnapps

NINJA (floater)
1/2 oz Dark Creme De Cacao
(bottom)
1/2 oz Melon Liqueur
1/2 oz Hazelnut Liqueur (top)

NINJA TURTLE
Fill glass with ice.
1 1/2 oz Gin
1/2 oz Blue Curacao
Fill with Orange Juice.
Stir.

NINJA TURTLE 2
Fill glass with ice.
1 oz Coconut Rum
1 oz Melon Liqueur
1 oz Pineapple Juice
Shake.
Strain into chilled glass.
Garnish with Cherry.

NINOTCHKA
Fill glass with ice.
1 1/2 oz Vodka
1/2 oz White Creme De Cacao
1 tsp Lemon Juice
Shake.
Serve or strain into chilled glass.

NO PROBLEM
Fill glass with ice.
1 oz Coconut Rum
1 oz Cherry Brandy
1 1/2 oz Apple Juice
1/2 oz Orange Juice
1/2 oz Lime Juice
1/2 oz Sugar Syrup
Shake.

NO TELL MOTEL
Fill glass with ice.
1 oz Bourbon
1 oz Mentholated Schnapps
Stir.
Strain into chilled glass.

NOCTURNAL
Fill glass with ice.
2 oz Bourbon
1 oz Dark Creme De Cacao
Fill with Cream or Milk.
Shake.

NORTHERN LIGHTS
Fill glass with ice.
2 oz Yukon Jack
Dash of Peach Schnapps (optional)
Fill with equal parts of Orange and
Cranberry Juice.
Stir.

NORTHERN LIGHTS 2
1 oz Yukon Jack
1 oz Orange Liqueur
Fill with hot Black Coffee.
Top with Whipped Cream.

NUCLEAR MELTDOWN aka
THREE MILE ISLAND
Fill glass with ice.
1/2 oz Vodka
1/2 oz Gin
1/2 oz Rum
1/2 oz Tequila
1/2 oz Triple Sec
Fill with Sour Mix
or Pineapple Juice.
Shake.
Top with 1/2 oz Melon Liqueur.

NUT AND HONEY (frozen)
In Blender:
1/2 cup of Ice
1 1/2 oz Vodka
1/2 oz Hazelnut Liqueur
1 Tbsp Honey
Scoop of Vanilla Ice Cream
Blend until smooth.
If too thick add milk.
If too thin add ice or ice cream.

NUTCRACKER
Fill glass with ice.
1 oz Vodka
1 oz Coffee Liqueur
1 oz Irish Cream
Shake.

NUTCRACKER 2
Fill glass with ice.
1 oz Vodka
1/2 oz Irish Cream
1/2 oz Amaretto
1/2 oz Hazelnut Liqueur
Shake.

NUTCRACKER (frozen)
In Blender:
1/2 cup of Ice
1 oz Vodka
1/2 oz Irish Cream
1/2 oz Amaretto
1/2 oz Hazelnut Liqueur
Scoop of Vanilla Ice Cream
Blend until smooth.
If too thick add milk or cream.
If too thin add ice or ice cream.

NUTS AND BERRIES
Fill glass with ice.
3/4 oz Black Raspberry Liqueur
3/4 oz Hazelnut Liqueur
3/4 oz Coffee Liqueur
Fill with Cream.
Shake.

NUTS AND BERRIES 2
Fill glass with ice.
1/2 oz Vodka
1/2 oz Irish Cream
1/2 oz Black Raspberry Liqueur
1/2 oz Hazelnut Liqueur
Shake.
Strain into chilled glass.

NUTTY CHINAMAN
Fill glass with ice.
1 oz Ginger Liqueur
1 oz Irish Cream
1 oz Hazelnut Liqueur
Stir.
Strain into chilled glass.

NUTTY COLADA (frozen)
In Blender:
1/2 cup of Ice
1 oz Amaretto
1 oz Rum
2 Tbsp Cream of Coconut
1/2 cup fresh or canned Pineapple
1 Tbsp Vanilla Ice Cream (optional)
Blend until smooth.
If too thick add fruit or juice.
If too thin add ice or ice cream.
Garnish with Pineapple, Cherry and
Shaved Almonds.

NUTTY IRISH COOLER
Fill glass with ice.
1 oz Irish Cream
1 oz Hazelnut Liqueur
Fill with Iced Coffee.
Shake.
Top with Whipped Cream.

NUTTY IRISHMAN
Fill glass with ice.
1 oz Irish Cream
1 oz Hazelnut Liqueur
Stir.

NUTTY IRISHMAN 2
Fill glass with ice.
1 oz Irish Whiskey
1 oz Hazelnut Liqueur
Fill with Milk or Cream.
Shake.

NUTTY IRISHMAN COFFEE
1 oz Irish Cream or Irish Whiskey
1 oz Hazelnut Liqueur
Fill with hot Black Coffee.
Top with Whipped Cream.
Sprinkle with Shaved Chocolate.

NUTTY JAMAICAN
Fill glass with ice.
1 oz Dark Rum
1 oz Hazelnut Liqueur
Stir.
Strain into chilled glass.

NUTTY RUSSIAN
Fill glass with ice.
1 oz Vodka
1 oz Hazelnut Liqueur
Fill with Milk or Cream.
Shake.

OATMEAL COOKIE
Fill glass with ice.
1/2 oz Jaegermeister
1/2 oz Cinnamon Schnapps
1/2 oz Irish Cream
1/2 oz Butterscotch Schnapps
Shake.
Strain into chilled glass.

OATMEAL COOKIE 2
Fill glass with ice.
3/4 oz Coffee Liqueur
3/4 oz Irish Cream
3/4 oz Cinnamon Schnapps
Dash of Milk or Cream
Shake.
Strain into chilled glass.

OCEAN VIEW SPECIAL
Fill glass with ice.
1 oz Vodka
1 oz Galliano
1 oz Green Creme De Menthe
Fill with Orange Juice.
Shake.

ODD McINTYRE
Fill glass with ice.
1 oz Brandy
1 oz Triple Sec
1 oz Lillet Blanc
1/2 oz Lemon Juice
Shake.
Strain into chilled glass.

OH, HENRY
Fill glass with ice.
1 1/2 oz Whiskey
1/4 oz Benedictine
3 oz Ginger Ale
Stir.
Garnish with Lemon.

OIL SLICK
Fill glass with ice.
1 oz Vodka
1 oz White Creme De Cacao
1 oz Milk
Shake.
Float 1 oz Dark Rum on top.

OIL SLICK 2
1 oz Peppermint Schnapps
1/2 oz Blue Curacao
Stir.
Float 1/2 oz Jaegermeister
on top.

OLD FASHIONED
Muddle together in glass:
Stemless Maraschino Cherry,
Orange Slice, 1/2 tsp Sugar,
4-5 dashes of Bitters.
Fill glass with ice.
2 oz Whiskey
Splash with Soda Water.
Stir.

OLD GROANER
Fill glass with ice.
1 1/2 oz Whiskey
1/2 oz Amaretto
Stir.

OLD GROANER'S WIFE
Fill glass with ice.
1 1/2 oz Whiskey
1/2 oz Amaretto
Fill with Cream or Milk.
Shake.

OLIVER TWIST
Fill glass with ice.
2 oz Gin or Vodka
1/2 oz Dry Vermouth
Stir.
Strain into chilled glass or pour
contents (with ice) into shot glass.
Garnish with Lemon Twist and
Olives.

OLYMPIC
Fill glass with ice.
1 oz Brandy
1 oz Curacao or Triple Sec
1 oz Orange Juice
Shake.

ONE SEVENTY
1 oz Brandy
Fill with Champagne.

OOM PAUL
Fill glass with ice.
1 oz Apple Brandy
1 oz Dubonnet Rouge
3 dashes of Bitters
Shake.

OPEN GRAVE
Fill glass with ice.
1/2 oz 151-Proof Rum
1/2 oz Dark Rum
1/2 oz Vodka
1/2 oz Southern Comfort
1/2 oz Peach Schnapps
Fill with equal parts Sour Mix,
Orange, Grapefruit, Pineapple
and Cherry Juice.

OPENING
Fill glass with ice.
1 1/2 oz Whiskey
1 tsp Sweet Vermouth
1 tsp Grenadine
Stir.
Strain into chilled glass.

OPERA
Fill glass with ice.
1 1/2 oz Gin
1/2 oz Dubonnet
1/2 oz Maraschino Liqueur
Stir.
Strain into chilled glass.
Garnish with Orange Twist.

ORANGE BLOSSOM
Fill glass with ice.
1 oz Gin
1 oz Orange Juice
1/4 tsp Sugar Syrup
or Powdered Sugar
Shake.
Strain into chilled glass.
Garnish with Orange.

ORANGE BUCK
Fill glass with ice.
1 1/2 oz Gin
1 oz Orange Juice
1 Tbsp Lime Juice
Shake.
Strain into chilled glass.
Top with Ginger Ale.

ORANGE DROP
Moisten inside of shot glass with
Orange Juice, then coat inside of
glass with Sugar.
Fill shot glass with chilled Vodka.

ORANGE DROP 2
Fill shot glass with Orange Vodka
Coat Orange wedge with Sugar.

ORANGE FREEZE (frozen)
In Blender:
1/2 cup of Ice
2 oz Vodka
Scoop of Orange Sherbet
Dash of Orange Juice
Blend until smooth.
If too thick add orange juice.
If too thin add sherbet.

ORANGE JULIUS (frozen)
In Blender:
1/2 cup of Ice
1 1/2 oz Vodka
1/2 oz Triple Sec or Curacao
Scoop of Orange Sherbet
1 Egg White
Blend until smooth.
If too thick add orange juice.
If too thin add ice or sherbet.

ORANGE KRUSH
Fill glass with ice.
1 1/2 oz Vodka
1/2 oz Triple Sec
1 oz Orange Juice
1 oz Lemon-Lime Soda
Stir.
Serve or strain into short glass.

ORANGE LIQUEUR
(type liqueur)
Mix together:
40 Coffee Beans
1 mashed ripe Orange
1 qt Vodka
1 1/2 cups Sugar
Store for 3 months.
Strain through cheesecloth.

ORANGE MARGARITA (frozen)
In Blender:
1/2 cup of Ice
1 1/2 oz Tequila
1/2 oz Triple Sec
or Orange Liqueur
Dash of Lime Juice
Scoop of Orange Sherbet
Blend until smooth.
If too thick add juice.
If too thin add ice or sherbet.
Garnish with Orange and Lime.

ORANGE OASIS
Fill glass with ice.
1 1/2 oz Gin
1/2 oz Cherry Brandy
4 oz Orange Juice
Stir.
Top with Ginger Ale.

ORANGE WHIP
In Blender:
1/2 cup of Ice
1 Egg White
Scoop of Orange Sherbet
2 oz Orange Juice
Blend until smooth.
If too thick add juice.
If too thin add sherbet or ice.

OR-E-OH COOKIE aka
COOKIES AND CREAM (frozen)
In Blender:
1/2 cup of Ice
1 oz Vodka
3/4 oz Dark Creme De Cacao
2 cookies
Scoop of Vanilla Ice Cream
Blend until smooth.
If too thick add milk or cream.
If too thin add ice or ice cream.
Garnish with a cookie.

ORIENT EXPRESS
Fill glass with ice.
3/4 oz Ginger Liqueur
1 tsp Sugar
Fill with espresso.

ORIENTAL
Fill glass with ice.
1 oz Whiskey
1/2 oz Triple Sec
1/2 oz Sweet Vermouth
1/2 oz Lime Juice
Shake.
Strain into chilled glass.

ORGASM aka
BURNT ALMOND,
ROASTED TOASTED ALMOND
Fill glass with ice.
1 oz Vodka
1 oz Coffee Liqueur
1 oz Amaretto
Fill with Cream or Milk.
Shake.

ORGASM 2
Fill glass with ice.
1/2 oz Vodka
1/2 oz Triple Sec
1/2 oz Amaretto
1/2 oz White Creme De Cacao
1 oz Cream
Shake.
Serve or strain into short glass.

ORGASM 3
Fill glass with ice.
3/4 oz Coffee Liqueur
3/4 oz Amaretto
3/4 oz Irish Cream
Fill with equal parts Milk or Cream
and Soda Water.

ORSINI (frozen)
In Blender:
1/2 cup of Ice
1 1/2 oz Gin
1/2 oz Triple Sec
Dash of Sour Mix
Dash of Orange Juice
Scoop of Vanilla Ice Cream.
Blend until smooth.
If too thick add milk or cream. If too
thin add ice or ice cream.

OSTEND FIZZ
Fill glass with ice.
1 oz Kirschwasser
1 oz Creme De Cassis
Stir.
Top with Soda Water.
Garnish with Lemon Twist.

OUT OF THE BLUE
Fill glass with ice.
1/4 oz Vodka
1/4 oz Blue Curacao
1/4 oz Blueberry Schnapps
Dash of Sour Mix
Shake.
Top with Soda Water.

OUTRIGGER
Fill glass with ice.
1 oz Light Rum
1/2 oz Amaretto
Fill with equal parts of Cranberry
and Pineapple Juice.
Top with Dark Rum.

O

OXBEND
Fill glass with ice.
1 oz Southern Comfort
1/2 oz Tequila
Dash of Grenadine
Fill with Orange Juice.
Stir.

OYSTER SHOT aka
LOUISIANA SHOOTER
In a shot glass:
1 raw oyster
1-3 dashes of Tabasco Sauce
1/4 tsp Horseradish
Fill with Vodka or Peppered Vodka.

OZARK MOUNTAIN PUNCH
Fill glass with ice.
1/2 oz Vodka
1/2 oz Gin
1/2 oz Tequila
1/2 oz Bourbon
Dash of Orgeat Syrup
Fill with Orange Juice.
Shake.
Top with 151-Proof Rum.

PACIFIC PACIFIER
Fill glass with ice.
1 oz Orange Liqueur or Triple Sec
1/2 oz Banana Liqueur
1/2 oz Cream
Shake.

PADDY COCKTAIL
Fill glass with ice.
1 1/2 oz Irish Whiskey
3/4oz Sweet Vermouth
3 dashes of Bitters
Shake.
Strain into chilled glass.

PAGO PAGO
Fill glass with ice.
1 1/2 oz Amber Rum
1/2 tsp White Creme De Cacao
1/2 tsp Green Chartreuse
1/2 oz Pineapple Juice
1/2 oz Lime Juice
Shake.

PAIN IN THE ASS (frozen)
In Blender:
1 cup of Ice
2 oz Rum
1/2 oz Banana Liqueur
1/2 oz Blackberry Brandy
Dash of Lime Juice
Dash of Grenadine
Dash of Cream of Coconut
1/2 cup fresh or canned Pineapple
Blend.

PAIR OF JACKS (floater)
1 oz Yukon Jack (bottom)
1 oz Bourbon (top)

PAISLEY MARTINI
Fill glass with ice.
2 oz Gin
1/2 tsp Dry Vermouth
1/2 tsp Scotch
Shake.
Strain into chilled glass.

PALL MALL
Fill glass with ice.
1 oz Gin
1 oz Dry Vermouth
1 oz Sweet Vermouth
1 tsp White Creme De Menthe
2 dashes of Orange Bitters
Stir.

PALMETTO
Fill glass with ice.
1 1/2 oz Rum
1 oz Sweet Vermouth
2 dashes of Bitters
Stir.
Serve or strain into chilled glass.
Garnish with Lemon Twist.

PANABRAITOR
Fill glass with ice.
1 oz Southern Comfort
1/2 oz Black Raspberry Liqueur
1/2 oz Triple Sec
Fill with equal parts Sour Mix and
Orange Juice.
Shake.

PANAMA
Fill glass with ice.
1 oz Dark Rum or Brandy
3/4 oz White Creme De Cacao
3/4 oz Cream
Shake.
Serve or strain into chilled glass.
Garnish with Nutmeg.

PANAMA JACK
Fill glass with ice.
2 oz Yukon Jack
Fill with equal parts Pineapple and
Cranberry Juice.

PANAMA RED
Fill glass with ice.
1 1/2 oz Gold Tequila
1/2 oz Triple Sec
Dash of Grenadine
Dash of Sour Mix
Shake.
Strain into chilled glass.

PANCHO VILLA
Fill glass with ice.
1 oz Rum
1 oz Gin
1 oz Apricot Brandy
1 tsp Cherry Brandy
1 tsp Pineapple Juice
Shake.

PANDA BEAR (frozen)
In Blender:
1/2 cup of Ice
1 oz Amaretto
1/2 oz White Creme De Cacao
1/2 oz White Creme De Menthe
Scoop of Vanilla Ice Cream
2-3 dashes of vanilla extract
Blend until smooth.
If too thick add milk or cream.
If too thin add ice or ice cream.
Dribble Chocolate Syrup on the
inside of glass before pouring in
drink.

PANTHER
Fill glass with ice.
2 oz Tequila
2 oz Sour Mix
Shake.

PANTOMIME
Fill glass with ice.
1 1/2 oz Dry Vermouth
3 drops of Orgeat Syrup
Dash of Grenadine
1/2 an Egg White
Shake.
Strain into chilled glass.

PANTY DROPPER
Fill glass with ice.
1 oz Vodka
1 oz Coffee Liqueur
1 oz Sloe Gin
Fill with Milk.
Shake.
Garnish with Cherry.

PARADISE
Fill glass with ice.
1 oz Gin
1 oz Apricot Brandy
1 oz Orange Juice
Stir.
Strain into chilled glass.

PARADISE PUNCH
Fill glass with ice.
1 oz Amber Rum
1 oz Dark Rum
1 oz Sour Mix
1 oz Cream of Coconut
1 oz Cream or Milk
Shake.

PARANOIA
Fill glass with ice.
1 oz Coconut Rum
1 oz Amaretto
Fill with equal parts Orange and
Pineapple Juice.
Shake.
Garnish with Pineapple or Orange.

PARFAIT
In Blender:
1/2 cup of Ice
2 oz Desired Liqueur
Scoop of Vanilla Ice Cream
Blend until smooth.
If too thick add Liqueur or Milk.
If too thin add ice or ice cream.

PARIS MATCH aka
PARIS IS BURNING
1 oz Cognac or Brandy
1 oz Black Raspberry Liqueur
Heat in microwave 10-15
seconds.

PARISIAN
Fill glass with ice.
1 oz Gin
1 oz Dry Vermouth
1 oz Creme De Cassis
Stir.
Strain into chilled glass.

PARISIAN BLONDE
Fill glass with ice.
1 oz Dark Rum
1 oz Triple Sec or Curacao
1 oz Cream
Shake.
Strain into chilled glass.

PARISIAN FRAPPE
Fill large stemmed glass (Red Wine
glass, Champagne saucer) with
crushed ice.
3/4 oz Dark Rum
3/4 oz Orange Liqueur
3/4 oz Cream

PARK AVENUE
Fill glass with ice.
1 1/2 oz Gin
1/2 oz Sweet Vermouth
1 oz Pineapple Juice
2-3 drops of Curacao (optional)
Stir.
Strain into chilled glass.

PASSIONATE POINT
Fill glass with ice.
3/4 oz Amber Rum
3/4 oz Peach Schnapps
3/4 oz Orange Liqueur
2 oz Orange Juice
2 oz Cranberry Juice
Shake.
Strain into chilled glass.

O
P

PASSIONATE SCREW

Fill glass with ice.
1 oz Vodka
1 oz Coconut Rum
1 oz Black Raspberry Liqueur
Dash of Grenadine
Fill with equal parts Orange and
Pineapple Juice.
Shake.
Garnish with Cherry and Orange or
Pineapple.

PEACH ALEXANDER (frozen)

In Blender:
1/2 cup of Ice
1 oz Peach Schnapps
1/2 oz White Creme De Cacao
1/2 fresh or canned Peach
1 1/2 oz Cream
or 1/2 scoop Vanilla Ice Cream
Blend until smooth.
If too thick add juice or milk.
If too thin add ice or ice cream.

PEACH BLASTER

Fill glass with ice
2 oz Peach Schnapps
Fill with Cranberry Juice.
Stir.

PEACH BLOW FIZZ

Fill glass with ice.
2 oz Gin
1 oz Cream
1 tsp Sugar Syrup
or Powdered Sugar
1 oz Lemon Juice
1/4 fresh ripe Peach (mashed with
no skin or pit)
Shake.
Top with Soda Water.

PEACH BREEZE

Fill glass with ice.
1 oz Vodka
1 oz Peach Schnapps
Fill with equal parts Cranberry and
Grapefruit Juice.
Shake.

PEACH BUCK

Fill glass with ice.
1 1/2 oz Vodka
1/2 oz Peach Schnapps
1/2 oz Lemon Juice
Shake.
Top with Ginger Ale.
Garnish with peach.

PEACH BULLDOG

Fill glass with ice.
1 oz Vodka
1 oz Peach Schnapps
Fill with Cranberry Juice.
Stir.

PEACH COBBLER

1 oz Rum
1 oz Peach Schnapps
Dash of Cinnamon Schnapps
Fill with hot Apple Cider.
Stir.
Top with Whipped Cream.

PEACH COLADA (frozen)

In Blender:
1/2 cup of Ice
2 oz Light Rum
2 Tbsp Cream of Coconut
1 cup of fresh or canned Peaches
1 Tbsp Vanilla Ice Cream (optional)
Blend until smooth.
If too thick add fruit or juice.
If too thin add ice or ice cream.
Garnish with peach and Cherry.

PEACH DAIQUIRI (frozen)

In Blender:
1 cup of Ice
1 oz Peach Schnapps
1 oz Rum
1/2 cup of fresh or canned Peaches
Dash of Lime Juice
Blend until smooth.

PEACH FUZZ

Fill glass with ice.
2 oz Peach Schnapps
Fill with equal parts Milk and
Cranberry Juice.
Shake.
Serve or strain into chilled glass.

PEACH MIMOSA

Fill glass with ice.
Fill 3/4 with Champagne.
Splash of Peach Schnapps
Fill with Orange Juice.
Garnish with Orange.

PEACH VELVET (frozen)

In Blender:
1/2 cup of Ice.
1 1/2 oz Peach Schnapps
1/2 oz White Creme De Cacao
1 scoop of Vanilla Ice Cream
1/2 fresh or canned Peach
Blend until smooth.

PEACHES AND CREAM

Fill glass with ice.
1 oz Irish Cream
1 oz Peach Schnapps
Splash of Cream
Shake.
Top with Soda Water.

PEANUT BUTTER AND JELLY
(frozen)
In Blender:
1/2 cup of Ice
1 oz Black Raspberry Liqueur
1 oz Hazelnut Liqueur
Dash of Irish Cream
3 Tbsp Cocktail Peanuts
3 Tbsp Grape Jelly
Scoop of Vanilla Ice Cream.
Blend until smooth.
If too thick add milk.
If too thin add ice or ice cream.

PEARL DIVER
Fill glass with ice.
1 1/2 oz Vodka
1/2 oz Orange Juice
Strain into chilled glass.
Dash of Grenadine
Splash of Lemon-Lime Soda
Garnish with stemless Cherry.

PEARL HARBOR
Fill glass with ice.
1 oz Vodka
1 oz Melon Liqueur
Fill with Pineapple Juice.
Shake.
Garnish with Cherry and Pineapple.

PEARL HARBOR (frozen)
In Blender:
1/2 cup of Ice
1 oz Vodka
1 oz Melon Liqueur
1/2 cup of fresh or canned
Pineapple
Scoop of Vanilla Ice Cream
Blend until smooth.
If too thick add fruit or juice.
If too thin add ice or ice cream.
Garnish with Cherry and Pineapple.

PEARL NECKLACE aka B. J.
(floater)
1/2 oz Cream (bottom)
1/2 oz White Creme De Cacao
1/2 oz Vodka (top)
Contents should mix slightly.
To drink, place hands behind back
and pick up using only mouth.

PECKERHEAD
Fill glass with ice.
1 oz Yukon Jack
1 oz Amaretto
1 oz Pineapple Juice
Shake.
Strain into chilled glass.

PEDRO COLLINS
Fill glass with ice.
2 oz Rum
Fill with Sour Mix.
Shake.
Splash of Soda Water
Garnish with Orange and Cherry.

PEGU CLUB
Fill glass with ice.
1 1/2 oz Gin
3/4 oz Orange Curacao
1 tsp Lime Juice
Dash of Bitters
Dash of Orange Bitters
Shake.
Strain into chilled glass.

PENDENNIS CLUB
Fill glass with ice.
1 1/2 oz Gin
3/4 oz Apricot Brandy
1/2 oz Lime Juice
1 tsp Sugar Syrup
3 dashes of Peychaud's Bitters
Shake.
Strain into chilled glass.

PENSACOLA (frozen)
In Blender:
1 cup of Ice
1 1/2 oz Rum
1/2 oz Guava Nectar
1/2 oz Orange Juice
1/2 oz Lemon Juice
Blend until smooth.
If too thick add juice.
If too thin add ice.

PEPPER MARTINI
Fill glass with ice.
2 oz Peppered Vodka
1/2 oz Dry Vermouth
Stir.
Strain into chilled glass or pour
contents (with ice) into short glass.
Garnish with a Jalapeno Pepper.

PEPPERMINT KISS aka
SNUGGLER, COCOANAPPS,
ADULT HOT CHOCOLATE
2 oz Peppermint Schnapps
Fill with Hot Chocolate.
Top with Whipped Cream.
Sprinkle with Shaved
Chocolate or Sprinkles.

PEPPERMINT PATTIE
Fill glass with ice.
1 oz White Creme De Cacao or
Dark Creme De Cacao
1 oz White Creme De Menthe
Stir.

PEPPERMINT PATTY
Fill glass with ice.
1 oz Peppermint Schnapps
1 oz Dark Creme De Cacao
2 oz Cream
Shake.

PEPPERMINT STINGER
Fill glass with ice.
1 1/2 oz Brandy
1/2 oz Peppermint Schnapps
Stir.
Serve or strain into chilled glass.

P

89

PERFECT MANHATTAN
Fill glass with ice.
2 oz Whiskey
1/4 oz Dry Vermouth
1/4 oz Sweet Vermouth
Stir.
Strain into chilled glass or pour
contents (with ice) into short glass.
Garnish with Cherry or Lemon
Twist.

PERNOD COCKTAIL
Fill glass with ice.
2 oz Pernod
3 dashes of Bitters
3 dashes of Sugar Syrup
1/2 oz Water
Stir.
Serve or strain into chilled glass.

PERNOD FLIP
Fill glass with ice.
1 oz Pernod
1/2 oz Orange Liqueur or Triple Sec
1/2 oz Lemon Juice
1 1/2 tsp Sugar Syrup
1 Egg
Shake.

PERNOD FLIP (frozen)
In Blender:
1 cup of Ice
1 1/2 oz Pernod
1 oz Heavy Cream
1/2 oz Sugar Syrup
or Orgeat Syrup
1 Egg
Blend until smooth.
Garnish with Nutmeg.

PERNOD FRAPPE
Fill glass with ice.
1 1/2 oz Pernod
1/2 oz Anisette
3 dashes of Bitters
Shake.
Strain into chilled glass.

PERSUADER
Fill glass with ice.
1 oz Brandy
1 oz Amaretto
Fill glass with Orange Juice.
Shake.

PETRIFIER
Fill glass with ice.
2 oz Vodka
2 oz Gin
2 oz Cognac
2 oz Triple Sec
3 dashes of Bitters
Dash of Grenadine
Shake.
Strain into chilled glass.
Fill with Ginger Ale.
Garnish with Orange and Cherry.

PHANTOM
Fill glass with ice.
1 1/2 oz Black Raspberry Liqueur
1/2 oz Black Sambuca
Stir.
Serve or strain into chilled glass.

PHOEBE SNOW
Fill glass with ice.
1 1/2 oz Cognac or Brandy
1 1/2 oz Dubonnet Rouge
2 dashes of Bitters
Stir.
Serve or strain into chilled glass.
Garnish with Lemon Twist.

PICON FIZZ
Fill glass with ice.
1 1/2 oz Amer Picon
1/4 oz Grenadine
3 oz Soda Water
Float 1/2 oz Cognac or Brandy on
top.

PICON ORANGE
Fill glass with ice.
2 oz Amer Picon
2 oz Orange Juice
Shake.
Fill with Soda Water.
Garnish with Orange.

PICON SOUR
Fill glass with ice.
1 1/2 oz Amer Picon
1 oz Sour Mix or Lemon Juice
1/2 tsp Powdered Sugar
or Sugar Syrup
Shake.
Strain into chilled glass.

PIERRE COLLINS
Fill glass with ice.
2 oz Cognac or Brandy
Fill with Sour Mix
Shake.
Splash with Lemon-Lime Soda.
Garnish with Orange and Cherry.

PILE DRIVER
Fill glass with ice.
2 oz Vodka
Fill with prune juice.
Stir.

PILOT BOAT
Fill glass with ice.
1 1/2 oz Dark Rum
1 oz Banana Liqueur
1 1/2 oz Sour Mix
Dash of Lime Juice
Shake.
Strain into chilled glass.

PIMLICO SPECIAL
Fill glass with ice.
1 1/2 oz Brandy
1/2 oz Amaretto
1/2 oz White Creme De Cacao
Shake.
Strain into chilled glass.

PIMM'S CUP
Fill glass with ice.
2 oz Pimm's cup No. 1
Fill with Lemon-Lime Soda.
Garnish with Lemon and/or
Cucumber.

PIÑA
Fill glass with ice.
1 1/2 oz Tequila
3 oz Pineapple Juice
1 oz Lime Juice
1 tsp Honey or Sugar Syrup
Shake.
Garnish with Lime.

PIÑA COLADA (frozen)
In Blender:
1/2 cup of Ice
2 oz Light Rum
2 Tbsp Cream of Coconut
1/2 cup fresh or canned Pineapple
1 Tbsp Vanilla Ice Cream (optional)
Blend until smooth.
If too thick add fruit or juice.
If too thin add ice or ice cream.
Garnish with Pineapple and Cherry.

PIÑATA
Fill glass with ice.
1 1/2 oz Tequila
1 oz Banana Liqueur
1 oz Lime Juice
Shake.
Serve or strain into chilled glass.

PINEAPPLE BOMB
Fill glass with ice.
1 1/2 oz Rum
1/2 oz Amaretto
Fill with Pineapple Juice.
Shake.

PINEAPPLE BOMBER
Fill glass with ice.
1 oz Spiced Rum
1 oz Southern Comfort
1 oz Amaretto
Fill with Pineapple Juice.
Shake.

PINEAPPLE BOMBER 2
Fill glass with ice.
1 oz Yukon Jack
1 oz Amaretto
Fill with Pineapple Juice.
Shake.

PINEAPPLE DAIQUIRI (frozen)
In Blender:
1/2 cup of Ice
1 2 oz Rum
1/2 oz Lime Juice
1/2 cup of fresh or canned
Pineapple
Blend until Smooth.
If too thick add juice.
If too thin add ice.

PINEAPPLE PASSION
Fill glass with ice.
1 1/2 oz Rum
1 oz Orange Curacao
2 oz Pineapple Juice
1 oz Passion Fruit Juice
Shake.

PINK ALMOND
Fill glass with ice.
1 oz Whiskey
1/2 oz Creme De Nouyax
1/2 oz Amaretto
1/2 oz Kirschwasser
1/2 oz Lemon Juice
Shake.
Garnish with Lemon.

PINK FLOYD (frozen)
In Blender:
1/2 cup of Ice
1 oz Vodka
1 oz Sloe Gin
1/2 cup fresh or canned Pineapple
Blend until smooth.
Top with Soda Water.
Garnish with Pineapple.

PINK GATOR
Fill glass with ice.
1 oz Light Rum
1 oz Amber Rum
1/2 oz Grenadine
Dash of Sour Mix
Fill with equal parts Orange and
Pineapple Juice.

PINK GIN
Fill glass with ice.
2 oz Gin
2 dashes of Bitters
Stir.
Serve or strain into chilled glass.

PINK LADY
Fill glass with ice.
1 1/2 oz Gin
1 1/2 oz Cream
1 tsp Grenadine
Shake.
Strain into chilled glass.

P

PINK LEMONADE
Fill glass with ice.
1 1/2 oz Vodka
1 oz Cranberry Juice
2 oz Sour Mix
Shake.
Fill with Lemon-Lime Soda.
Garnish with Lemon.

PINK LEMONADE 2
Fill glass with ice.
2 oz Citrus Vodka
Dash of Grenadine
Shake.
Strain into chilled glass.

PINK PANTHER
Fill glass with ice.
3/4 oz Gin
3/4 oz Dry Vermouth
1/2 oz Creme De Cassis
1/2 oz Orange Juice
1/2 Egg White
Shake.
Strain into chilled glass.

PINK PANTHER 2
Fill glass with ice.
2 oz Rum
Dash of Lemon Juice
Dash of Cream
Dash of Grenadine
Shake.
Strain into chilled glass.

PINK PANTHER 3
Fill glass with ice.
2 oz Gin
2 oz Apple Juice
Dash of Grenadine
Fill with Grapefruit Juice.
Shake.

PINK PARADISE
Fill glass with ice.
1 oz Coconut Rum
1 oz Amaretto
2 oz Pineapple Juice
Fill with Cranberry Juice.
Stir.

PINK PUSSYCAT
Fill glass with ice.
1 1/2 oz Gin or Vodka
1/2 oz Grenadine
Fill with Pineapple or Grapefruit
Juice.
Shake.

PINK ROSE
Fill glass with ice.
1 1/2 oz Gin
1 tsp Lemon Juice
1 tsp Heavy Cream
1 Egg White
3 dashes of Grenadine
Shake.
Strain into chilled glass.

PINK SLIP
1 oz Coconut Rum
1 oz Cranberry juice
Fill with Champagne.

PINK SQUIRREL
Fill glass with ice.
1 oz Creme De Nouyax.
1 oz White Creme De Cacao
1 oz Cream or Milk
Shake.
Strain into chilled glass.

PINK VERANDA
Fill glass with ice.
1 oz Amber Rum
1/2 oz Dark Rum
1 1/2 oz Cranberry Juice
1/2 oz Lime Juice
1 tsp Sugar
1/2 Egg White
Shake.

PINK WHISKERS
Fill glass with ice.
1 oz Apricot Brandy
1/2 oz Dry Vermouth
1 oz Orange Juice
1 tsp Grenadine
3 dashes of White Creme De
Menthe
Shake.
Float 1 oz Port on top.

PISCO PUNCH
Fill glass with ice.
3 oz Brandy
1 tsp Lime Juice
1 tsp Pineapple Juice
2 oz cold Water (optional)
Stir.
Garnish with Pineapple.

PISCO SOUR
Fill glass with ice.
2 oz Brandy
1 oz Sour Mix
1/2 Egg White
Dash of Lime Juice
Shake.
Strain into chilled glass.
2-3 dashes of Bitters

PLANTER'S PUNCH
Fill glass with ice.
1 1/2 oz Light Rum
Dash of Grenadine
Fill with equal parts Sour Mix and
either Orange or
Pineapple Juice.
Shake.
Top with 1/2 oz Dark Rum.
Garnish with Orange and Cherry.

PLANTER'S PUNCH 2
Fill glass with ice.
1 oz Dark Rum
1 oz Amber Rum
Dash of Brandy
Dash of Sweet Vermouth
Dash of Bitters
1 tsp of Cherry Juice
or Grenadine
Fill with equal parts Sour Mix and
Pineapple Juice.
Shake.
Louis Steede

PLATINUM BLOND
Fill glass with ice.
1 1/2 oz Rum
3/4 oz Orange Liqueur or Curacao
or Triple Sec
Fill with Milk or Cream.
Shake.

PLAZA
Fill glass with ice.
3/4 oz Gin
3/4 oz Dry Vermouth
3/4 oz Sweet Vermouth
1 Tbsp Pineapple Juice (optional)
Shake.
Strain into chilled glass.

P. M. S.
Fill glass with ice.
3/4 oz Peach Schnapps
3/4 oz Coconut Rum
3/4 oz Russian Vodka
Stir.
Strain into chilled glass.

POINT (floater)
3/4 oz Drambuie (bottom)
3/4 oz White Creme De Menthe
3/4 oz Irish Cream (top)

POINSETTIA aka
NANTUCKET RED
Fill glass 3/4 with ice.
Fill 3/4 with Champagne.
Fill with Cranberry Juice.
Garnish with Lime.

POKER
Fill glass with ice.
1 1/2 oz Amber Rum
1 oz Dry Vermouth
Stir.
Strain into chilled glass.
Garnish with Orange Twist.

POLLYANNA
Fill glass with ice.
1 1/2 oz Gin
1/4 oz Sweet Vermouth
1/4 oz Grenadine
Shake.
Strain into chilled glass.

POLLY'S SPECIAL
Fill glass with ice.
1 1/2 oz Scotch
1/2 oz Triple Sec
1/2 oz Grapefruit Juice
Shake.

POLO
Fill glass with ice.
1 1/2 oz Gin
1 Tbsp Orange Juice
1 Tbsp Lemon or Grapefruit Juice
Stir.
Serve or strain into chilled glass.

POLYNESIAN
Fill glass with ice.
1 1/2 oz Vodka
3/4 oz Cherry Brandy
3/4 oz Lime Juice
Shake.
Rub rim of second glass with Lime
and dip rim in Powdered Sugar.
Strain into second glass.

POND SCUM
Fill glass with ice.
2 oz Vodka
Fill with Soda Water.
Float 1/4oz Irish Cream on top.

POOP DECK
Fill glass with ice.
1 oz Blackberry Brandy
1/2 oz Brandy
1/2 oz Port
Shake.
Strain into chilled glass.

POPPER
In shot glass:
1 oz Desired Liqueur or Liquor
1 oz Ginger Ale
or Lemon-Lime Soda
Cover glass with napkin and hand,
then slam on bar top.
Drink while foaming.

POP-SICLE
Fill glass with ice.
2 oz Amaretto
Fill with equal parts Cream
and Orange Juice.
Shake.

POP-SICLE 2
Fill glass with ice.
1 1/2 oz Southern Comfort
1/2 oz Amaretto
Dash of Grenadine
1 oz Orange Juice
Fill with Lemon-Lime Soda.

P

POP-SICLE 3
Fill glass with ice.
1 1/2 oz Vodka
1/2 oz Triple Sec
Dash of Milk or Cream
Fill with Orange Juice.
Shake.

PORCH CLIMBER
Fill glass with ice.
1 oz Rum
1/2 oz Apricot Brandy
1/2 oz Cherry Brandy
Fill with Sour Mix.
Shake.
Princely Masters

PORT IN A STORM
Fill glass with ice.
1 oz Brandy or Cognac
2 oz Port
Fill with Red Wine
Strain.
Garnish with mint sprig.

PORT AND STARBOARD (floater)
1 oz Green Creme De Menthe
(bottom)
1 oz Grenadine (top)

PORT ANTONIO
Fill glass with ice.
1 oz Amber Rum
1/2 oz Dark Rum
1/2 oz Lime Juice
1/2 oz Tia Maria
1 tsp Falernum
Shake.
Garnish with Lime.

PORT PELICAN
Fill glass with ice.
1 oz Rum
1/2 oz Banana Liqueur
1/2 oz Galliano
Fill with Orange Juice.
Shake.

PORT SANGAREE
Fill glass with ice.
2 oz Port
1/2 tsp Powdered Sugar
1 oz Water
Fill with Soda Water.
Stir.
Float 1 tsp Brandy on top
(optional).

POUSSE CAFÉ
A glass of liqueurs arranged
in layers.

POUSSE CAFÉ (floater)
Layer ingredients in order and in
equal amounts.
1/4 oz Grenadine (bottom)
1/4 oz Coffee Liqueur
1/4 oz White Creme De Cacao
1/4 oz Blue Curacao
1/4 oz Galliano
1/4 oz Green Chartreuse
1/4 oz Brandy (top)

PRADO
Fill glass with ice.
1 1/2 oz Tequila
1/2 oz Maraschino Liqueur
3/4 oz Lime Juice
1/2 Egg White
1 tsp Grenadine
Shake.
Garnish with Cherry.

PRAIRIE FIRE
2 oz Tequila
Add Tabasco Sauce until pink.

PRAIRIE OYSTER
1 oz Brandy or Whiskey
1 unbroken Egg Yolk
Dash of Wine Vinegar
Dash of Tabasco Sauce
1 tsp Worcestershire Sauce
2 oz Tomato Juice
Pinch of Salt
Stir gently.

PREAKNESS
Fill glass with ice.
1 1/2 oz Whiskey
1/4 oz Benedictine
1/4 oz Sweet Vermouth
Dash of Bitters
Stir.
Strain into chilled glass.
Garnish with Lemon Twist.

PRESIDENTE
Fill glass with ice.
1 1/2 oz Rum
1/2 oz Dry Vermouth
1/2 oz Curacao
Dash of Grenadine
Shake.
Serve or strain into chilled glass.
Garnish with Lemon Twist.

PRESS
Fill glass with ice.
2 oz Whiskey
Fill with equal parts Ginger Ale and
Soda Water.

PRINCE EDWARD
Fill glass with ice.
1 1/2 oz Scotch
1/2 oz Lillet Blanc
1/4 oz Drambuie
Shake.
Serve or strain into chilled glass.
Garnish with Orange.

PRINCE IGOR aka HIGH ROLLER
Fill glass with ice.
1 1/2 oz Vodka
3/4 oz Orange Liqueur
Dash of Grenadine
Fill with Orange Juice.
Shake.
Garnish with Orange and Cherry.

PRINCE OF WALES
Fill glass with ice.
1 oz Brandy
1 oz Madeira
or any sweet Red Wine
1/4 oz Curacao
3 dashes of Bitters
Shake.
Strain into wine glass.
Fill with Champagne.
Garnish with Orange.

PRINCESS MARY'S PRIDE
Fill glass with ice.
1 1/2 oz Apple Brandy
3/4 oz Dubonnet Rouge
1/2 oz Dry Vermouth
Shake.
Strain into chilled glass.

PRINCE'S SMILE
Fill glass with ice.
1 oz Gin
1/2 oz Apricot Brandy
1/2 oz Apple Brandy
1/4 oz Lemon Juice
Shake.
Strain into chilled glass.

PRINCETON
Fill glass with ice.
1 1/2 oz Gin
3/4 oz Port
3 dashes of Orange Bitters
Shake.
Strain into chilled glass.
Garnish with Lemon Twist.

PROVINCETOWN
Fill glass with ice.
2 oz Vodka
2 oz Cranberry Juice
2 oz Grapefruit Juice
Strain into chilled glass.
Fill with Soda Water.
Garnish with Lemon wedge.

PTERODACTYL
Fill glass with ice.
1/2 oz Vodka
1/2 oz Rum
1/2 oz Triple Sec
1/2 oz Amaretto
1/2 oz Southern Comfort
Dash of Grenadine
Fill with Orange Juice.
Shake.
Garnish with Orange.

PUCCINI
Fill glass with ice.
1 1/2 oz Vodka
1 oz Melon Liqueur
1/2 oz Tuaca
Fill with Orange Juice.
Shake

PUERTO RICAN SCREW
Fill glass with ice.
2 oz Rum
Fill with Orange Juice.

PUMPKIN PIE (floater)
1/2 oz Coffee Liqueur (bottom)
1/2 oz Irish Cream
1/2 oz Cinnamon Schnapps (top)

PUNT E MES NEGRONI
Fill glass with ice.
1/2 oz Gin or Vodka
1/2 oz Punt e Mes
1/2 oz Sweet Vermouth
Shake.
Strain into chilled glass.
Garnish with Orange Twist.

PURPLE ARMADILLO
Fill glass with ice.
1 1/2 oz Rum
1/2 oz Blue Curacao
Fill with equal parts Sour Mix and
Cranberry Juice.
Shake.
Top with Lemon-Lime Soda.

PURPLE BUNNY
Fill glass with ice.
1 oz Cherry Brandy
1/2 oz White Creme De Cacao
1 oz Cream or Milk
Shake.
Strain into chilled glass.

PURPLE DREAM
Fill glass with ice.
1 oz Black Raspberry Liqueur
1 oz White Creme De Cacao
Fill with Milk or Cream.
Shake.

PURPLE FLIRT
Fill glass with ice.
1 1/2 oz Amber Rum
1/2 oz Blue Curacao
Dash of Pineapple Juice
Dash of Cranberry Juice
Dash of Sour Mix
Dash of Grenadine
Shake.
Strain into chilled glass.

PURPLE HAZE
Fill glass with ice.
1 1/2 oz Vodka
1/2 oz Black Raspberry Liqueur
Fill with equal parts Sour Mix and
Pineapple Juice.
Shake.

P

PURPLE HAZE 2
Fill glass with ice.
1 oz Vodka
1 oz Black Raspberry Liqueur
1 oz Cranberry Juice
Stir.
Strain into chilled glass.

PURPLE HEATHER
Fill glass with ice.
1 1/2 oz Scotch
1/2 oz Creme De Cassis
Fill with Soda Water.

PURPLE HOOTER or
PURPLE KAMIKAZE
Fill glass with ice.
2 oz Vodka
1/2 oz Black Raspberry Liqueur
1/2 oz Lime Juice
Stir.
Strain into shot glass.

PURPLE MARGARITA
Fill glass with ice.
1 oz Tequila
1/2 oz Sloe Gin
1/2 oz Blue Curacao
Dash of Lime Juice
3 oz Sour Mix
Shake.

PURPLE MATADOR
Fill glass with ice.
1 1/2 oz Amaretto
1 oz Black Raspberry Liqueur
1/2 oz Pineapple Juice
Shake.
Strain into chilled glass.

PURPLE NASTY
1/2 oz Creme De Cassis
Fill with equal parts Hard Cider and
Ale.

PURPLE NIPPLE (floater)
1/2 oz Black Raspberry Liqueur
(bottom)
1/2 oz Irish Cream (top)

PURPLE PASSION aka
TRANSFUSION
Fill glass with ice.
2 oz Vodka
Fill with equal parts grape juice and
Ginger Ale or Soda Water.

PURPLE PASSION 2
Fill glass with ice.
2 oz Vodka
Fill with Grape Cool Aid.

PURPLE RAIN
Fill glass with ice.
1/2 oz Vodka
1/2 oz Gin
1/2 oz Rum
1/2 oz Tequila
1/2 oz Triple Sec
Fill with Sour Mix.
Shake.
Top with Black Raspberry Liqueur.
Garnish with Lime.

PURPLE RAIN 2
Fill glass with ice.
1 1/2 oz Vodka
1/2 oz Blue Curacao
1 oz Cranberry Juice
Stir.
Strain into chilled glass.

PURPLE RUSSIAN
Fill glass with ice.
1 1/2 oz Vodka
1/2 oz Black Raspberry Liqueur
Stir.

PURPLE THUNDER
Fill glass with ice.
1 oz Light Rum
1 oz Amber Rum
1/2 oz Blue Curacao
Fill with equal parts Grape and
Cranberry Juice.
Shake.
Strain into chilled glass.
Fill with Soda Water.

PUSSER'S PAINKILLER
Shake without ice.
2 oz Pusser's Rum
1 oz Cream of Coconut
1 oz Orange Juice
4 oz Pineapple Juice
Pour over ice.
Garnish with a pinch of
Cinnamon and Nutmeg.

PUSSY GALORE (floater)
1/2 oz Banana Liqueur
(bottom)
1 oz White Creme De Cacao
1/2 oz Irish Cream (top)

QUAKER
Fill glass with ice.
1 1/2 oz Brandy
3/4 oz Rum
1/2 oz Lemon Juice
1/2 oz Raspberry Syrup
Shake.
Strain into chilled glass.
Garnish with Lemon Twist.

QUAKER CITY COOLER
Fill glass with ice.
1 oz Vodka
3 oz Chablis
1/2 oz Sugar Syrup
1/2 oz Lemon Juice
3 dashes of Vanilla Extract
Stir.
Top with 1/4 oz Grenadine.

QUARTER DECK
Fill glass with ice.
1 1/2 oz Rum
1/3 oz Sherry
1 tsp Lime Juice
Shake.
Serve or strain into chilled glass.

QUEBEC
Fill glass with ice.
1 1/2 oz Canadian Whiskey
1/2 oz Amer Picon
1/2 oz Maraschino Liqueur
1/2 oz Dry Vermouth
Shake.
Strain into chilled glass.

QUEEN
Muddle 1/2 cup Pineapple in glass.
Fill glass with ice.
1 1/2 oz Gin
1/2 oz Dry Vermouth
Stir.
Strain into chilled glass.

QUEEN ELIZABETH
Fill glass with ice.
1 oz Gin
1/2 oz Orange Liqueur
1/2 oz Lemon Juice
1 tsp Pernod
Stir.
Strain into chilled glass.

QUEEN ELIZABETH WINE
Fill glass with ice.
1 1/2 oz Benedictine
3/4 oz Dry Vermouth
3/4 oz Lemon Juice
Shake.
Strain into chilled glass.

QUELLE VIE
Fill glass with ice.
1 1/2 oz Brandy
3/4 oz Kummel
Stir.
Strain into chilled glass.

QUICKIE
Fill glass with ice.
1 oz Bourbon
1 oz Rum
1/4 oz Triple Sec
Stir.
Strain into chilled glass.

QUIET NUN
Fill glass with ice.
1 oz Benedictine
1 oz Tripe Sec
1 oz Cream or Milk
Shake.
Strain into chilled glass.

QUWAYLUDE
Fill glass with ice.
1/2 oz Vodka
1/2 oz Coffee Liqueur
1/2 oz Hazelnut Liqueur
1/2 oz Dark Creme De Cacao
1/2 oz Orange Liqueur
Fill with Milk or Cream.
Shake.

QUWAYLUDE 2
Fill glass with ice.
1 oz Southern Comfort
1 oz Bourbon
Splash of Orange Juice
Fill with Pineapple Juice.
Shake.

RACQUET CLUB
Fill glass with ice.
1 1/2 oz Gin
3/4 oz Dry Vermouth
Dash of Bitters
Stir.
Strain into chilled glass.

RAINBOW (floater)
1/2 oz Dark Creme De Cacao
(bottom)
1/2 oz Creme De Violette
1/2 oz Yellow Chartreuse
1/2 oz Maraschino Liqueur
1/2 oz Benedictine
1/2 oz Green Chartreuse
1/2 oz Cognac (top)

RAINBOW 2 (floater)
1/2 oz Creme De Nouyax
(bottom)
1/2 oz Melon Liqueur
1/2 oz White Creme De Cacao
(top)

RAINFOREST (frozen)
In Blender:
1 cup of Ice
1 oz Dark Rum
1 oz Melon Liqueur
1 Tbsp Cream of Coconut
1 oz Passion Fruit Liqueur
Blend until smooth.

P
Q
R

RAMOS FIZZ
Fill glass with ice.
1 1/2 oz Gin
1/2 oz Cream
1 1/2 oz Sour Mix
1 Egg White
1 tsp Triple Sec or Curacao
or Orange Juice
Shake.
Strain into chilled glass.
Fill with Soda Water.

RANCH VALENCIA
RUM PUNCH
Fill glass with ice.
1 oz Light Rum
1 oz Amber Rum
2 dashes of Bitters
Fill with equal parts Orange and
Pineapple Juice.
Shake.
Strain into glass.
Float 1/2 oz Dark Rum on top.
Garnish with Orange and/or
Pineapple.

RASBARETTA (frozen)
In Blender:
1/2 cup of Ice
1 oz Raspberry Liqueur
1 oz Amaretto
Scoop of Vanilla Ice Cream
Blend until smooth.
If too thick add liqueur or milk. If too
thin add ice or ice cream.

RASPBERRY COLADA (frozen)
In Blender:
1/2 cup of Ice
1 oz Rum
1 oz Black Raspberry Liqueur
2 Tbsp Cream of Coconut
1/2 cup fresh or frozen Raspberries
1 Tbsp Vanilla Ice Cream (optional)
Blend until smooth.

RASPBERRY DAIQUIRI
(frozen)
In Blender:
1 cup of Ice
1 1/2 oz Rum
3/4 oz Raspberry Liqueur
Dash of Lime Juice
1/2 cup of fresh or frozen
Raspberries
or 2 Tbsp Raspberry Jam
Blend until smooth.
If too thick add berries.
If too thin add ice.
Garnish with Lime.

RASPBERRY GIMLET aka
PURPLE HOOTER
Fill glass with ice.
2 oz Vodka
1/2 oz Black Raspberry Liqueur
1/2 oz Lime Juice
Stir.
Strain into shot glass.

RASPBERRY KISS
Fill glass with ice.
1 oz Black Raspberry Liqueur
1 oz Dark Creme De Cacao
1 oz Milk or Cream
Shake.
Strain into chilled glass.

RASPBERRY LIME RICKEY
Fill glass with ice.
1 1/2 oz Vodka or Gin or Rum or
Whiskey
1/2 oz Black Raspberry Liqueur
Dash of Lime Juice
Fill with Soda Water
Garnish with Lime.

RASPBERRY MARGARITA
(frozen)
In Blender:
1/2 cup of Ice
1 1/2 oz Tequila
1/2 oz Black Raspberry Liqueur
1/2 cup fresh or frozen
Raspberries or 2 Tbsp of
Raspberry Jam
Dash of Lime Juice
Blend until smooth.
If too thick add juice or alcohol.
If too thin add ice.
Garnish with Lime.

RASPBERRY SHERBET
Fill glass with ice.
1 1/2 oz Vodka
1/2 oz Black Raspberry Liqueur
Dash of Grenadine
Dash of Orange Juice
Dash of Lime Juice
Fill with Sour Mix.
Shake.
Nick G. Zeroulias

RASPBERRY SMASH aka
HOLLYWOOD
Fill glass with ice.
1 1/2 oz Vodka
1/2 oz Black Raspberry Liqueur
Fill with Pineapple Juice.
Garnish with Pineapple.
Shake.

RASPBERRY SODA
Fill glass with ice.
2 oz Vodka
1/2 oz Black Raspberry Liqueur
Fill with Raspberry Flavored
Sparkling Water.
Garnish with Orange.

RASPBERRY SOMBRERO
Fill glass with ice.
2 oz Black Raspberry Liqueur
Fill with Milk or Cream.
Shake.

RASPBERRY TORTE
Fill glass with ice.
1 oz Vodka
1 oz Black Raspberry Liqueur
Stir.

RASPBERRY VODKA
(type liqueur)
In a screw top jar mix together:
1 qt Vodka
1 lb fresh Raspberries
2 cups of Sugar (optional)
Store in cool dark place for
2 months (optional)
Stir weekly.
Strain when ready.

RASTA MAN (floater)
1/2 oz Coffee Liqueur (bottom)
1/2 oz Myer's Rum Cream
1/2 oz Chocolate Liqueur (top)

RATTLER
Fill glass with ice.
1 1/2 oz Tequila
1/2 oz Triple Sec
Fill with Grapefruit Juice.
Garnish with Lime.

RATTLESNAKE
Fill glass with ice.
1 1/2 oz of Whiskey
1/2 Egg White
1/4 tsp Pernod
1 tsp Powdered Sugar
or Sugar Syrup
1 tsp Lemon Juice
Shake.

RATTLESNAKE 2
Fill glass with ice.
1 1/2 oz Southern Comfort
or Yukon Jack
1/2 oz Blackberry Brandy
1/4 oz Sugar Syrup
Stir.

RATTLESNAKE 3
Fill glass with ice.
1/2 oz Coffee Liqueur
1/2 oz Irish Cream
1/2 oz Peppermint Schnapps
Stir.
Strain into chilled glass.

RAZORBACK HOGCALLER
Fill glass with ice.
1 oz 151- Proof Rum
1 oz Green Chartreuse
Strain into chilled glass.

RAZZLE DAZZLE
Fill glass with ice.
1 oz Vodka
1 oz Black Raspberry Liqueur
Fill with equal parts Orange and
Cranberry Juice.
Shake.
Hilary

RED APPLE
Fill glass with ice.
1 oz Vodka
1 oz Apple Juice
1/2 oz Lemon Juice
3-4 dashes of Grenadine
Shake.
Serve or strain into chilled glass.

RED BEER
2 oz Tomato Juice
Fill with Beer.
Add Salt to taste.

RED BEER SHOOTER
In shot glass:
Dash of Tabasco
Dash of Tomato Juice
Fill with Beer.

RED CLOUD
Fill glass with ice.
1 1/2 oz Gin
1/2 oz Apricot Liqueur
1/2 oz Lemon Juice
1 tsp Grenadine
Dash of Bitters
Shake.
Strain into chilled glass.

RED DEATH aka RED DEVIL
Fill glass with ice.
1/2 oz Vodka
1/2 oz Southern Comfort
1/2 oz Amaretto
1/2 oz Triple Sec
1/2 oz Sloe Gin
1/2 oz Lime Juice
Fill with Orange Juice.
Shake.

RED DEATH 2
Fill glass with ice.
1/2 oz Vodka
1/2 oz 151-Proof Rum
1/2 oz Yukon Jack
1/2 oz Cinnamon Schnapps
Stir.
Strain into chilled glass.

RED EYE
1 1/2 oz Vodka
1 Egg
2 oz Bloody Mary Mix
Fill with cold Beer.
Shake.

RED LION
Fill glass with ice.
1 oz Gin
1 oz Orange Liqueur
1/2 oz Orange Juice
1/2 oz Lemon Juice
Shake.
Strain into chilled glass.

R

RED NEEDLE
2 oz Tequila
Fill to 1/2 inch from top with Ginger Ale.
Top with Cranberry Juice.
Garnish with Lime.

RED PANTIES
Fill glass with ice.
1 1/2 oz Vodka
1/2 oz Peach Schnapps
Dash of Grenadine
1 oz Orange Juice
1 oz Cranberry Juice
Shake.
Strain into chilled glass.

RED ROOSTER
Fill 1 shot glass with Gold Tequila.
Fill 1 shot glass with Orange Juice.
Fill 1 shot glass with Bloody Mary mix.
Drink in order given, one after the other.

RED RUBY
Fill glass with ice.
2 oz Amaretto
2 tsp Grenadine
1 1/2 oz Orange Juice
1 1/2 oz Cranberry Juice
Fill with Ginger Ale.

RED RUM SONIC
Fill glass with ice.
2 oz Amber Rum
2 oz Cranberry Juice
Fill with equal parts Soda Water and Tonic Water.
Garnish with a Lemon.
Orville Giddings

RED RUSSIAN aka SNOWBERRY
Fill glass with ice.
1 oz Vodka
1 oz Strawberry Liqueur
Fill with Milk or Cream.
Shake.

RED SILK PANTIES
Fill glass with ice.
1 1/2 oz Vodka
1/2 oz Peach Schnapps
1 oz Cranberry Juice
Stir.
Strain into chilled glass.

RED SNAPPER
Fill glass with ice.
2 oz Gin
1 tsp of Horseradish
3 dashes of Tabasco Sauce
3 dashes of Worcestershire Sauce
Dash of Lime Juice
3 dashes of Celery Salt
3 dashes of Pepper
1 oz Clam Juice (optional)
Fill with Tomato Juice.
Shake.
Garnish with Lemon or Lime, Celery or Cucumber and/or Cocktail Shrimp.

RED WINE COOLER
Fill glass 3/4 with ice.
Fill 3/4 with Desired Red Wine.
Fill with Lemon-Lime Soda or Ginger Ale.
Stir.
Garnish with Lime.

RED ZIPPER
Fill glass with ice.
1 oz Vodka
1 oz Galliano
Fill with Cranberry Juice.
Stir.
Garnish with Lime.

REFORM
Fill glass with ice.
1 1/2 oz Dry Sherry
3/4 oz Dry Vermouth
1-2 dashes of Orange Bitters
Stir.
Strain into chilled glass.

RELEASE VALVE
Fill glass with ice.
1 oz Vodka
1 oz Rum
Fill with Pineapple Juice.
Top with 1/2 oz Grenadine.

RENAISSANCE COCKTAIL
Fill glass with ice.
1 1/2 oz Gin
1/2 oz Dry Sherry
1 Tbsp Cream
Shake.
Strain into chilled glass.
Sprinkle with Nutmeg.

RENDEZVOUS
Fill glass with ice.
1 1/2 oz Gin
1/2 oz Kirschwasser
1/2 oz Campari
Shake.
Strain into chilled glass.
Garnish with Lemon Twist.

RESTORATION
Fill glass with ice.
1 oz Brandy
1 oz Black Raspberry Liqueur
Dash of Sour Mix
Fill with Red Wine.
Shake.
Strain into wine glass.
Garnish with Lemon Twist.

REVEREND
Fill glass with ice.
2 oz Bourbon
2 oz Sour Mix
Shake and strain.
Fill with Beer.

RHETT BUTTLER
Fill glass with ice
1 1/2 oz Southern Comfort
1 tsp Curacao
1/2 oz Lime Juice
1/2 oz Lemon Juice
1 tsp Sugar
Shake.
Strain into chilled glass.

RICKEY
Fill glass with ice.
2 oz Desired Liqueur
Fill with Soda Water.
Stir.

RIGOR MORTIS
Fill glass with ice.
1 1/2 oz Vodka
1 oz Amaretto
Fill with equal parts Orange and
Pineapple Juice.
Shake.

RITZ FIZZ
Fill glass with ice.
1 oz Amaretto
1/2 oz Blue Curacao
1 oz Sour Mix
Shake.
Strain into chilled glass.
Fill with Champagne.
Garnish with Orange.

RITZ PICK-ME-UP
1 oz Cognac or Brandy
1 oz Orange Liqueur
2 oz Orange Juice
Fill with Champagne.

RIVER BERRY
Fill glass with ice.
1 oz Vodka
1 oz Wilderberry Schnapps
4 oz Sour Mix
Shake.
Drop of Grenadine
Splash of Soda Water

RIVIERA
Fill glass with ice.
3/4 oz Rum
3/4 oz Orange Liqueur
3/4 oz Black Raspberry Liqueur
Stir.

ROASTED TOASTED ALMOND
aka BURNT ALMOND, ORGASM
Fill glass with ice.
1 oz Vodka
1 oz Coffee Liqueur
1 oz Amaretto
Fill with Milk or Cream.
Shake.

ROASTED TOASTED ALMOND
(frozen)
In Blender:
1/2 cup of Ice
1 oz Vodka
1 oz Coffee Liqueur
1 oz Amaretto
Scoop of Vanilla Ice Cream
Blend until smooth.
If too thick add milk or cream.
If too thin add ice or ice cream.

ROB ROY
(*CAUTION:* DRY can mean either
make drink with Dry Vermouth or
less Sweet Vermouth than usual.
PERFECT means use equal
amounts of Sweet and Dry
Vermouth.
SWEET means use more
Sweet Vermouth than usual.)
Fill glass with ice.
2 oz Scotch Whiskey
1/2 oz Sweet Vermouth
Stir.
Strain into chilled glass or pour
contents (with ice) into short glass.
Garnish with Cherry or Lemon
Twist.

ROBSON
Fill glass with ice.
1 1/2 oz Jamaican Rum
1 Tbsp Orange Juice
1 1/2 tsp Lemon Juice
1 tsp Grenadine
Shake.
Serve or strain into chilled glass.

ROCK LOBSTER (frozen)
In Blender:
1 cup of Ice.
1 oz Coconut Rum
1/2 oz Banana Liqueur
Dash of Grenadine
1/2 ripe peeled Banana
Dash of Pineapple and Orange
Juice
Blend until smooth.
Top with Dark Rum.

R

ROCKAWAY BEACH
Fill glass with ice.
1 1/2 oz Light Rum
1/2 oz Dark Rum
1/2 oz Tequila
1 oz Orange Juice
1/2 oz Pineapple Juice
1/2 oz Cranberry Juice
1 tsp Creme De Nouyax
Shake.
Garnish with Cherry.

ROCKET
Fill glass with ice.
2 oz Yukon Jack
Fill with Lemonade.
Float 1/2 oz 151-Proof Rum
on top.

ROCKY ROAD
Fill glass with ice.
1 oz Hazelnut Liqueur
1 oz Creme De Cacao
Fill with Milk or Cream.
Shake.

ROMAN CANDLE
Fill glass with ice.
1 oz Sambuca
1 oz Amaretto
Dash of Grenadine
Fill with Orange Juice.
Shake.
Top with Soda Water.

ROMAN CAPPUCCINO
1 1/2 oz Sambuca
Fill with Espresso.
Top with steamed Milk.
Garnish with 3 Coffee Beans.

ROMAN CAPPUCCINO (frozen)
In Blender:
1/2 cup of Ice
2 oz Sambuca
3 oz Espresso
Scoop of Vanilla or Coffee Ice
Cream
Blend until smooth.

ROMAN COFFEE
2 oz Sambuca
Fill with hot Black Coffee.
Top with Whipped Cream.
Garnish with 3 Coffee Beans.

ROMAN HOLIDAY
Fill glass with ice.
3/4 oz Amaretto
3/4 oz Sambuca
3/4 oz Blackberry Brandy
Fill with Milk.
Shake.

ROMAN ICED TEA
Fill glass with ice.
1/2 oz Vodka
1/2 oz Gin
1/2 oz Rum
1/2 oz Triple Sec
1/2 oz Amaretto
Fill with equal parts Cranberry
Juice and Sour Mix.
Shake.
Top with Lemon-Lime Soda.

ROMAN RASTA COFFEE
1 oz Sambuca
1 oz Dark Rum
Fill with hot Black Coffee.
Top with Whipped Cream.

ROOT BEER
Fill glass with ice.
3/4 oz Vodka
3/4 oz Coffee Liqueur
3/4 oz Galliano
Fill with Cola.
Stir.

ROOT BEER FLOAT
Fill glass with ice.
1 oz Vodka
1 oz Root Beer Schnapps
1 oz Cream
Shake.
Top with 2 oz Cola.

ROOT BEER FLOAT 2
Place a scoop of Vanilla Ice Cream
in large glass.
2 oz Dark Rum
Fill with Root Beer.

ROSÉ COOLER
Fill glass 3/4 with ice.
Fill 3/4 with Rosé Wine.
Fill with Ginger Ale
or Lemon-Lime Soda.
Garnish with Lime.

ROSE HALL
Fill glass with ice.
1 1/2 oz Dark Rum
1/2 oz Banana Liqueur
1 oz Orange Juice
1 tsp Lime Juice
Shake.
Serve or strain into chilled glass.
Garnish with a Lime.

ROSÉ SPRITZER
Fill glass 3/4 with ice.
Fill glass 3/4 with Rosé Wine.
Fill with Soda Water.
Garnish with Lime.

ROXANNE
Fill glass with ice.
1 oz Vodka
1/2 oz Peach Schnapps
1/2 oz Amaretto
Fill with equal parts Orange Juice
and Cranberry Juice.
Shake.
Strain into chilled glass.

ROYAL CANADIAN
Fill glass with ice.
1/2 oz Canadian Whiskey
1/2 oz Coffee Liqueur
1/2 oz Amaretto
Strain into chilled glass.

ROYAL GIN FIZZ
Fill glass with ice.
2 oz Gin
1/2 oz Orange Liqueur
1 Egg
1 oz Lemon Juice or Sour Mix
1 tsp Sugar Syrup
Shake.
Fill with Soda Water.

ROYAL SCREW
Fill glass 3/4 with ice.
2 oz Cognac
2 oz Orange Juice
Fill with Champagne.

ROYAL SHEET COFFEE
1 oz Amaretto
1 oz Coffee Liqueur
Fill with hot Black Coffee.
Top with Whipped Cream.
Sprinkle with Shaved Almonds.

ROYAL SMILE
Fill glass with ice.
1 oz Apple Brandy
1/2 oz Gin
1/2 oz Lemon Juice
1 tsp Grenadine
Shake.
Strain into chilled glass.

ROYAL SPRITZER
Fill glass 3/4 with ice.
1 oz Black Raspberry Liqueur
Fill 3/4 with Champagne.
Fill with Soda.
Garnish with Lime.

R. ROGERS
Fill glass with ice.
Fill with Cola.
Dash of Grenadine
Garnish with Cherry.

R. ROYCE
Fill glass with ice.
1 1/2 oz Gin
1/2 oz Dry Vermouth
1/2 oz Sweet Vermouth
Stir.
Strain into chilled glass.

RUBY FIZZ
Fill glass with ice.
2 1/2 oz Sloe Gin
1/2 Egg White
1 tsp Grenadine
1 tsp Sugar Syrup
or Powdered Sugar
1 oz Lemon Juice
Shake.
Fill with Soda Water.

RUBY RED
Fill glass with ice.
1 1/2 oz Vodka
1/2 oz Grenadine or Campari
Fill with Grapefruit Juice.
Shake.

RUDDY MIMOSA
1/2 oz Peach Schnapps
1 oz Orange Juice
1 oz Cranberry Juice
Fill with Champagne.
Garnish with Orange.

RUM AND COKE
Fill glass with ice.
2 oz Rum
Fill with Cola.
Garnish with Lime.

RUMBALL
1 oz Dark Rum
1 oz Chocolate Liqueur
Stir.

RUM MADRAS aka
BOG FOG
Fill glass with ice.
2 oz Rum
Fill with equal parts Orange and
Cranberry Juice.
Garnish with Lime.

RUM PUNCH
Fill glass with ice.
2 oz Rum
Dash of Grenadine
Fill with equal parts Orange and
Pineapple Juice.
Shake
Splash with Lemon-Lime Soda.
Garnish with Lime.

RUM RUNNER
Fill glass with ice.
1/2 oz Light Rum
1/2 oz Dark Rum
1/2 oz Banana Liqueur
1/2 oz Blackberry Brandy
Dash of Grenadine
Dash of Sour Mix
Dash of Orange Juice
Shake.
Float 1/2 oz 151-Proof Rum
on top.

R

RUM RUNNER (frozen)
In Blender:
1 cup of Ice
1 oz Rum
1 oz Banana Liqueur
1/2 oz Blackberry Brandy
Dash of Grenadine
Dash of Lime Juice
Blend until smooth.
If too thick add liqueur or juice.
If too thin add ice.

RUM-LACED CIDER
1 oz Dark Rum
1 oz Spiced Rum
Fill with hot Apple Cider.
Float Pat of Butter on top.
Sprinkle Cinnamon and whole
Cloves on top.

RUMPLESTILTSKIN
1 oz 100-Proof Peppermint
Schnapps
1 oz Bourbon
Potter

RUN, SKIP AND GO NAKED
Fill glass with ice.
1/2 oz Gin
1/2 oz Rum
1/2 oz Brandy
1/2 oz Triple Sec
Fill with Sour Mix (leaving 1/2 inch
from top).
Shake.
Top with Beer.

RUPTURED DUCK
Fill glass with ice.
1 oz Banana Liqueur
1 oz Creme De Nouyax
1 oz Cream
Shake.
Strain into chilled glass.

RUSSIAN
Fill glass with ice.
3/4 oz Vodka
3/4 oz Gin
3/4 oz White Creme De Cacao
Shake.
Strain into chilled glass.

RUSSIAN BANANA
Fill glass with ice.
3/4 oz Vodka
3/4 oz Banana Liqueur
3/4 oz Dark Creme De Cacao
1 oz Cream or Milk
Shake.
Strain into chilled glass.

RUSSIAN BEAR
Fill glass with ice.
1 oz Vodka
1 oz Dark Creme De Cacao
1 oz Heavy Cream
Shake.
Strain into chilled glass.

RUSSIAN COFFEE
2 oz Vodka
Fill with hot Black Coffee.
1/2 tsp of Sugar (optional)
Stir.
Top with Whipped Cream.
Garnish with Orange.

RUSSIAN NIGHTS aka
FLYING MADRAS
Fill glass with ice.
2 oz Vodka
2 oz Cranberry Juice
2 oz Orange Juice
Fill with Champagne.
Garnish with Orange.

RUSSIAN QUWAYLUDE
Fill glass with ice.
1 oz Vodka
1 oz Irish Cream
1 oz Hazelnut Liqueur
Fill with Milk.
Shake.

RUSSIAN QUWAYLUDE 2
Fill glass with ice.
1/2 oz Vodka
1/2 oz Coffee Liqueur
1/2 oz Amaretto
1/2 oz Hazelnut Liqueur
1/2 oz Irish Cream
1 oz Milk (optional)
Shake.

RUSSIAN QUWAYLUDE (floater)
1 oz Hazelnut Liqueur (bottom)
1 oz Irish Cream
1 oz Vodka (top)

RUSSIAN QUWAYLUDE (frozen)
In Blender:
1/2 cup of Ice
1/2 oz Vodka
1/2 oz Coffee Liqueur
1/2 oz Irish Cream
1/2 oz Hazelnut Liqueur
1/2 oz Tia Maria
1/2 oz Amaretto
Scoop of Vanilla Ice Cream
Blend until smooth.
If too thick add milk or cream.
If too thin add ice or ice cream.
Garnish with Shaved Chocolate or
Sprinkles.

RUSSIAN ROSE
Fill glass with ice.
2 oz Vodka
1/2 oz Grenadine
Dash of Orange Bitters
Shake.
Strain into chilled glass.

RUSSIAN ROULETTE
Fill glass with ice.
1 oz Vodka
1/2 oz Drambuie
1/2 oz Galliano
Fill with equal parts Sour Mix and
Orange Juice.
Shake.
Garnish with Lemon.
Teddy Chan

RUSSIAN ROULETTE 2
Fill glass with ice.
1/2 oz Vodka
1/2 oz Brandy or Cognac
1/2 oz Banana Liqueur
1 oz Sour Mix
1 oz Orange Juice
Shake.
Strain into chilled glass.

RUSSIAN SUNRISE
Fill glass with ice.
2 oz Vodka
Fill with Orange Juice.
Pour 1/2 oz Grenadine down spoon
to bottom of glass.
Garnish with Orange.

RUSTY NAIL
Fill glass with ice.
1 1/2 oz Scotch
1/2 oz Drambuie
Stir.

RUSTY NAIL COFFEE aka
HEATHER COFFEE
1 oz Scotch
1 oz Drambuie
Fill with hot Black Coffee.
Top with Whipped Cream.
Sprinkle with Cinnamon.

SAINT MORITZ (floater)
1/2 oz Black Raspberry Liqueur
(bottom)
1/2 oz Milk or Cream (top)

SAKETINI
Fill glass with ice.
2 oz Gin
1/2 oz Sake
Stir.
Strain into chilled glass
or pour contents (with ice)
into short glass.
Garnish with Lemon Twist
or Olives.

SALTY BULL
Fill glass with ice.
2 oz Tequila
Fill with Grapefruit Juice.
Rub rim of second glass with Lime.
Dip rim in Kosher Salt.
Pour contents of first glass into
salted glass.
Garnish with Lime.

SALTY DOG
Fill glass with ice.
2 oz Gin or Vodka
Fill with Grapefruit Juice.
Rub rim of second glass with Lime.
Dip rim in kosher salt.
Pour contents of first glass into
salted glass.
Garnish with Lime.

SALTY DOGITRON
Fill glass with ice.
2 oz Citrus Vodka
Dash of Grenadine
Fill with Grapefruit Juice.

SAMARI
Fill glass with ice.
1 1/2 oz Citrus Vodka
1/2 oz Triple Sec
Stir.
Garnish with a Lemon.

SAN FRANCISCO
Fill glass with ice.
3/4 oz Sloe Gin
3/4 oz Dry Vermouth
3/4 oz Sweet Vermouth
Dash of Bitters
Dash of Orange Bitters
Shake.
Strain into chilled glass.

SAN JUAN (frozen)
In Blender:
1 cup of Ice
1 1/2 oz Amber Rum
1 oz Grapefruit Juice
1 oz Lime Juice
1/2 oz Cream of Coconut
Blend until smooth.
If too thick add juice.
If too thin add ice.
Float tsp 151-Proof Rum
on top.
Garnish with Lime.

SAN JUAN SUNSET
Fill glass with ice.
2 oz Rum
Fill with Orange Juice.
Float 1/2 oz Cherry Brandy
on top.

SAN SEBASTIAN
Fill glass with ice.
1 oz Gin
1 1/2 tsp Rum
1/2 tsp Triple Sec
1 Tbsp Grapefruit Juice
1 Tbsp Lemon Juice
Shake.
Strain into chilled glass.

SANCTUARY
Fill glass with ice.
1 1/2 oz Dubonnet Rouge
3/4 oz Amer Picon
3/4 oz Orange Liqueur
Shake.
Serve or strain into chilled glass.

SAND BLASTER
Fill glass with ice.
1 oz Rum
1 oz Jaegermeister
Fill with Cola.
Stir.

SAND FLEA
Fill glass with ice.
1 oz Rum
1/2 oz Apricot Brandy
1/2 oz Orange Liqueur
Dash of Grenadine.
Fill with equal parts Orange Juice
and Sour Mix.

SANGRIA
(Chill all ingredients prior to
mixing.)
In a large punch bowl with a cake
of ice in it, mix:
2 750ml bottles of desired
Red Wine
3 oz Curacao or Triple Sec
2 oz Brandy
1/2 cup Orange Juice
1/4 cup Lemon Juice
1/4 cup Sugar
2 oz Water
Stir until sugar dissolves.
Add an Orange and a Lemon sliced
thinly.
Add 1 qt Soda Water.

SANGRIA
Fill glass with ice.
1 oz Orange Liqueur
1/2 oz Brandy
Dash of Sour Mix
Dash of Orange Juice
Pinch Sugar
Fill with desired Red Wine.
Shake.
Splash with Soda Water.
Garnish with Orange and Lemon.

SANTIAGO
Fill glass with ice.
1 oz Light Rum
1 oz Dark Rum
1 oz Triple Sec
1 oz Sour Mix
1/2 oz Lime Juice
2-3 dashes of Bitters
Shake.
Strain into chilled glass.
Garnish with Lime.

SANTIAGO 2
Fill glass with ice.
3/4 oz Light Rum
3/4 oz Dark Rum
3/4 oz Triple Sec
1 oz Sour Mix
1/2 oz Lime Juice
2-3 dashes of Bitters
Shake.
Strain into tall chilled glass.
Fill with Champagne.
Garnish with Lime.

SARATOGA
Fill glass with ice.
2 oz Brandy
1 oz crushed fresh or canned
Pineapple
1/2 tsp Maraschino Liqueur
2 or 3 dashes of Bitters
Shake.
Strain into chilled glass.

SATURN'S RING (floater)
1/2 oz Anisette (bottom)
1/2 oz Grenadine
1/2 oz Southern Comfort (top)

SAUCY SUE
Fill glass with ice.
2 oz Apple Brandy
1/2 tsp Apricot Brandy
1/2 tsp Pernod
Stir.
Strain into chilled glass.

SAVANNAH
Fill glass with ice.
2 oz Gin
1 Egg White
1 oz Orange Juice
Shake.
Strain into chilled glass.
Top with 1/2 oz White Creme De
Cacao.

SAVE THE PLANET
Fill glass with ice.
1 oz Vodka
1 oz Melon Liqueur
1/2 oz Blue Curacao
Shake.
Strain into chilled glass.
Float 1/2 oz Green Chartreuse on
top.

SAVOY HOTEL (floater)
1/2 oz White Creme De Cacao
(bottom)
1/2 oz Benedictine
1/2 oz Brandy (top)

SAVOY TANGO
Fill glass with ice.
1 1/2 oz Apple Brandy
1 oz Sloe Gin
Stir.
Strain into chilled glass.

SAZERAC
Fill glass with ice.
2 oz Bourbon
1 tsp Sugar
2 dashes of Bitters
Stir until sugar dissolves.
Coat inside of second glass with
Pernod.
Strain mixture into coated glass.
Garnish with Lemon Twist.

SCARLET LETTER aka CHAM CRAN CHAM, BRUT AND BOGS
Fill glass 3/4 with ice.
Fill glass 3/4 with Champagne.
Dash of Black Raspberry Liqueur
Fill with Cranberry Juice.

SCARLET O'HARA
Fill glass with ice.
2 oz Southern Comfort
Dash of Lime Juice (optional)
Fill with Cranberry Juice.
Garnish with Lime.

SCORPION (frozen)
In Blender:
1/2 cup of Ice
1 oz Light Rum
1 oz Gin
1 oz Brandy
1 oz Orange Juice
1 oz White wine
1 oz Lemon Juice
1/2 oz Creme De Nouyax or Orgeat
Syrup
Blend until smooth.
Float 1/2 oz Dark Rum on top.
Garnish with gardenia.

SCORPION (floater)
1/2 oz Grenadine (bottom)
1 oz Blackberry Brandy
1/2 oz Vodka (top)

SCOTCH COLLINS aka JOE COLLINS
Fill glass with ice.
2 oz Scotch
Fill with Sour Mix.
Shake.
Splash with Soda Water.
Garnish with Orange and Cherry.

SCOTCH SOUR
Fill glass with ice.
2 oz Scotch
Fill with Sour Mix.
Shake.
Garnish with Orange and Cherry.

SCOTTISH COFFEE
2 oz Drambuie or Scotch
or 1 oz of each
Fill with hot Black Coffee.
Top with Whipped Cream.
Sprinkle with Shaved Chocolate.

SCREAMER
Fill glass with ice.
1 1/2 oz Greek Brandy
1/2 oz Green Chartreuse
Stir.
Strain into chilled glass.

SCREAMING BANSHEE
Fill glass with ice.
1 oz Vodka
1 oz Banana Liqueur
1/2 oz White Creme De Cacao
Fill with Milk or Cream.
Shake.

SCREAMING NAZI
Fill glass with ice.
1 oz 100-Proof Peppermint
Schnapps
1 oz Jaegermeister
Stir.
Strain into chilled glass.

SCREAMING O.
Fill glass with ice.
1/2 oz Vodka
1/2 oz Coffee Liqueur
1/2 oz Amaretto
1/2 oz Irish Cream
Fill with equal parts Milk
or Cream and Soda Water.

SCREAMING VIKING aka SKYSCRAPER
Fill glass with ice.
2 oz Bourbon
2-3 dashes of Bitters
1/2 oz Lime Juice
Fill with Cranberry Juice.
Stir.
Garnish with Cucumber.

SCREAMING YELLOW MONKEY
Fill glass with ice.
1 oz Vodka
1 oz Banana Liqueur
1/2 oz White Creme De Cacao
Fill with Milk or Cream.
Shake.

SCREWDRIVER
Fill glass with ice.
2 oz Vodka
Fill with Orange Juice.
Garnish with Orange or Lime.

SCREW-UP
Fill glass with ice.
2 oz Vodka
Splash of Orange Juice
Fill with Lemon-Lime Soda.
Garnish with Orange.

S

SEA BREEZE aka
CAPE GRAPE
Fill glass with ice.
2 oz Vodka
Fill with equal parts Cranberry and
Grapefruit Juice
Garnish with Lime.

SELF-STARTER
Fill glass with ice.
1 oz Gin
1/2 oz Lillet Blanc
1 tsp Apricot Brandy
2-3 dashes of Pernod
Shake.
Strain into chilled glass.

SEPARATOR aka
DIRTY MOTHER
Fill glass with ice.
1 1/2 oz Brandy
3/4 oz Coffee Liqueur
1 oz Cream (optional)
Stir.

SEPTEMBER MORN
Fill glass with ice.
2 1/2 oz Rum
1/2 oz Lime Juice
1 tsp Grenadine
1 Egg White
Shake.
Strain into chilled glass.

SEVEN AND SEVEN
Fill glass with ice.
2 oz Seagram's 7 Whiskey
Fill with 7-up.
Garnish with Lemon.

SEVENTH AVENUE
Fill glass with ice.
1 oz Amaretto
1 oz Drambuie
1 oz Chocolate Liqueur
Fill with Milk or Cream.
Shake.

SEVENTH HEAVEN
Fill glass with ice.
1 1/2 oz Whiskey
1/2 oz Amaretto
Fill with Orange Juice.
Stir.

727
Fill glass with ice.
1/2 oz Vodka
1/2 oz Coffee Liqueur
1/2 oz Irish Cream
1/2 oz Orange Liqueur
Shake.

747 (floater)
1/2 oz Coffee Liqueur (bottom)
1/2 oz Irish Cream
1/2 oz Hazelnut Liqueur (top)

SEVILLA
Fill glass with ice.
1 oz Dark Rum
1 oz Sweet Vermouth
Shake.
Strain into chilled glass.
Garnish with Orange Twist.

SEVILLA 2
Fill glass with ice.
1 1/2 oz Rum
1 1/2 oz Port
1 egg
1/2 tsp Powdered Sugar
or Sugar Syrup
Shake.
Sprinkle Nutmeg on top.

SEX
Fill glass with ice.
1 oz Coffee Liqueur
1 oz Orange Liqueur
Stir.
Garnish with Orange.

SEX AT MY HOUSE
Fill glass with ice.
1 oz Amaretto
1 oz Black Raspberry Liqueur
Fill with Pineapple Juice.
Shake.
Garnish with Pineapple.

SEX AT THE BEACH
Fill glass with ice.
1/2 oz Vodka
1/2 oz Southern Comfort
1/2 oz Peach Schnapps
1/2 oz Apple Brandy
1/2 oz Orange Liqueur
1/2 oz Orange Juice
1/2 oz Cranberry Juice
1/2 oz Milk or Cream
Shake.
Strain into chilled glass.

SEX IN A HOT TUB
Fill glass with ice.
1 oz Vodka
1/2 oz Peach Schnapps
1/2 oz Black Raspberry Liqueur
Dash of Cranberry Juice
Dash of Pineapple Juice
Shake.
Fill with Champagne.

SEX IN THE WOODS
Fill glass with ice.
1 oz Vodka
1/2 oz Amaretto
1/2 oz Coffee Liqueur
Fill with Pineapple Juice.
Shake.

SEX ON THE BEACH
Fill glass with ice.
1 1/2 oz Vodka
1/2 oz Peach Schnapps
Fill with equal parts Cranberry and
Orange or Pineapple Juice.
Garnish with Orange or Pineapple.

SEX ON THE BEACH 2
Fill glass with ice.
1 oz Vodka
1/2 oz Melon Liqueur
1/2 oz Black Raspberry Liqueur
Fill with Pineapple Juice or equal
parts Pineapple and Cranberry
Juice.
Shake.
Garnish with Pineapple.

SEX ON THE BEACH 3
Fill glass with ice.
1 oz Vodka
1/2 oz Coffee Liqueur
1/2 oz Black Raspberry Liqueur
Fill with Pineapple Juice.
Shake.

SEX ON THE BEACH IN WINTER
Fill glass with ice.
1 oz Vodka
1 oz Peach Schnapps
1/2 tsp Cream of Coconut
Fill with equal parts Pineapple and
Cranberry Juice.
Shake.

SEXY
Fill glass with ice.
1 oz Coffee Liqueur
1 oz Orange Liqueur
Fill with Milk or Cream.
Shake.
Garnish with Orange.

SHADY LADY
Fill glass with ice.
1 oz Tequila
1 oz Melon Liqueur
Fill with Grapefruit Juice.

SHANGHAI
Fill glass with ice.
1 1/2 oz Dark Rum
1/2 oz Sambuca or Anisette
1/2 oz Lemon Juice
1 tsp Grenadine
Shake.
Strain into chilled glass.

SHANTE'GAF
Fill glass 3/4 with Ale or Beer.
Fill with Ginger Beer or
Lemon-Lime Soda.

SHARK ATTACK
Fill glass with ice.
2 oz Light Rum
Fill with Lemonade.
Float 1/2 oz Blue Curacao
on top.

SHARK BITE
Fill glass with ice.
2 oz Dark Rum
Dash of Grenadine
Fill with Orange Juice.
Shake.
Garnish with Orange and Cherry.

SHARK BITE 2
Fill glass with ice.
1 oz Vodka
1 oz Coconut Rum
Fill with Pineapple Juice.
Shake.
Top with Cranberry Juice.
Shawn Sullivan

SHARK'S TOOTH
Fill glass with ice.
1 1/2 oz Dark Rum
1/2 oz Lime Juice
1/2 oz Lemon Juice
1/4 oz Grenadine
Shake.
Fill with Soda Water.

SHARK'S TOOTH 2
Fill glass with ice.
2 oz Dark Rum
Fill with Sour Mix.
Shake.
Top with 1/2 oz Grenadine.

SHARKY PUNCH
Fill glass with ice.
1 1/2 oz Apple Brandy
1/2 oz Whiskey
1 tsp Sugar Syrup
Shake.
Fill with Soda Water.

SHERRY COCKTAIL
Fill glass with ice.
2 1/2 oz Cream Sherry
Dash of Bitters
Stir.
Strain into chilled glass.
Garnish with Orange Twist.

SHERRY TWIST
Fill glass with ice.
3 oz Sherry
1 oz Brandy
1 oz Dry Vermouth
1/2 tsp Curacao or Triple Sec
3 dashes of Lemon Juice
Shake.
Strain into chilled glass.
Sprinkle with Cinnamon.

S

SHILLELAGH aka BUSHWACKER
Fill glass with ice.
1 oz Irish Whiskey or Irish Mist
1 oz Irish Cream
Stir.

SHIPWRECK
Fill glass with ice.
2 oz Coconut Rum
Fill with Pineapple Juice.
Top with 1/2 oz 151-Proof Rum.
Garnish with Pineapple.

SHIRLEY TEMPLE
Fill glass with ice.
Fill with Ginger Ale or
Lemon-Lime Soda.
Dash of Grenadine
Garnish with Cherry.

SHIVER SHOT
Find an attractive, desirable, ample bust.
Ask permission to use it.
If yes, fill shot glass with Tequila.
Lick upper chest, and salt
moistened location.
Place Lime wedge between desired lips.
Place shot glass in cleavage.
Lick salt, drink shot, take Lime.
(No Hands)

SHOT IN THE DARK
1/2 oz Yukon Jack
1/2 oz Orange Liqueur
1/2 oz hot Black Coffee

SIBERIAN
Fill glass with ice.
1 1/2 oz Vodka
1/2 oz Coffee Liqueur
1/2 oz Brandy
Stir.

SICILIAN COFFEE
1 oz Southern Comfort
1 oz Amaretto
Fill glass with hot Black Coffee.
Top with Whipped Cream.
Sprinkle with Shaved Almonds.

SICILIAN KISS
Fill glass with ice.
1 1/2 oz Southern Comfort
1/2 oz Amaretto
Stir.

SIDECAR
Fill glass with ice.
1 1/2 oz Brandy
1/2 oz Triple Sec
Fill with Sour Mix.
Shake.
Garnish with Orange and Cherry.

SILK PANTIES
Fill glass with ice.
3/4 oz Peach Schnapps
3/4 oz Sambuca or Vodka
Stir.
Strain into chilled glass.

SILK PANTIES 2 aka WOO WOO
Fill glass with ice.
3/4 oz Vodka
3/4 oz Peach Schnapps
1 oz Cranberry Juice
Stir.
Strain into chilled glass.

SILK SHORTS
3/4 oz Vodka
3/4 oz Peach Schnapps
Stir.

SILKEN VEIL
Fill glass with ice.
1 oz Vodka
1 oz Dubonnet Rouge
Stir.
Garnish with twist.

SILVER BULLET
Fill glass with ice.
1 1/2 oz Tequila
1/2 oz White Creme De Menthe
Stir.
Serve or strain into chilled glass.

SILVER CLOUD
Fill glass with ice.
1/2 oz Vodka
1/2 oz Coffee Liqueur
1/2 oz White Creme De Cacao
1/ oz Amaretto
Fill with Milk.
Shake.
Top with Whipped Cream.

SILVER FIZZ
Fill glass with ice.
2 oz Gin
1 Egg White
2 oz Sour Mix
Shake.
Strain into chilled glass.
Fill with Soda Water.

SILVER FIZZ 2
Fill glass with ice.
2 oz Gin
1 Egg White
1/2 oz Sugar Syrup
or 1 tsp Sugar
1 oz Sour Mix
2 oz Cream or Milk
Shake.
Strain into chilled glass.
Splash with Soda Water.
Garnish with Orange and Cherry.

SILVER KING
Fill glass with ice.
1 1/2 oz Gin
1 Egg White
1 oz Lemon Juice
1/2 tsp Sugar Syrup
or Powdered Sugar
2 dashes of Orange Bitters
Shake.
Serve or strain into chilled glass.

SILVER SPIDER
Fill glass with ice.
1/2 oz Vodka
1/2 oz Light Rum
1/2 oz Triple Sec
1/2 oz White Creme De Menthe
Stir.
Serve or strain into chilled glass.

SILVERADO
Fill glass with ice.
1 1/2 oz Vodka
1/2 oz Campari
Fill with Orange or Grapefruit Juice.
Shake.

SIMPLY EXQUISITE
Fill glass with ice.
3/4 oz Orange Liqueur
3/4 oz Banana Liqueur
3/4 oz Hazelnut Liqueur
Fill with Milk or Cream.
Shake.
Garnish with Orange and Banana.

SINGAPORE SLING
Fill glass with ice.
2 oz Gin
Splash Sloe Gin
3 oz Sour Mix
Shake.
Splash of Soda Water
Top with Cherry Brandy.
Garnish with Cherry and Lemon.

SINGAPORE SLING 2
Fill glass with ice.
1 1/2 oz Gin
1/2 oz Triple Sec
Dash of Lime Juice
Fill with equal parts Orange,
Pineapple Juice and Sour Mix.
Shake.
Top with Cherry Brandy
Garnish with Orange and Cherry.

SINK OR SWIM
Fill glass with ice.
1 1/2 oz Brandy
1/2 oz Sweet Vermouth
3 dashes of Bitters
Shake.
Strain into chilled glass.

SIR WALTER
Fill glass with ice.
1 1/2 oz Brandy
3/4 oz Light Rum
1 tsp Curacao
1 tsp Grenadine
1 tsp Lemon or Lime Juice
Shake.
Serve or strain into chilled glass.

S. O. M. F. (floater)
1/2 oz Coffee Liqueur (bottom)
1/2 oz Irish Cream
1/2 oz Hazelnut Liqueur (top)

S. O. M. F. 2 (floater)
1/2 oz Blackberry Brandy
(bottom)
1/2 oz Amaretto
1/2 oz Triple Sec
1/2 oz Lime Juice (top)

SKINNY DIPPING
Fill glass with ice.
1 1/2 oz Vodka
1/2 oz Peach Schnapps
1/2 oz Amaretto
Fill with equal parts Orange and
Cranberry Juice.
Stir.
Garnish with Orange.

SKIP AND GO NAKED
Fill glass with ice.
2 oz Gin
Fill with Orange Juice
(leaving 1/2 inch from top).
Float Beer on top.
Garnish with Orange.

SKIP AND GO NAKED 2
Fill glass with ice.
2 oz Gin or Vodka
Dash of Grenadine
Fill with Sour Mix
(leaving 1/2 inch from top).
Float Beer on top.
Garnish with Lemon.

SKULL CRACKER
Fill glass with ice.
4 oz Rum
1 oz White Creme De Cacao
1 oz Pineapple Juice
1 oz Lemon Juice
Shake.
Garnish with Lime.

SKYSCRAPER aka
SCREAMING VIKING
Fill glass with ice.
2 oz Bourbon
2-3 dashes of Bitters
1/2 oz Lime Juice
Fill with Cranberry Juice.
Stir.
Garnish with Cucumber.

S

SLEDGEHAMMER
Fill glass with ice.
1 oz Brandy
1 oz Apple Brandy
1 oz Dark Rum
2 dashes of Pernod
Shake.
Strain into chilled glass.

SLEDGEHAMMER 2
Fill glass with ice.
1 oz Gin
1 oz Coconut Rum
Dash of Grenadine
Fill with equal parts Pineapple and
Orange Juice.
Shake.

SLEDGEHAMMER (floater)
1 oz Sambuca (bottom)
1 oz Cognac or Brandy (top)

SLEEPY HEAD
Fill glass with ice.
3 oz Brandy
Fill with Ginger Ale.
Garnish with Orange Twist.

SLIM JIM
Fill glass with ice.
2 oz Vodka
Fill with Diet Soda.
Garnish with Lime.

SLIMEBALL
Make Lime Flavored Gelatin.
Replace 1 cup of water in the
recipe with:
6 oz Vodka
2 oz Melon Liqueur
Chill until it coagulates.

SLIPPERY BLACK NIPPLE
(floater)
1 1/2 oz Black Sambuca
(bottom)
1/2 oz Irish Cream (top)
Carefully drip a single drop of
Grenadine in center (optional).

SLIPPERY DICK (floater)
1 1/2 oz Banana Liqueur
(bottom)
1/2 oz Irish Cream (top)

SLIPPERY NIPPLE
Fill glass with ice.
1 1/2 oz Sambuca
1/2 oz Irish Cream
Shake.

SLIPPERY NIPPLE (floater)
1 1/2 oz Sambuca (bottom)
1/2 oz Irish Cream (top)
Carefully drop a single drop of
Grenadine in center (optional).

SLIPPERY NIPPLE 2 (floater)
1 1/2 oz Peppermint Schnapps
1/2 oz Irish Cream
Carefully drip a single drop of
Grenadine in center (optional).

SLOE BALL
Fill glass with ice.
1 oz Sloe Gin
1/2 oz Vodka
1/2 oz Gin
Dash of Sour Mix
1 oz Orange Juice
Shake.
Strain into chilled glass.

SLOE BOAT TO CHINA
Fill glass with ice.
1 1/2 oz Ginger Liqueur
1/2 oz Sloe Gin
Stir.
Fill with Lemon-Lime Soda.

SLOE BRANDY
Fill glass with ice.
2 oz Brandy
1/2 oz Sloe Gin
1 tsp Lemon Juice
Shake.
Strain into chilled glass.
Garnish with Lemon Twist.

SLOE COMFORTABLE SCREW
Fill glass with ice.
1 oz Vodka
1 oz Southern Comfort
1/2 oz Sloe Gin
Fill with Orange Juice.
Garnish with Orange.

SLOE COMFORTABLE SCREW
AGAINST THE WALL
Fill glass with ice.
1 oz Vodka
1 oz Southern Comfort
1/2 oz Sloe Gin
Fill with Orange Juice.
Shake.
Top with Galliano.
Garnish with Orange.

SLOE DOG
Fill glass with ice.
1 1/2 oz Vodka
1/2 oz Sloe Gin
Fill with Grapefruit Juice.
Shake.

SLOE GIN FIZZ
Fill glass with ice.
2 oz Sloe Gin
Fill with Sour Mix.
Shake.
Splash with Soda Water.
Garnish with Lemon.

SLOE POKE
Fill glass with ice.
2 oz Sloe Gin
Fill with Cola.

SLOE SCREW
Fill glass with ice.
1 1/2 oz Sloe Gin
or 3/4 oz Vodka
and 3/4 oz Sloe Gin
Fill with Orange Juice.
Stir.
Garnish with Orange.

SLOE TEQUILA
Fill glass with ice.
1 1/2 oz Tequila
1/2 oz Sloe Gin
1 tsp Lime Juice
Shake.
Strain into chilled glass.
Garnish with Cucumber Peel.

SLOPPY JOE
Fill glass with ice.
3/4 oz Rum
3/4 oz Dry Vermouth
1/4 oz Triple Sec
1/4 oz Grenadine
1 oz Lime Juice
Shake.
Serve or strain into chilled glass.

SLOPPY JOE'S
Fill glass with ice.
1 oz Brandy
1 oz Port
1/2 tsp Triple Sec
1 oz Pineapple Juice
1/2 tsp Grenadine
Shake.
Strain into chilled glass.

SMITH AND KERNS
Fill glass with ice.
2 oz Coffee Liqueur
1 oz Cream
Shake.
Fill with Soda Water.

SMOOTH DRIVER
Fill glass with ice.
2 oz Vodka
Fill with Orange Juice.
Float 1/2 oz Orange Liqueur on top.

SMURF P.
Fill glass with ice.
1 oz Light Rum
1/2 oz Blueberry Schnapps
1/2 oz Blue Curacao
1 oz Sour Mix
Shake.
Strain into chilled glass.
Splash with Lemon-Lime Soda.

SNAKE BITE
Fill glass with ice.
2 oz Yukon Jack
Dash of Lime Juice
Shake.
Serve or strain into chilled glass.
Garnish with Lime.

SNAKE BITE 2
Fill glass with ice.
1 1/2 oz Bourbon
or Canadian Whiskey
1/2 oz Peppermint Schnapps
Stir.
Strain into chilled glass.

SNAKE BITE 3
Fill glass 3/4 with Hard Cider.
Fill glass with Ale.

SNEAKY PETE
Fill glass with ice.
2 oz Tequila
1/2 oz White Creme De Menthe
1 oz Pineapple Juice
Dash of Lime Juice
Shake.
Strain into chilled glass.
Garnish with Lime.

SNICKER
Fill glass with ice.
1 oz Hazelnut Liqueur
1 oz Irish Cream
1 oz Dark Creme De Cacao
Fill with Milk or Cream.
Shake.

SNICKER AT THE BAR (frozen)
In Blender:
1/2 cup of Ice
3/4 oz Coffee Liqueur
3/4 oz Irish Cream
3/4 oz Hazelnut Liqueur
1/4 cup peanuts
1 scoop of Vanilla Ice Cream
Blend until smooth.
If too thick add Milk.
If too thin add ice or ice cream.

SNOWBALL
Fill glass with ice.
1 oz Gin
1/2 oz White Creme De Menthe
1/2 oz Anisette
Fill with Milk or Cream.
Shake.

SNOWBALL 2
Fill glass with ice.
3/4 oz Brandy
3/4 oz Peppermint Schnapps
3/4 oz White Creme De Cacao
Shake.
Strain into shot glass.

S

SNOWBALL 3
Fill glass with ice.
1 oz Sambuca
1 oz White Creme De Cacao
1 oz Cream
Shake.
Strain into chilled glass.

SNOWBERRY aka
RED RUSSIAN
Fill glass with ice.
1 oz Vodka
1 oz Strawberry Liqueur
Fill with Milk or Cream.
Shake.

SNOWBLOWER
Fill glass with ice.
1 oz Rum
1 oz Cranberry Liqueur
Fill with Orange Juice.
Shake.

SNOWBLOWER 2
Fill glass with ice.
1 oz Gin
3/4 oz Peppermint Schnapps
2 oz Cream of Coconut
Fill with Pineapple Juice.
Shake.

SNOWCAP (floater)
3/4 oz Tequila (bottom)
3/4 oz Irish Cream (top)

SNOWSHOE GROG
Fill glass with ice.
1 1/2 oz Bourbon or Brandy
1/2 oz Peppermint Schnapps
Stir.

SNUGGLER aka COCOANAPPS, ADULT HOT CHOCOLATE, PEPPERMINT KISS
2 oz Peppermint Schnapps
Fill with Hot Chocolate.
Top with Whipped Cream.
Sprinkle with Shaved Chocolate or
Chocolate Sprinkles.

SOMBRERO
Fill glass with ice.
2 oz Coffee Liqueur
or Coffee Brandy
Fill with Milk or Cream.
Shake.

S. O. B.
1/3 oz Orange Liqueur or Triple Sec
1/3 oz Brandy
1/3 oz 151-Proof Rum

S. O. B. 2 (floater)
1 oz Orange Liqueur (bottom)
1 oz Southern Comfort (top)
Serve with Lemon or Lime wedge.
Bite fruit before drinking.

SONIC
Fill glass with ice.
1 oz desired Liquor or Liqueur
Fill with equal parts Soda Water
and Tonic Water.

SOUL KISS
Fill glass with ice.
1 oz Whiskey
1 oz Dry Vermouth
1/2 oz Dubonnet
3/4 oz Orange Juice
Shake.
Serve or strain into chilled glass.

SOUR
Fill glass with ice.
2 oz desired liquor or liqueur
Fill with Sour Mix.
Shake.
Garnish with Orange and Cherry.

SOUR BALL
Fill glass with ice.
1 oz Vodka
1 oz Apricot Brandy
Fill with equal parts Sour Mix and
Orange Juice.
Shake.
Garnish with Orange and Cherry.

SOUR GRAPES
Fill glass with ice.
3/4 oz Vodka
3/4 oz Black Raspberry Liqueur
3/4 oz Sour Mix
Shake.
Strain into chilled glass.

SOUR MIX
In Blender:
1 Egg White
1 cup of Water
1 cup of Lemon Juice
3 Tbsp Sugar
Blend until sugar is liquefied.

SOUTH OF FRANCE
Fill glass with ice.
1 oz Rum
1 oz B&B
1 Tbsp Cream of Coconut
Fill with Pineapple Juice.
Shake.

SOUTHERN BELLE
Fill glass with ice.
1 oz Southern Comfort
1 oz Irish Cream

SOUTHERN BRIDE
1 1/2 oz Gin
1 oz Grapefruit Juice
Dash of Grenadine
Shake.
Strain into chilled glass.

SOUTHERN BRIDE 2
Fill glass with ice.
2 oz Gin
1/2 tsp Triple Sec or Curacao
2 dashes of Orange Bitters
Stir.
Strain into chilled glass.
Garnish with Lemon Twist.

SOUTHERN BULLDOG
Fill glass with ice.
1 oz Southern Comfort
1 oz Coffee Liqueur
Fill with Milk or Cream.
Shake.

SOUTHERN COMFORT MANHATTAN
Fill glass with ice.
2 oz Southern Comfort
1/2 oz Dry Vermouth
Stir.
Strain into chilled glass or pour
contents (with ice) into short glass.
Garnish with Cherry or Lemon
Twist.

SOUTHERN COMFORT OLD FASHIONED
Muddle together in glass:
Stemless Maraschino Cherry
Orange Slice
1/2 tsp Sugar
4 or 5 dashes of Bitters
Fill glass with ice.
2 oz Southern Comfort
Splash of Soda Water
Stir.

SOUTHSIDE
Muddle together in glass:
6 Mint Leaves
1 tsp Sugar
Dash of Water
1 Tbsp Lemon Juice.
Fill glass with crushed ice.
2 oz Bourbon
Fill with Spring Water.
Stir vigorously.

SOVEREIGN COFFEE
1 oz Black Raspberry Liqueur
1 oz Dark Creme De Cacao
Fill with hot Black Coffee.
Top with Whipped Cream.
Sprinkle with Shaved Chocolate or
Sprinkles.

SOVIET COCKTAIL
Fill glass with ice.
1 1/2 oz Vodka
1/2 oz Amontillato Sherry
1/2 oz Dry Vermouth
Shake.
Serve or strain into chilled glass.
Garnish with Lemon Twist.

SPANISH COFFEE
1 oz Coffee Liqueur
1 oz Cognac or Brandy
Fill with hot Black Coffee.
Top with Whipped Cream.
Garnish with Orange.

SPANISH COFFEE 2
3/4 oz Coffee Liqueur
3/4 oz Brandy
3/4 oz Orange Liqueur
Fill with hot Black Coffee.
Top with Whipped Cream.
Garnish with Orange.

SPANISH COFFEE 3
2 oz Tequila
Fill with hot Black Coffee.
Top with Whipped Cream.
Garnish with Lime.

SPANISH DYNAMITE
Fill glass with ice.
1 oz Tequila
1/2 oz Licor 43
1/2 oz Orange Liqueur or Triple Sec
Shake.
Strain into chilled glass.
Garnish with Cinnamon Stick.

SPANISH FLY
Fill glass with ice.
1 oz Tequila
1 oz Amaretto
Stir.

SPANISH ICED COFFEE
Fill glass with ice.
1 oz Coffee Liqueur
1 oz Cognac or Brandy
Fill with Iced Coffee.
Add cream or milk and sugar or
sweetener to taste.

SPANISH MOSS
Fill glass with ice.
1 1/2 oz Tequila
1 oz Coffee Liqueur
or Coffee Brandy
Shake.
Strain into chilled glass.
Add 3 drops of Green Creme De
Menthe.

SPARKS
Fill glass 3/4 full with ice.
1 oz Peppered Vodka
Fill with Champagne.

SPATS
Fill glass with ice.
1 1/2 oz Rum
1/2 oz Melon Liqueur
Fill with equal parts Orange and
Pineapple Juice.
Shake.
Float 1/2 oz Sloe Gin on top.
Garnish with Orange or Pineapple
and Cherry.

S

SPECIAL ROUGH
Fill glass with ice.
1 1/2 oz Brandy
1 1/2 oz Apple Brandy
2 dashes of Pernod
Stir.
Strain into chilled glass.

SPEEDY GONZALAS
Fill glass with ice.
2 oz 151-Proof Rum
Dash of Lime Juice
Fill with Jolt Cola.
Stir.
Garnish with Lime.

SPERM WHALE (floater)
1 1/2 oz Tequila (bottom)
1/2 oz Irish Cream (top)

SPERM WHALE AT THE BANK
(floater)
1/2 oz Irish Cream (bottom)
1/2 oz White Creme De Cacao
1/2 oz Amaretto (top)
Place 1 drop of Grenadine in center
of glass.

SPHINX
Fill glass with ice.
2 oz Gin
2 tsp Dry Vermouth
2 tsp Sweet Vermouth
Stir.
Strain into chilled glass.

SPIKE
Fill glass with ice.
2 oz Tequila
Fill with Grapefruit Juice.
Stir.
Garnish with Lime.

SPILT MILK
1/2 oz Light Rum
1/2 oz Blended Whiskey
1/2 oz Irish Cream
1/2 oz Creme De Nouyax
or Amaretto
1 oz Milk or Cream
Shake.
Strain into chilled glass.

SPLEEF
Fill glass with ice.
2 oz Dark Rum
2 oz Orange Juice
Fill with Pineapple Juice.
Stir.
Garnish with Lime.

SPRING ACTION
Fill glass with ice.
3/4 oz Southern Comfort
3/4 oz Apricot Brandy
3/4 oz Sloe Gin
Fill with Orange Juice.
Shake.

SPRING BREAK
Fill glass with ice.
2 oz Coconut Rum
Fill with equal parts Cranberry
Juice and Lemon-Lime Soda.

SPRING FLING
Fill glass with ice.
1/2 oz Vodka
1/2 oz Triple Sec
1/2 oz Apricot Brandy
Fill with equal parts Orange Juice
and Sour Mix.
Shake.

SPRING THAW (floater)
1 1/4 oz Yukon Jack (bottom)
1/2 oz Irish Cream
1/4 oz Vodka (top)
Nick G. Zeroulias

SPRITZER
Fill glass 3/4 with ice.
Fill 3/4 with desired Wine.
Fill with Soda Water.
Garnish with Lime.

SPY'S DEMISE
Fill glass with ice.
1/2 oz Vodka
1/2 oz Gin
1/2 oz Rum
1/2 oz Sloe Gin
1 oz Sour Mix
Shake.
Strain into chilled glass.
Fill with Lemon-Lime Soda.

STAR
Fill glass with ice.
1 1/2 oz Apple Brandy
1 1/2 oz Sweet Vermouth
2 dashes of Bitters
Stir.
Strain into chilled glass.

STAR WARS
Fill glass with ice.
3/4 oz Vodka
3/4 oz Southern Comfort
3/4 oz Orange Liqueur
Fill with Orange Juice.
Dash of Grenadine
Shake.
Garnish with Orange.

STARBOARD TACK
Fill glass with ice.
1 oz Spiced Rum
1 oz Coconut Rum
Fill with equal parts Cranberry and
Orange Juice.
Garnish with Orange.

STARLIGHT
Fill glass with ice.
1 1/2 oz Vodka
1/2 oz Black Sambuca
Stir.
Strain into chilled glass.
Garnish with Lemon Twist.

STARS AND STRIPES (floater)
1 oz Grenadine (bottom)
1 oz Heavy Cream
1 oz Blue Curacao (top)

STEALTH (floater)
1/2 oz Coffee Liqueur (bottom)
1/2 oz Banana Liqueur
1/2 oz Irish Cream
1/2 oz Orange Liqueur (top)

STEEL HELMET
Fill glass with ice.
1 oz Vodka
1 oz Coffee Liqueur
Fill with Milk or Cream.
Shake.
Top with Galliano.

STEEPLE JACK
Fill glass with ice.
2 oz Apple Brandy
2 oz Apple Cider
or Apple Juice
Dash of Lime Juice
Shake.
Strain into chilled glass.
Fill with Soda Water.
Garnish with Cinnamon Stick and
Lime.

STILETTO
Fill glass with ice.
1 oz Rum
1/2 oz Amaretto
1/2 oz Banana Liqueur
Fill with equal parts Orange Juice
and Pineapple Juice.
Shake.

STINGER
Fill glass with ice.
1 1/2 oz Brandy
1/2 oz White Creme De Menthe
Stir.
Serve or strain into chilled glass.

STOCK MARKET ZOO
Fill glass with ice.
1/2 oz Gin
1/2 oz Rum
1/2 oz Tequila
1/2 oz Bourbon
Dash of Grenadine
Dash of Orange Juice
Fill with Pineapple Juice.
Shake.
Strain into chilled glass.

STONE FENCE
Fill glass with ice.
2 oz Apple Brandy or Scotch
2 dashes of Bitters
Fill glass with cold cider.

STONEWALL
Fill glass with ice.
1 oz Dark Rum
2 oz Apple Cider
Stir.

STORM CLOUD
Fill glass with ice.
1 oz 151-Proof Rum
1 oz Coffee Liqueur
Stir.

STRAIGHT LAW
Fill glass with ice.
2 oz Dry Sherry
1 oz Gin
Stir.
Strain into chilled glass.
Garnish with Lemon Twist.

STRAWBERRY BLONDE (frozen)
In Blender:
1/2 cup of Ice
1 oz Strawberry Liqueur
1 oz White Creme De Cacao
1/2 cup fresh or frozen
Strawberries
Scoop of Vanilla Ice Cream
Blend until smooth.
If too thick add Milk or berries. If too
thin add ice or ice cream.

STRAWBERRY COLADA
(frozen)
In Blender:
1/2 cup of Ice
2 oz Rum
2 Tbsp Cream of Coconut
1/2 cup fresh or frozen
Strawberries
1 Tbsp Vanilla Ice Cream
Blend until smooth.
If too thick add fruit or juice.
If too thin add ice or ice cream.
Garnish with strawberry.

STRAWBERRY DAIQUIRI
(frozen)
In Blender:
1 cup of Ice
1 1/2 oz Rum
1/2 oz Strawberry Liqueur
1/2 oz Lime Juice
1/2 cup fresh or frozen
Strawberries
Blend until smooth.
If too thick add berries or juice.
If too thin add ice.
Garnish with Lime and/or
strawberry.

S

117

STRAWBERRY LIQUEUR
(type liqueur)
Bring 2 cups of Water and
2 cups Granulated Sugar
to a boil.
Simmer for 5 minutes.
Let cool.
Add: 1 1/3 cups Vodka
2 tsp Strawberry Extract
6 drops of Red Food Coloring
Store in a glass jar in the dark for 1
week.

STRAWBERRY MARGARITA
(frozen)
In Blender:
1 cup of Ice
1 1/2 oz Tequila
1/2 oz Triple Sec
1/2 oz Lime Juice
1/2 cup fresh or frozen
Strawberries
Blend until smooth.
If too thick add juice or berries.
If too thin add ice.
Garnish with Lime and/or
strawberry.

STRAWBERRY SHORTCAKE
(frozen)
In Blender:
1/2 cup of Ice
1 oz Vodka
1 oz Strawberry Liqueur
1/2 cup fresh or frozen
Strawberries
Scoop of Vanilla Ice Cream
Blend until smooth.
If too thick add fruit or Milk.
If too thin add ice or ice cream.
Top with Whipped Cream.
Garnish with strawberry.

STREGA SOUR
Fill glass with ice.
1 1/2 oz Gin
1/2 oz Strega
2 oz Sour Mix
Shake.
Strain into chilled glass.

STUFFED TOILET (floater)
1/2 oz Coffee Liqueur (bottom)
1/2 oz Irish Cream
1/2 oz Tuaca (top)

STUMBLING F.
Fill glass with ice.
1 oz 151-Proof Rum
1 oz Jaegermeister
1 oz 100-Proof Peppermint
Schnapps
Stir.
Strain into shot glass.

STUMP BUSTER
Fill glass with ice.
1/2 oz Vodka
1/2 oz Gin
1/2 oz Rum
1/2 oz Tequila
Dash of Grenadine
Fill with Orange Juice.
Shake.
Garnish with Orange.

STUPID CUBE
Fill glass with ice.
1/2 oz Light Rum
1/2 oz Spiced Rum
1/2 oz Dark Rum
1/2 oz Amber Rum
Fill with equal parts Orange,
Grapefruit and Cranberry Juice.
Garnish with Lime, Lemon, Orange
and Cherry.

SUFFERING BASTARD
Fill glass with ice.
1 1/2 oz Dark Rum
1 oz 151-Proof Rum
1/2 oz Orange Curacao
or Triple Sec
1/2 oz Orgeat Syrup
Fill with equal parts Orange and
Lemon Juice.
Shake.
Garnish with Lime.

SUGAR APPLE
Fill glass with ice.
2 oz Spiced Rum
Fill with Apple Juice.
Garnish with Cinnamon Stick.
John Adams

SUGAR DADDY
Fill glass with ice.
1 oz Butterscotch Schnapps
1 oz Irish Cream
Dash of Coffee Liqueur
1 oz Milk
Shake.

SUGAR SYRUP
Mix 1 part Water
with 2 parts Sugar
(Works much better with hot water
and superfine sugar.)

SUISSESSE
Fill glass with ice.
1 1/2 oz Pernod
2 oz Sour Mix
Shake.
Strain into chilled glass.
Fill with Soda Water.
Garnish with Lemon and Cherry.

SUMMER BREEZE
Fill glass with ice.
2 oz Rum
Fill with equal parts Cranberry and
Grapefruit Juice.
Garnish with Lime.

SUMMER SHARE
Fill glass with ice.
1 oz Vodka
1 oz Rum
1/2 oz Tequila
1 oz Orange Juice
1 oz Cranberry Juice
Dash of Apricot Brandy
Shake.
Fill with Lemon-Lime Soda.
Garnish with Orange.

SUMMER SOLSTICE
SUNRISE
Fill glass with ice.
1 oz Vodka
1 oz Rum
Fill glass leaving 1/4 inch from top
with Orange, Pineapple and
Cranberry Juice.
Top with 1/2 oz Cherry Brandy.

SUN STROKE
Fill glass with ice.
1 1/2 oz Vodka
1/4 oz Orange Liqueur
Fill with Grapefruit Juice.
Shake.

SUNBURST
Fill glass with ice.
1 1/2 oz Vodka
1/2 oz Triple Sec
Fill with Grapefruit Juice.
Dash of Grenadine
Shake.

SUNDOWNER
Fill glass with ice.
2 oz Rum
Dash of Triple Sec
1 tsp Grenadine
3/4 oz Sour Mix
Shake.
Strain into chilled glass.
Fill with Tonic Water.

SUNNY DAY DREAM
Fill glass with ice.
2 oz Southern Comfort
Fill with Iced Tea.
Garnish with Lemon.
Mary Beth Dallas

SUNTAN
Fill glass with ice.
2 oz Coconut Rum
Fill with Iced Tea.
Garnish with Lemon and Lime.

SUPER COFFEE aka
SPANISH COFFEE
1 oz Coffee Liqueur
1 oz Brandy
Fill with hot Black Coffee.
Top with Whipped Cream.
Garnish with Orange.

SURFER TAKING A TRIP
Fill glass with ice.
1 oz Coconut Rum
1 oz Jaegermeister
Fill with Pineapple Juice.
Shake.

SUSIE TAYLOR
Fill glass with ice.
2 oz Light Rum
1/2 oz Lime Juice
Fill with Ginger Ale.
Stir.
Garnish with Lemon.

SWAMP WATER
Fill glass with ice.
2 oz Rum
1/4 oz Blue Curacao
1 oz Orange Juice
1/2 oz Lemon Juice
Shake.

SWAMP WATER 2
Fill glass with ice.
2 oz Green Chartreuse
Fill with Pineapple Juice or
Grapefruit Juice.
Shake.

SWEATY MEXICAN
LUMBERJACK
Fill glass with ice.
1 oz Tequila
1 oz Yukon Jack
3 dashes of Tabasco Sauce
Strain into shot glass.

SWEET CREAM (floater)
1 1/2 oz Coffee Liqueur (bottom)
1/2 oz Irish Cream (top)

SWEET PATOOTIE
Fill glass with ice.
1 oz Gin
1/2 oz Triple Sec
1/2 oz Orange Juice
Shake.
Strain into chilled glass.

SWEET RELEASE
Fill glass with ice.
1 oz Vodka
1 oz Rum
Fill with Pineapple Juice.
Top with Sloe Gin.

S

SWEET TART
Fill glass with ice.
1 1/2 oz Vodka
1/2 oz Black Raspberry Liqueur
2 oz Sour Mix
2 oz Cranberry Juice
Shake.
Fill with Lemon-Lime Soda.

SWEET TART 2
Fill glass with ice.
1 oz Vodka
1/2 oz Orange Liqueur
1/2 oz Amaretto
Dash of Grenadine
Dash of Lime Juice
Fill with equal parts Sour Mix and
Lemon-Lime Soda.
Shake.

SWEDISH BEAR
Fill glass with ice.
1 1/2 oz Vodka
1/2 oz Dark Creme De Cacao
Fill with Milk or Cream.
Shake.

SWEDISH LULLABY
Fill glass with ice.
1 1/2 oz Swedish Punch
1 oz Cherry Liqueur
1/2 oz Lemon juice
Shake.
Strain into chilled glass.

TAHITI CLUB
Fill glass with ice.
2 oz Amber Rum
1/2 oz Lime Juice
1/2 oz Lemon Juice
1/2 oz Pineapple Juice
1/4 oz Maraschino Liqueur
Shake.
Garnish with Orange.

TAHITIAN APPLE
Fill glass with ice.
2 oz Light Rum
Fill with Apple Juice.

TAHITIAN ITCH
Fill glass with ice.
1 oz Bourbon
1 oz Rum
1/2 oz Orange Liqueur
2 oz Pineapple Juice
2 Tbsp Lime Sherbet
Fill with Ginger Ale.

TAM-O-SHANTER
Fill glass with ice.
1 oz Irish Whiskey
1 oz Coffee Liqueur
Fill with Milk or Cream.
Shake.

TAMPA BAY SMOOTHIE
Fill glass with ice.
1 1/2 oz Vodka
1/2 oz Orange Liqueur
Dash of Grenadine
1 oz Orange Juice
Shake.
Strain into chilled glass.
Garnish with Orange and Cherry.

TANGERINE
Fill glass with ice.
2 oz Gin
1 tsp Grenadine
1 tsp Lime Juice
Fill with Sour Mix.

TANGERINE 2
Fill glass with ice.
1 oz Vodka
1/2 oz Orange Liqueur
1/2 oz Amaretto
Dash of Grenadine
Fill with Orange Juice.
Shake.

TANGO
Fill glass with ice.
1 1/2 oz Gin
1/4 oz Dry Vermouth
1/4 oz Sweet Vermouth
1/2 tsp Curacao or Triple Sec
3/4 oz Orange Juice
Shake.
Serve or strain into chilled glass.
Garnish with Orange.

TANTALUS
Fill glass with ice.
1 oz Brandy
1 oz Forbidden Fruit
1 oz Lemon Juice
Shake.
Strain into chilled glass.

TARA
Fill glass with ice.
3/4 oz Coconut Rum
3/4 oz Melon Liqueur
3/4 oz Black Raspberry Liqueur
Fill with Cranberry Juice.
Shake.
Tara Phipps

TARNISHED BULLET
Fill glass with ice.
1/2 oz Tequila
1/2 oz Green Creme De Menthe
Stir.

TAWNY RUSSIAN aka
GOD MOTHER
Fill glass with ice.
1 1/2 oz Vodka
1/2 oz Amaretto
Stir.

T-BIRD

Fill glass with ice.
1/2 oz Vodka
1/2 oz Orange Liqueur
1/2 oz Amaretto
2 oz Pineapple Juice
Dash of Cream (optional)
Shake.
Strain into chilled glass.

TEACHER'S PET aka AGGRAVATION

Fill glass with ice.
1 oz Scotch
1 oz Coffee Liqueur
or Coffee Brandy
Fill with Milk or Cream.
Shake.

TEAR DROP

3 oz White Zinfandel
1 oz Peach Schnapps
Dash of Sour Mix
Fill with Soda Water.
Garnish with Lemon.

TEMPTATION

Fill glass with ice.
1 1/2 oz Whiskey
1/4 oz Triple Sec or Curacao
1/4 oz Dubonnet Rouge
1/4 oz Pernod
Shake.
Strain into chilled glass.
Garnish with Orange Twist and
Lemon Twist.

TEMPTER

Fill glass with ice.
1 1/2 oz Apricot Brandy
1 1/2 oz Port
Shake.
Serve or strain into chilled glass.

TENNESSEE

Fill glass with ice.
2 oz Whiskey
3/4 oz Maraschino Liqueur
1/2 oz Lemon Juice
Shake.

TENNESSEE LEMONADE

Fill glass with ice.
2 oz Bourbon
Fill with Lemonade.
Shake.

TENNESSEE MUD

1 oz Bourbon
1 oz Amaretto
Fill with hot Black Coffee.
Top with Whipped Cream.
Sprinkle with Brown Sugar.

TENNESSEE TEA

Fill glass with ice.
1/2 oz Bourbon
1/2 oz Dark Creme De Cacao
Fill with Cranberry Juice.
Stir.
Garnish with Lemon.

TEQUILA COLLINS

Fill glass with ice.
2 oz Tequila
Fill with Sour Mix.
Shake.
Splash of Soda Water
Garnish with Cherry and Orange.

TEQUILA GIMLET

Fill glass with ice.
2 oz Tequila
1 oz Lime Juice
Stir.
Serve or strain into chilled glass.
Garnish with Lime.

TEQUILA MANHATTAN

Fill glass with ice.
2 oz Tequila
1/2 oz Sweet Vermouth
Stir.
Strain into chilled glass
or pour contents (with ice)
into short glass.
Garnish with Cherry.

TEQUILA MARTINI aka TEQUINI

Fill glass with ice.
2 oz Tequila
1/2 oz Dry Vermouth
Stir.
Strain into chilled glass
or pour contents (with ice)
into short glass.
Garnish with Lemon Twist or
Orange Twist.

TEQUILA OLD FASHIONED

Muddle together in glass:
Stemless Maraschino Cherry
Orange Slice
1/2 tsp Sugar
4-5 dashes of Bitters
Fill glass with ice.
2 oz Tequila
Fill with Soda Water.
Stir.

TEQUILA POPPER

In shot glass:
1 oz Tequila
1 oz Ginger Ale
Cover glass with napkin and hand,
then slam on bar top.
Drink while foaming.

S
T

TEQUILA QUENCHER
Fill glass with ice.
2 oz Tequila
Fill with equal parts Orange Juice
and Soda Water.
Garnish with Lime.

TEQUILA ROSE
Fill glass with ice.
2 oz Tequila
1/2 oz Lime Juice
Fill with Grapefruit Juice.
Shake.
Float 1/2 oz Grenadine on top.

TEQUILA SHOOTER
Fill shot glass with Tequila.
Lick hand and pour small amount
of salt on moistened skin.
Have wedge of Lime or Lemon
ready.
1. Lick off salt
2. Drink shot
3. Bite and suck fruit wedge

TEQUILA SLAMMER
In Shot glass:
1 oz Tequila
1/2 tsp Cream of Coconut
1/2 tsp Strawberries in syrup
Fill with Ginger Ale.
Place hand and/or napkin over
glass. Slam on bar to make foam.
Drink.

TEQUILA SOUR
Fill glass with ice.
2 oz Tequila
Fill with Sour Mix.
Shake.
Garnish with Cherry and Orange.

TEQUILA STINGER
Fill glass with ice.
1 1/2 oz Tequila
1/2 oz White Creme De Menthe
Stir.
Strain into chilled glass.

TEQUILA SUNRISE
Fill glass with ice.
2 oz Tequila
Fill with Orange Juice.
Pour 1/2 oz Grenadine down spoon
to bottom of glass.
Garnish with Orange.

TEQUILA SUNSET
Fill glass with ice.
2 oz Tequila
Fill with Orange or Grapefruit Juice.
Pour 1/2 oz Blackberry Brandy
down spoon to bottom of glass.

TEQUINI aka
TEQUILA MARTINI
Fill glass with ice.
2 oz Tequila
1/2 oz Dry Vermouth
Stir.
Strain into chilled glass
or pour contents (with ice)
into short glass.
Garnish with Lemon Twist or
Orange Twist.

TERMINAL ICED TEA
Fill glass with ice.
1/2 oz Premium Vodka
1/2 oz Premium Gin
1/2 oz Premium Rum
1/2 oz Premium Tequila
1/2 oz Premium Orange Liqueur
2 oz Sour Mix
Top with Cola.
Garnish with Lemon.

TERMINATOR
Fill glass with ice.
1 oz Yukon Jack
1 oz Amaretto
1/2 oz Coconut Rum
1/2 oz Blue Curacao
Dash of Orange Juice
Shake.
Fill with Lemon-Lime Soda.

TEST-TUBE BABE
Fill glass with ice.
1 oz Tequila
or Southern Comfort
1 oz Amaretto
Strain into chilled glass.
Add 3-4 drops of Irish Cream or
Milk.

TEXAS TEA
Fill glass with ice.
1 oz Tequila
1/2 oz Vodka
1/2 oz Rum
1/2 oz Triple Sec
1 oz Sour Mix
Splash with Cola.
Garnish with Lemon.

THANKSGIVING
Fill glass with ice.
3/4 oz Gin
3/4 oz Dry Vermouth
3/4 oz Apricot Brandy
1/4 oz Lemon Juice
Shake.
Strain into chilled glass.
Garnish with Cherry.

THIRD DEGREE
Fill glass with ice.
1 1/2 oz Gin
1/2 oz Dry Vermouth
1/2 tsp Pernod
Stir.
Strain into chilled glass.

THIRD RAIL
Fill glass with ice.
3/4 oz Brandy
3/4 oz Apple Brandy
3/4 oz Light Rum
1/4 tsp Pernod
Shake.
Strain into chilled glass.

THISTLE
Fill glass with ice.
1 1/2 oz Scotch
3/4 oz Sweet Vermouth
3 dashes of Bitters
Stir.
Strain into chilled glass.

38TH PARALLEL COFFEE
1/2 oz Brandy
1/2 oz Irish Cream
1/2 oz Dark Creme De Cacao
1/2 oz Black Raspberry Liqueur
Fill with hot Black Coffee.
Top with Whipped Cream.
Drizzle Chocolate Syrup on top.

THREE AMIGOS
Fill glass with ice.
3/4 oz Jose Cuervo
3/4 oz Ron Bacardi
3/4 oz Jack Daniels
Stir.
Strain into shot glass.

THREE MILES
Fill glass with ice.
1 oz Brandy
1 oz Rum
1 tsp Grenadine
1/4 tsp Lemon Juice
Shake.
Strain into chilled glass.

THREE MILE ISLAND aka NUCLEAR MELTDOWN
Fill glass with ice.
1/2 oz Vodka
1/2 oz Gin
1/2 oz Rum
1/2 oz Tequila
1/2 oz Triple Sec
Fill with Sour Mix
or Pineapple Juice.
Shake.
Top with 1/2 oz Melon Liqueur.

THREE STORY HOUSE ON FIRE (floater)
1/2 oz Creme De Nouyax (bottom)
1/2 oz Banana Liqueur
1/2 oz Melon Liqueur
1/2 oz 151-Proof Rum (top)
Ignite.

THREE STRIPES
Fill glass with ice.
1 oz Gin
1/2 oz Dry Vermouth
1/2 oz Orange Juice
Shake.
Strain into chilled glass.

THREE WISE MEN
Fill glass with ice.
3/4 oz Johnnie Walker
3/4 oz Jim Beam
or Jack Daniels
3/4 oz Ron Bacardi
Stir.
Strain into chilled glass.

THUMPER
Fill glass with ice.
1 1/2 oz Cognac or Brandy
1/2 oz Tuaca
Stir.
Garnish with Lemon Twist.

THUNDER
Fill glass with ice.
1 1/2 oz Brandy
1 tsp Sugar Syrup
or Powdered Sugar
1 Egg Yolk
1 pinch Cayenne Pepper
Shake.
Serve or strain into chilled glass.

THUNDER AND LIGHTNING
In shot glass:
1 oz 151-Proof Rum
1 oz 100-Proof Peppermint Schnapps

TIA TIA
Fill glass with ice.
1 oz Rum
1/2 oz Dark Rum
1/2 oz Dark Creme De Cacao
2 oz Pineapple Juice
1/2 oz Lime Juice
1/2 oz Sugar Syrup
Shake.

TIC TAC
Fill glass with ice.
1 oz Peppermint Schnapps
1 oz Anisette or Sambuca
Stir.
Strain into chilled glass.

TIDAL WAVE
Fill glass with ice.
1 oz Coconut Rum
1 oz Blackberry Brandy
Dash of Grenadine
Fill with Pineapple Juice.
Shake.

T

TIDAL WAVE 2
Fill glass with ice.
1 oz Vodka
1 oz Light Rum
1 oz Spiced Rum
1 oz Sour Mix
Fill with Cranberry Juice.
Shake.

TIDAL WAVE (frozen)
In Blender:
1/2 cup of Ice
3/4 oz Vodka
3/4 oz Gin
3/4 oz Southern Comfort
Dash of Grenadine
Scoop of Orange Sherbet
Blend until smooth.
If too thick add orange juice.
If too thin add ice or sherbet.

TIDBIT (frozen)
In Blender:
1/2 cup of Ice
1 oz Gin
1/4 oz Dry Sherry
Scoop of Vanilla Ice Cream
Blend until smooth.
If too thick add Milk.
If too thin add ice or ice cream.

TIGER'S MILK
Fill glass with ice.
1 oz Amber or Dark Rum
1 oz Cognac or Brandy
4 oz Cream
1/4 oz Sugar Syrup
Shake.
Garnish with grated Nutmeg or
Cinnamon.

TIGER'S MILK 2
Fill glass with ice.
2 oz Tuaca
Fill with Milk.
Shake.

TIGER'S TAIL
Fill glass with ice.
1 1/2 oz Pernod or Ricard
Dash of Curacao
or Triple Sec
Fill with Orange Juice.
Stir.
Garnish with Lime.

TIJUANA BULLDOG
Fill glass with ice.
1 1/2 oz Tequila
1/2 oz Coffee Liqueur
Fill with equal parts Milk and Cola.
Shake.

TIJUANA SUNRISE
Fill glass with ice.
2 oz Tequila
Fill with Orange Juice.
Stir.
Pour 1/4 oz Bitters down spoon to
bottom of glass.

TIKI BOWL
Fill glass with ice.
3/4 oz Light Rum
3/4 oz Dark Rum
1/2 oz Cherry Brandy
Fill with equal parts Orange and
Pineapple Juice.
Shake.

TIME BOMB
Fill glass with ice.
1 1/2 oz Melon Liqueur
1/2 oz Coconut Rum
Dash of Cranberry Juice
Fill with Pineapple Juice.
Shake.
Garnish with Cherry and Orange.
Kevin Cuniff

TINTORETTO
Puree 1/2 cup of fresh or canned
pears.
Pour into glass.
1/2 oz Pear Brandy
Fill with chilled Champagne.

TINY BOWL
1 1/2 oz Vodka
1 or 2 drops Blue Curacao
Garnish with 2 Raisins.

TIPPERARY
Fill glass with ice.
3/4 oz Irish Whiskey
3/4 oz Sweet Vermouth
3/4 oz Green Chartreuse
Stir well.
Strain into chilled glass.

TIVOLI
Fill glass with ice.
1 1/2 oz Bourbon
1/2 oz Aquavit
1/2 oz Sweet Vermouth
Dash of Campari
Shake.
Strain into chilled glass.

T. K. O.
Fill glass with ice.
2 oz Tequila
1 oz Coffee Liqueur
1 oz Ouzo
Stir.

T. N. T.

Fill glass with ice.
2 oz Tequila
Fill with Tonic Water.
Garnish with Lime.

T.N.T. can also mean a Tangueray
Gin and Tonic

TO HELL YOU RIDE

Fill shot glass with Vodka
7-10 dashes of hot sauce

TOASTED ALMOND

Fill glass with ice.
1 oz Coffee Liqueur
1 oz Amaretto
Fill with Milk or Cream.
Shake.

TOASTED ALMOND (frozen)

In Blender:
1/2 cup of Ice
1 oz Coffee Liqueur
1 oz Amaretto
Scoop of Vanilla Ice Cream
Blend until smooth.
If too thick add milk or cream.
If too thin add ice or ice cream.

TOASTED MARSHMALLOW

Fill glass with ice.
3/4 oz Amaretto
3/4 oz Galliano
3/4 oz Banana Liqueur
Fill with Milk or Cream.
Shake.
Top with Soda Water.

TOKYO EXPRESS (frozen)

In Blender:
1 cup of Ice
2 oz Dark Rum
1 oz Peach Schnapps
Dash of Grenadine
1 oz Sour Mix
2 oz Orange Juice
Blend 3-6 seconds on low speed.
Garnish with Orange, Lemon and
Cherry.

TOM AND JERRY

Beat an Egg White and an Egg Yolk
separately.
Fold together and place into mug.
1/2 oz Sugar Syrup
or 1 tsp Powdered Sugar
1 oz Dark Rum
1 oz Cognac or Brandy
Fill with hot Milk or hot Water.
Stir.
Garnish with Nutmeg.

TOM COLLINS

Fill glass with ice.
2 oz Gin
Fill with Sour Mix.
Shake.
Splash of Soda Water
Garnish with Orange and Cherry.

TOM MIX HIGH

Fill glass with ice.
2 oz Blended Whiskey
Dash of Grenadine
Dash of Bitters
Fill with Soda Water.
Garnish with Lemon.

TOOL

Fill glass with ice.
1 1/2 oz Tequila
Dash of Grenadine
Fill with Orange Juice.
Shake.
Float 1/2 oz Southern Comfort on
top.

TOOTSIE

Fill glass with ice.
2 oz Coffee Liqueur or Sabra
or Dark Creme De Cacao
Fill with Orange Juice.
Shake.
Garnish with Orange.

TOP GUN

Fill glass with ice.
Dash of Vodka
Dash of Dark Rum
Dash of Coconut Rum
Dash of Southern Comfort
Dash of Peach Schnapps
Dash of Amaretto
Dash of Triple Sec
Fill with equal parts Orange and
Cranberry Juice.
Shake.

TOP HAT

Fill glass with ice.
1 oz Orange Liqueur
1 oz Cherry Liqueur
Stir.

TOREADOR

Fill glass with ice.
1 1/2 oz Tequila
1/2 oz White Creme De Cacao
1/2 oz Cream
Shake.
Strain into chilled glass.
Top with Whipped Cream.
Sprinkle with Cocoa or Shaved
Chocolate.

T

TOREADOR 2
Fill glass with ice.
2 oz Brandy
1 oz Coffee Liqueur
1/2 Egg White
Shake.

TORPEDO
Fill glass with ice.
1 1/2 oz Apple Brandy
3/4 oz Brandy
Shake.
Strain into chilled glass.

TORQUE WRENCH
1 oz Melon Liqueur
1 oz Orange Juice
Fill with Champagne.
Garnish with Orange.

TOVARICH
Fill glass with ice.
1 1/2 oz Vodka
3/4 oz Kummel
1/4 oz Lime Juice
Shake.
Strain into chilled glass.

TOXIC WASTE
Fill glass with ice.
1/2 oz Coffee Liqueur
1/2 oz Galliano
1/2 oz Apricot Brandy
Fill with Orange Juice
(leaving 1/2 inch from top).
Shake.
Top with Cream.

TRADE WIND
Fill glass with ice.
1/2 oz Rum
1/2 oz Galliano
1/2 oz Apricot Brandy
1/2 oz Orange Liqueur
Fill with Milk or Cream.
Shake.

TRADE WINDS (frozen)
In Blender:
1/2 cup of Ice
2 oz Amber Rum
1/2 oz Plum Brandy
1/2 oz Lime Juice
2 tsp Sugar Syrup
Blend until smooth.

TRAFFIC LIGHT (floater)
1/2 oz Green Creme De Menthe
(bottom)
1/2 oz Banana Liqueur
1/2 oz Sloe Gin (top)

TRAFFIC LIGHT 2 (floater)
1/2 oz Creme De Nouyax
(bottom)
1/2 oz Galliano
1/2 oz Melon Liqueur (top)

TRANSFUSION aka
PURPLE PASSION
Fill glass with ice.
2 oz Vodka
Fill with equal parts
Grape Juice and Ginger Ale
or Soda Water.

TRAPPIST FRAPPE
Fill large stemmed glass (Red Wine
glass, Champagne saucer) with
crushed ice.
3/4 oz Coffee Liqueur
3/4 oz Hazelnut Liqueur
3/4 oz Irish Cream

TRAPPIST MONK
3/4 oz Coffee Liqueur
3/4 oz Hazelnut Liqueur
3/4 oz Irish Cream
Fill with hot Black Coffee.
Top with Whipped Cream.

TRAVELING WILD BERRIES
Fill glass with ice.
3/4 oz Peach Schnapps
3/4 oz Black Raspberry Liqueur
3/4 oz Melon Liqueur
Fill with equal parts Orange and
Cranberry Juice.
Shake.
H. R. C.

TREE CLIMBER
Fill glass with ice.
1 oz Rum
1/2 oz Amaretto
1/2 oz White Creme De Cacao
Fill with Milk or Cream.
Shake.

TRILBY
Fill glass with ice.
1 1/2 oz Bourbon
1/2 oz Sweet Vermouth
2 dashes of Orange Bitters
Stir.
Strain into chilled glass.

TROIS RIVIERES
Fill glass with ice.
1 1/2 oz Canadian Whiskey
3/4 oz Dubonnet Rouge
1/2 oz Triple Sec
Shake.
Serve or strain into chilled glass.
Garnish with Orange Twist.

TROLLEY
Fill glass with ice.
2 oz Bourbon
Fill with equal parts Cranberry and
Pineapple Juice.
Stir.

TROPHY ROOM COFFEE
1/2 oz Amaretto
1/2 oz Vandermint
1/2 oz Dark Rum
Fill with hot Black Coffee.
Top with Whipped Cream.
Dribble Coffee Liqueur on top.

TROPICAL BREEZE (frozen)
In Blender:
1/2 cup of Ice
1 1/2 oz Banana Liqueur
1 1/2 oz Creme De Nouyax
1/2 cup fresh or frozen
Strawberries
Scoop of Vanilla Ice Cream
Blend until smooth.
If too thick add berries or juice.
If too thin add ice or ice cream.
Top with Whipped Cream.

TROPICAL COCKTAIL
Fill glass with ice.
3/4 oz White Creme De Cacao
3/4 oz Maraschino Liqueur
3/4 oz Dry Vermouth
Dash of Bitters
Stir.
Strain into chilled glass.

TROPICAL GOLD
Fill glass with ice.
1 1/2 oz Rum
1/2 oz Banana Liqueur
Fill with Orange Juice.
Shake.

TROPICAL HOOTER
Fill glass with ice.
1 1/2 oz Coconut Rum
1/2 oz Melon Liqueur
Dash of Cranberry Juice
Dash of Pineapple Juice
Shake.
Strain into chilled glass.

TROPICAL MOON (frozen)
In Blender:
1/2 cup of Ice
1 oz Dark Rum
1 oz coconut Rum
1/2 cup fresh or canned Pineapple
Scoop of Vanilla Ice Cream
Blend until smooth.
Float 1/2 oz Amaretto on top.
Garnish with Pineapple.

TROPICAL STORM
Fill glass with ice.
1/2 oz Vodka
1/2 oz Gin
1/2 oz Rum
1/2 oz Tequila
1/2 oz Triple Sec
Dash of Cherry Brandy
Dash of Sour Mix
Shake.

TROPICAL STORM 2
Fill glass with ice.
1 1/2 oz Rum
1/2 oz Blackberry Brandy
Fill with Grapefruit Juice.
Shake.
Garnish with Lime.

TROPICAL STORM 3
Fill glass with ice.
1 oz Dark Rum
1/4 oz Amber Rum
1/4 oz Coconut Rum
1/4 oz Galliano
1/4 oz Grenadine
Fill with equal parts Sour Mix,
Pineapple and Orange Juice.
Shake.
Garnish with Orange and Cherry.

TROPICAL STORM 4
Fill glass with ice.
1 oz Orange Vodka
1 oz Coconut Rum
Dash of Triple Sec
Fill with equal parts Orange and
Cranberry Juice.
Stir.
*Tracy Moude, PT's Late Night, Key
West*

TUACA COCKTAIL
Fill glass with ice.
1 oz Vodka
1 oz Tuaca
2 Tbsp Lime Juice
Shake.
Strain into chilled glass.

TULIP
Fill glass with ice.
3/4 oz Apple Brandy
3/4 oz Sweet Vermouth
1 1/2 tsp Apricot Brandy
1 1/2 tsp Lemon Juice
Shake.
Strain into chilled glass.

TUMBLEWEED
Fill glass with ice.
1/2 oz Coffee Liqueur
1/2 oz Brandy
1/2 oz White Creme De Cacao
1/2 oz Hazelnut Liqueur
Fill with Milk.
Shake.

TUMBLEWEED (frozen)
In Blender:
1/2 cup of Ice
1/2 oz Coffee Liqueur
1/2 oz Brandy
1/2 oz White Creme De Cacao
1/2 oz Hazelnut Liqueur
Scoop of Vanilla Ice Cream
Blend until smooth.
If too thick add cream or milk.
If too thin add ice or ice cream.
Top with Whipped Cream.
Sprinkle with Shaved Chocolate or
Sprinkles.

T

TURF
Fill glass with ice.
1 oz Gin
3/4 oz Dry Vermouth
1/4 oz Maraschino Liqueur
(optional)
1/4 oz Anisette
1/4 oz Bitters
Stir.
Strain into chilled glass.

TURKEY SHOOT (floater)
3/4 oz 101-Proof Bourbon (bottom)
1/4 oz White Creme De Menthe
(top)

TUXEDO
Fill glass with ice.
2 oz Fino Sherry
1/2 oz Anisette
1/4 oz Maraschino Liqueur
1/4 oz Bitters
Stir.
Strain into chilled glass.

24 KARAT NIGHTMARE aka 911
Fill glass with ice.
1 oz 100-Proof Cinnamon
Schnapps
1 oz 100-Proof Peppermint
Schnapps
Stir.

TWIN HILLS
Fill glass with ice.
1 1/2 oz Whiskey
2 tsp Benedictine
1 1/2 tsp Lemon Juice
1 1/2 tsp Lime Juice
1 tsp Sugar Syrup
or Powdered Sugar
Shake.
Strain into chilled glass.

TWIN SIX
Fill glass with ice.
1 oz Gin
1/2 oz Sweet Vermouth
1 tsp Grenadine
1 Tbsp Orange Juice
1 Egg White
Shake.
Strain into chilled glass.

TWISTER
Fill glass with ice.
2 oz Vodka
1/2 oz Lime Juice
Fill with Lemon-Lime Soda.
Stir.
Garnish with Lime.

TYPHOON
Fill glass with ice.
1/2 oz Gin
1/2 oz Sambuca
Dash of Lime Juice
Fill with Champagne.
Garnish with Lime.

UGLY DUCKLING
Fill glass with ice.
2 oz Amaretto
Fill with equal parts Milk or Cream
and Soda Water.
Stir.

ULANDA
Fill glass with ice.
1 1/2 oz Gin
3/4 oz Orange Liqueur or Triple Sec
1/4 tsp Pernod
Shake.
Strain into chilled glass.

UNCLE SAM
1 oz Bourbon
1 oz Peach Schnapps
Dash of Lime Juice
Stir.

UNION JACK
Fill glass with ice.
1 1/2 oz Gin
3/4 oz Sloe Gin
1/2 tsp Grenadine
Shake.
Strain into chilled glass.

UNION JACK 2
Fill glass with ice.
1 1/2 oz Gin
1/4 oz Creme De Yvette
Stir.
Strain into chilled glass.

UNION LEAGUE
Fill glass with ice.
1 1/2 oz Gin
1 oz Port
2-3 dashes of Orange Bitters
Stir.
Strain into chilled glass.
Garnish with Orange Twist.

UNIVERSAL
Fill glass with ice.
3/4 oz Vodka
3/4 oz Amaretto
3/4 oz Melon Liqueur
Fill with Grapefruit
or Pineapple Juice.
Shake.

UNPUBLISHED HEMINGWAY
2 oz Cognac
1/2 oz Orange Liqueur

UPSIDE DOWN MARGARITA aka HEAD REST
Rest head on bar.
Have friend pour ingredients into
mouth.
1 oz Tequila
1/2 oz Triple Sec
Dash of Lime Juice
Dash of Sour Mix
Dash of Orange Juice
Slosh around mouth.
Swallow!

URINALYSIS

Fill glass with ice.
1 1/2 oz Southern Comfort
1/2 oz Peppermint Schnapps
Stir.
Strain into chilled glass.

URINE SAMPLE

Fill glass with ice.
2 oz Amber Rum
1 oz Sour Mix
1 oz Pineapple Juice
Fill with Lemon-Lime Soda.

UZI (floater)

1/2 oz Coffee Liqueur (bottom)
1/2 oz Apricot Brandy
1/2 oz Ouzo (top)

VALENCIA

Fill glass with ice.
2 oz Apricot Brandy
1 oz Orange Juice
2-3 dashes of Orange Bitters
Shake.
Strain into chilled glass.
Add 3 oz chilled Champagne
(optional).

VANCOUVER

Fill glass with ice.
2 oz Canadian Whiskey
1 oz Dubonnet Rouge
1/2 oz Lemon Juice
1/2 oz Egg White
1/2 tsp Maple or Sugar Syrup
3 dashes of Orange Bitters
Shake.

VANDERBILT

Fill glass with ice.
1 1/2 oz Brandy
3/4 oz Cherry Brandy
1 tsp Sugar Syrup
2 dashes of Bitters
Stir.
Strain into chilled glass.

VANITY FAIR

Fill glass with ice.
1 1/2 oz Apple Brandy
1/2 oz Cherry Brandy
1/2 oz Cherry Liqueur
Shake.
Float 1 tsp Creme De Nouyax or
Amaretto on top.

VATICAN COFFEE

1 oz Cognac or Brandy
1 oz Hazelnut Liqueur
Fill with hot Black Coffee.
Top with Whipped Cream.

VELVET GAF

Fill glass 1/2 with Porter.
Fill glass 1/2 with Champagne.

VELVET GLOVE

Fill glass with ice.
1 oz Sloe Gin
1 oz White Creme De Menthe
1 oz Cream or Milk
Shake.
Strain into chilled glass.

VELVET HAMMER

Fill glass with ice.
1 oz Triple Sec or Curacao
1 oz White Creme De Cacao
1 oz Cream or Milk
Shake.
Strain into chilled glass.

VELVET HAMMER (frozen)

In Blender:
1/2 cup of Ice
1 oz Triple Sec or Curacao
1 oz White Creme De Cacao
Scoop of Vanilla Ice Cream
Blend until smooth.
If too thick add milk or cream.
If too thin add ice or ice cream.
Sprinkle with Shaved Chocolate.
Garnish with Orange.

VELVET KISS

Fill glass with ice.
1 oz Gin
1/2 oz Banana Liqueur
1/2 oz Pineapple Juice
1 oz Cream
Dash of Grenadine (optional)
Shake.
Strain into chilled glass.

VENETIAN COFFEE

1 oz Brandy
1/2 oz Galliano
1/2 oz Triple Sec
Fill with hot Black Coffee.
Top with Whipped Cream.
Sprinkle with Cinnamon.

VENETIAN FRAPPE

Fill large stemmed glass (Red Wine
glass, Champagne saucer) with
crushed ice.
3/4 oz Brandy
3/4 oz Galliano
3/4 oz Triple Sec

VENETIAN SUNRISE

Fill glass with ice.
1 1/2 oz Grappa or Brandy
Fill with Orange Juice.
Pour 1/2 oz Campari down spoon
to bottom of glass.
Garnish with Orange.

T
U
V

VERMOUTH CASSIS

Fill glass with ice.
2 oz Sweet or Dry Vermouth
1 oz Creme De Cassis
Fill with Soda Water.
Stir.
Garnish with Lemon Twist.

VERONA

Fill glass with ice.
1 oz Gin
1 oz Amaretto
1/2 oz Sweet Vermouth
1 or 2 dashes of Lemon Juice
Shake.
Garnish with Orange.

VERY JOLL-E RANCHER

Fill glass with ice.
1 oz Vodka
1/2 oz Apple Brandy
1/2 oz Peach Schnapps
Fill with Cranberry Juice.
Shake.

VIA VENETO

Fill glass with ice.
1 1/2 oz Brandy
1/2 oz Sambuca
1/2 oz Lemon Juice
1 tsp Sugar Syrup
1/2 Egg White
Shake.

VICTOR

Fill glass with ice.
1 1/2 oz Gin
1/2 oz Brandy
1/2 oz Sweet Vermouth
Shake.
Strain into chilled glass.

VICTORY

Fill glass with ice.
1 1/2 oz Pernod
3/4 oz Grenadine
Shake.
Fill with Soda Water.

VIKING

Fill glass with ice.
1 1/2 oz Swedish Punch
1 oz Aquavit
1 oz Lime Juice
Shake.

VIRGIN

Fill glass with ice.
1 oz Gin
1/2 oz White Creme De Menthe
1 oz Forbidden Fruit
Shake.
Strain into chilled glass.
Garnish with Cherry.

VIRGIN MARY

Fill glass with ice.
1 tsp Horseradish
3 dashes of Tabasco Sauce
3 dashes of Worcestershire Sauce
Dash of Lime Juice
3 dashes of Celery Salt
3 dashes of Pepper
1 oz Clam Juice (optional)
Fill with Tomato Juice.
Pour from one glass to
another until mixed.
Garnish with Lemon and/or Lime,
Celery and /or Cucumber and /or
Cocktail Shrimp.

VIRGIN PIÑA COLADA

(frozen)
In Blender:
1 cup of Ice
2 Tbsp Cream of Coconut
1 cup fresh or canned Pineapple
1 tsp Vanilla Ice Cream (optional)
Blend until smooth.
If too thick add fruit or juice.
If too thin add ice.
Garnish with Pineapple and Cherry.

VIRGIN STRAWBERRY DAIQUIRI

(frozen)
In Blender:
1 cup of Ice
Dash of Lime Juice
1 cup of fresh or frozen
Strawberries
Blend until smooth.
If too thick add berries or juice.
If too thin add ice.
Garnish with Strawberry and/or
Lime.

VISITOR

Fill glass with ice.
1 oz Vodka
1/2 oz Orange Liqueur
1/2 oz Banana Liqueur
Fill with Orange Juice.
Shake.

VODKA COLLINS

Fill glass with ice.
2 oz Vodka
Fill with Sour Mix.
Shake.
Splash with Soda Water.
Garnish with Orange and Cherry.

VODKA COOLER

Fill glass with ice.
2 oz Vodka
1/2 oz Sweet Vermouth
Dash of Sour Mix
1/2 oz Sugar Syrup
or Powdered Sugar
Shake.
Fill with Soda Water.

VODKA GIBSON
(*CAUTION:* DRY usually means less Vermouth than usual. EXTRA DRY can mean even less Vermouth than usual or no Vermouth at all.)
Fill glass with ice.
2 oz Vodka
1/2 oz Dry Vermouth
Stir.
Strain into chilled glass
or pour contents (with ice)
into short glass.
Garnish with Cocktail Onion.

VODKA GIMLET
Fill glass with ice.
2 oz Vodka
1/2 oz Lime Juice
Stir.
Strain into chilled glass
or pour contents (with ice)
into short glass.
Garnish with Lime.

VODKA GRAND MARNIER
Fill glass with ice.
1 1/2 oz Vodka
1/2 oz Orange Liqueur
1/2 oz Lime Juice
Shake.
Strain into chilled glass.
Garnish with Orange.

VODKA GRASSHOPPER aka FLYING GRASSHOPPER
Fill glass with ice.
1 oz Vodka
3/4 oz Green Creme De Menthe
3/4 oz White Creme De Cacao
Fill with Milk or Cream.
Shake.
Serve or strain into chilled glass.

VODKA MARTINI
(*CAUTION:* DRY usually means less Vermouth than usual. EXTRA DRY can mean even less Vermouth than usual or no Vermouth at all.)
Fill glass with ice.
2 oz Vodka
1/2 oz Dry Vermouth
Stir.
Strain into chilled glass
or pour contents (with ice)
into short glass.
Garnish with Lemon Twist or Olives.

VODKA SAKETINI
Fill glass with ice.
2 oz Vodka
1/2 oz Sake
Stir.
Strain into chilled glass
or pour contents (with ice)
into short glass.
Garnish with Lemon Twist or Olives
or Cocktail Onions.

VODKA SLING
Fill glass 1/2 way with ice.
Place 2 fresh Sliced Pitted Cherries around the inside of the glass.
2 oz Vodka
1/2 oz Lime Juice
Fill glass with crushed ice.
Top with 1/2 oz Cherry Brandy.

VODKA SODA
Fill glass with ice.
2 oz Vodka
Fill with Soda Water.
Garnish with Lemon or Lime.

VODKA SONIC
Fill glass with ice.
2 oz Vodka
Fill with equal parts Soda and Tonic Water.
Garnish with Lemon or Lime.

VODKA SOUR
Fill glass with ice.
2 oz Vodka
Fill with Sour Mix.
Shake.
Garnish with Cherry and Orange.

VODKA STINGER
Fill glass with ice.
1 1/2 oz Vodka
1/2 oz White Creme De Menthe
Stir.
Serve or strain into chilled glass.

VODKA TONIC
Fill glass with ice.
2 oz Vodka
Fill with Tonic Water.
Garnish with Lime.

VOLCANO
Fill glass with ice.
1 1/2 oz Brandy
1 oz Orange Juice
1 oz Pineapple Juice
1 oz Sour Mix
Dash of Grenadine
Dash of Lime Juice
Shake.
Top with 1/2 oz 151-Proof Rum.
Ignite.
Pour in 1/2 oz Champagne.

V

VOLGA BOATMAN
Fill glass with ice.
1 1/2 oz Vodka
1 oz Cherry Liqueur
1 oz Orange Juice
Shake.
Strain into chilled glass.
Garnish with Cherry.

VOO DOO (floater)
1/2 oz Coffee Liqueur (bottom)
1/2 oz Irish Cream
1/2 oz Dark Rum (top)

VOO DOO 2 (floater)
1/2 oz Coffee Liqueur (bottom)
1/2 oz Dark Rum
1/2 oz 151-Proof Rum (top)

VULCAN
Fill glass with ice.
1/2 oz Vodka
1/2 oz Gin
1/2 oz Coconut Rum
1/2 oz Southern Comfort
Fill with equal parts Grapefruit
Juice and Lemon-Lime Soda.
Stir.

VULCAN MIND MELT
1 oz Sambuca
1 oz 151-Proof Rum
Ignite.

VULCAN MIND PROBE
Fill glass with ice.
1/2 oz Vodka
1/2 oz Gin
1/2 oz Coconut Rum
1/2 oz Melon Liqueur
Dash of Lime Juice
Shake.
Strain into chilled glass.

VULCAN MIND PROBE 2
Fill glass with ice.
1/2 oz Gin
1/2 oz Rum
1/2 oz Brandy
1/2 oz Triple Sec or Curacao
Fill with equal parts Sour Mix and
Beer.

WADKINS GLEN
Fill glass with ice.
1 oz Vodka
1/2 oz Black Raspberry Liqueur
1/2 oz Banana Liqueur
Dash of Orange Juice
Dash of Cranberry Juice
Dash of Pineapple Juice
Shake.
Strain into chilled glass.
Garnish with Lime.

WAGON WHEEL
Fill glass with ice.
2 oz Southern Comfort
1 oz Cognac or Brandy
1 oz Sour Mix
1/2 oz Grenadine
Shake.
Strain into chilled glass.

WALDORF
Fill glass with ice.
1 1/2 oz Bourbon
3/4 oz Pernod
1/2 oz Sweet Vermouth
Dash of Bitters
Stir.
Strain into chilled glass.

WALL STREET LIZARD
Fill glass with ice.
1/2 oz Vodka
1/2 oz Gin
1/2 oz Rum
1/2 oz Melon Liqueur
1/2 oz Blue Curacao
Stir.
Serve or strain into chilled glass.

WALTZING MATILDA
Fill glass with ice.
2 oz Vodka
1 tsp Horseradish
3 dashes of Tabasco Sauce
3 dashes of Worcestershire Sauce
Dash of Lime Juice
3 dashes of Celery Salt
3 dashes of Pepper
1 oz Clam Juice (optional)
Fill with Tomato Juice.
Pour from one glass to
another until mixed.
Garnish with Lemon and/or Lime,
Celery and/or Cucumber
and/or Cocktail Shrimp.

WANDERING MINSTREL
Fill glass with ice.
1/2 oz Vodka
1/2 oz Coffee Liqueur
1/2 oz Brandy
1/2 oz White Creme De Menthe
Stir.
Strain into chilled glass.

WANNA PROBE YA
Fill glass with ice.
1 oz Spiced Rum
1 oz Coconut Rum
Fill with equal parts Pineapple and
Cranberry Juice.
Stir.
Garnish with Lime.

WARD EIGHT
Fill glass with ice.
2 oz Whiskey
Dash of Grenadine
Fill with Sour Mix.
Shake.
Garnish with Cherry and Orange.

WARDAY'S COCKTAIL
Fill glass with ice.
1 oz Gin
1 oz Sweet Vermouth
1 oz Apple Brandy
1 tsp Yellow Chartreuse
Shake.
Strain into chilled glass.

WARSAW
Fill glass with ice.
1 1/2 oz Vodka
1/2 oz Blackberry Liqueur
1/2 oz Dry Vermouth
1/4 oz Lemon Juice
Shake.
Strain into chilled glass.
Garnish with Lemon Twist.

WASHINGTON
Fill glass with ice.
1 1/2 oz Dry Vermouth
3/4 oz Brandy
1/2 tsp Sugar Syrup
2-3 dashes of Bitters
Stir.
Strain into chilled glass.

WATERBURY COCKTAIL
Fill glass with ice.
2 oz Cognac or Brandy
1/2 oz Lemon Juice
1 tsp Sugar Syrup
1/2 Egg White
2-3 dashes of Bitters
Shake.
Strain into chilled glass.

WATERFALL
Fill shot glass with desired Liquor
or Liqueur. (Tequila, Peppermint
Schnapps, Jaegermeister, Whiskey)
Fill shot glass with desired chaser.
(beer, soda, juice, water, espresso)
Hold 1st glass between thumb and
forefinger. Hold 2nd glass between
forefinger and middle finger. Drink
from first glass and let second
glass flow into first glass.

WATERGATE COFFEE
1 oz Coffee Liqueur
1 oz Orange Liqueur
Fill with hot Black Coffee.
Top with Whipped Cream.

WATERMELON
Fill glass with ice.
1 oz Southern Comfort
1/2 oz Sloe Gin
Dash of Orange Juice
Fill with Pineapple Juice.
Shake.

WATERMELON 2
Fill glass with ice.
1 oz Vodka or Amaretto
1 oz Melon Liqueur
Fill with Cranberry Juice.
Stir.

WATERMELON 3
Fill glass with ice.
1 oz Vodka
1 oz Strawberry Liqueur
1 oz Sour Mix
1 oz Orange Juice
Shake.

WEDDING BELLE
Fill glass with ice.
3/4 oz Gin
3/4 oz Dubonnet Rouge
1/2 oz Cherry Brandy
1/2 oz Orange Juice
Shake.
Serve or strain into chilled glass.

WEEK ON THE BEACH
Fill glass with ice.
1 oz Rum
1/2 oz Peach Schnapps
1/2 oz Apple Brandy
Fill with equal parts Orange,
Cranberry and Pineapple Juice.
Shake.

WEEKEND AT THE BEACH
Fill glass with ice.
1 oz Rum
1 oz Peach Schnapps
Fill with equal parts Pineapple and
Orange Juice.
Shake.

WEEP NO MORE
Fill glass with ice.
3/4 oz Brandy
3/4 oz Dubonnet
3/4 oz Lime Juice
1/4 tsp Cherry Liqueur
(optional)
Shake.
Strain into chilled glass.

WELL RED RHINO (frozen)
In Blender:
1 cup of Ice
1 oz Vodka
1 oz Rum
1 oz Cream of Coconut
1 oz fresh or frozen
Strawberries
Dash of Cranberry, Lime and
Pineapple Juice
Blend until smooth.

WEMBLEY
Fill glass with ice.
1 1/2 oz Gin
3/4 oz Dry Vermouth
1/2 oz Apple Brandy
1/4 oz Apricot Brandy (optional)
Stir.
Strain into chilled glass.

WEST INDIAN FRAPPE
Fill large stemmed glass (Red Wine
glass, Champagne saucer) with
crushed ice.
3/4 oz Light Rum
3/4 oz Banana Liqueur
3/4 oz Orange Liqueur

WEST INDIES YELLOWBIRD
Fill glass with ice.
1 oz Rum
1 oz Banana Liqueur
Splash Galliano
1/2 tsp Sugar
Dash of Cream
Fill with equal parts Orange and
Pineapple Juice.
Shake.

WET DREAM
1 oz Vodka
1/2 oz Black Raspberry Llqueur
1/2 oz Banana Liqueur
Fill with equal parts of Orange
Juice and Milk.
Shake.

WHALE'S TAIL
Fill glass with ice.
1 oz Vodka
1 oz Spiced Rum
1/2 oz Blue Curacao
1 oz Sour Mix
Fill with Pineapple Juice.
Shake.

WHARF RAT
Fill glass with ice.
1 oz Rum
1/2 oz Apricot Brandy
Dash of Grenadine
2 oz Sour Mix
Fill with Orange Juice.
Shake.
Garnish with Lime and Black
Licorice Whip.

WHEN HELL FREEZES OVER
(frozen)
In Blender:
1 cup of Ice
1 oz Cinnamon Schnapps
1 oz Banana Liqueur
1/2 ripe peeled Banana
Dash of Orange Juice
Dash of Cranberry Juice
Pinch ground Cinnamon
Blend until smooth.

WHIP COCKTAIL
Fill glass with ice.
1 1/2 oz Brandy
3/4 oz Sweet Vermouth
3/4 oz Dry Vermouth
1/2 tsp Curacao or Triple Sec
1/4 tsp Pernod
Stir.
Strain into chilled glass.

WHIPPET
Fill glass with ice.
1 1/2 oz Whiskey
1/2 oz Peppermint Schnapps
1/2 oz White Creme De Cacao
Shake.
Strain into chilled glass.

WHIRLAWAY
Fill glass with ice.
1 1/2 oz Bourbon
3/4 oz Curacao
2-3 dashes of Bitters
Shake.
Top with Soda Water.

WHISKEY AND WATER
Fill glass with ice.
2 oz Whiskey
Fill with Water.
Stir.

WHISKEY COLLINS
Fill glass with ice.
2 oz Whiskey
Fill with Sour Mix.
Shake.
Splash with Soda Water.
Garnish with Cherry and Orange.

WHISKEY DAISY
Fill glass with ice.
2 oz Whiskey
1 tsp Raspberry Syrup
or Grenadine or Red Currant Syrup
1/2 oz Lemon Juice
Shake.
Fill with Soda Water.
Float 1 tsp Yellow Chartreuse on
top.
Garnish with Lemon wedge.

WHISKEY FIX
Fill glass with ice.
2 oz Blended Whiskey
or Blended Scotch Whiskey
1 oz Lemon Juice
1 tsp Powdered Sugar
Stir.
Garnish with Lemon.

WHISKEY HIGHBALL
Fill glass with ice.
2 oz Whiskey
Fill with Water or Soda Water
or Ginger Ale.

WHISKEY RICKEY
Fill glass with ice.
1 1/2 oz Whiskey
1/2 oz Lime Juice
1 tsp Sugar Syrup (optional)
Fill with Soda Water.
Stir.
Garnish with Lime.

WHISKEY SOUR
Fill glass with ice.
2 oz Whiskey
Fill with Sour Mix.
Shake.
Garnish with Cherry and Orange.

WHISPER (frozen)
In Blender:
1/2 cup of Ice
1/2 oz Coffee Liqueur
1/2 oz Creme De Cacao
1/2 oz Brandy
Scoop of Vanilla Ice Cream
Blend until smooth.
If too thick add cream or milk.
If too thin add ice or ice cream.
Sprinkle with Shaved Chocolate.

WHITE BABY
Fill glass with ice.
1 oz Gin
1 oz Triple Sec
1 oz Heavy Cream
Shake.
Strain into chilled glass.

WHITE BULL
Fill glass with ice.
1 oz Tequila
1 oz Coffee Liqueur
Fill with Milk or Cream.
Shake.

WHITE CADILLAC
Fill glass with ice.
2 oz Scotch
Fill with Milk or Cream.
Stir.

WHITE CADILLAC 2
Fill glass with ice.
1 oz Triple Sec
1 oz White Creme De Cacao
1 oz Milk or Cream
Shake.
Strain into chilled glass.

WHITE CARGO (frozen)
In Blender:
1/2 cup of Ice
2 1/2 oz Gin
1/2 oz Maraschino Liqueur
1/2 oz Dry White Wine
Scoop of Vanilla Ice Cream
Blend until smooth.
If too thick add milk or cream. If too
thin add ice or ice cream.

WHITE CLOUD
Fill glass with ice.
2 oz Sambuca
Fill with Soda Water.
Stir.

WHITE DEATH
Fill glass with ice.
1 oz Vodka
1/2 oz White Creme De Cacao
1/2 oz Raspberry Schnapps
Stir.
Strain into chilled glass.

WHITE ELEPHANT
Fill glass with ice.
1 oz Vodka
1 oz White Creme De Cacao
Fill with Milk.
Shake.

WHITE GHOST (frozen)
In Blender:
1 cup of Ice
1 1/2 oz Hazelnut Liqueur
3/4 oz White Creme De Cacao
1/4 oz Black Raspberry Liqueur
2 oz Cream
Blend.

WHITE HEART
Fill glass with ice.
1/2 oz Sambuca
1/2 oz White Creme De Cacao
2 oz Cream or Milk
Shake.
Strain into chilled glass.

WHITE HEAT
Fill glass with ice.
1 oz Gin
1/2 oz Triple Sec
1/2 oz Dry Vermouth
1 oz Pineapple Juice
Shake.

W

WHITE JAMAICAN
Fill glass with ice.
1 oz Rum
1 oz Coffee Liqueur
Fill with Milk or Cream.
Shake.

WHITE KNIGHT
Fill glass with ice.
3/4 oz Scotch
3/4 oz Drambuie
3/4 oz Coffee Liqueur
Fill with Milk or Cream.
Shake.

WHITE LADY
Fill glass with ice.
1 1/2 oz Gin
1/4 oz Cream
1 tsp Sugar Syrup
or Powdered Sugar
1/2 Egg White
Shake.
Strain into chilled glass.

WHITE LADY 2
Fill glass with ice.
1 oz Gin
1 oz Triple Sec
1 oz Cream or Milk
Shake.
Strain into chilled glass.

WHITE LILY
Fill glass with ice.
1 oz Gin
1 oz Rum
1 oz Triple Sec
1/4 tsp Pernod
Shake.
Serve or strain into chilled glass.

WHITE LION
Fill glass with ice.
1 1/2 oz Rum
3/4 oz Lemon juice
1 tsp Powdered Sugar
1/2 tsp Grenadine
2-3 dashes of Bitters
Shake.
Strain into chilled glass.

WHITE MINK
Fill glass with ice.
1 oz Vodka
1/2 oz White Creme De Menthe
1/2 oz Galliano
Fill with Cream or Milk.
Shake.

WHITE MINK 2
Fill glass with ice.
1 oz Galliano
1 oz Triple Sec
1 oz Cream or Milk
Shake.
Strain into chilled glass.

WHITE MINNESOTA
Fill glass with ice.
2 oz White Creme De Menthe
Fill with Soda Water.
Stir.

WHITE OUT
Fill glass with ice.
1 1/2 oz Gin
1 oz White Creme De Cacao
Fill with Milk.
Shake.

WHITE ROMAN
Fill glass with ice.
1 oz Sambuca
1 oz Coffee Liqueur
Fill with Milk or Cream.
Shake.

WHITE ROSE
Fill glass with ice.
1 1/2 oz Gin
3/4 oz Cherry Liqueur
2 oz Orange Juice
1/2 oz Lime Juice
1 tsp Sugar Syrup
1/2 Egg White
Shake.
Strain into chilled glass.

WHITE RUSSIAN
Fill glass with ice.
1 oz Vodka
1 oz Coffee Liqueur
Fill with Milk or Cream.
Shake.

WHITE RUSSIAN (frozen)
In Blender:
1/2 cup of Ice
1 oz Vodka
1 oz Coffee Liqueur
Scoop of Vanilla Ice Cream
Blend until smooth.
If too thick add milk or cream.
If too thin add ice or ice cream.
Sprinkle with Shaved Chocolate or
Sprinkles.

WHITE SPANIARD
Fill glass with ice.
1 oz Brandy
1 oz Coffee Liqueur
Fill with Milk or Cream.
Shake.

WHITE SPIDER
Fill glass with ice.
2 oz Vodka
1 oz White Creme De Menthe
Shake.
Strain into chilled glass.

WHITE SWAN
Fill glass with ice.
2 oz Amaretto
2 oz Milk or Cream
Shake.

WHITE WATER
Fill glass with ice.
1/2 oz Triple Sec
1 oz Pineapple Juice
Fill with White Wine.
Top with Lemon-Lime Soda.

WHITE WITCH
Fill glass with ice.
1 oz Light Rum
1/2 oz White Creme De Cacao
1/2 oz Triple Sec
Squeeze 1/2 Lime into drink.
Fill with Soda Water.
Garnish with Mint Sprigs
dusted with Powdered Sugar.

WHY NOT
Fill glass with ice.
1 oz Gin
1 oz Apricot Brandy
or Dry Vermouth
1/2 oz Dry Vermouth
or Apricot Brandy
1 tsp Lemon Juice
Shake.
Strain into chilled glass.

WIDOW'S DREAM
Fill glass with ice.
2 oz Benedictine
1 Egg
Shake.
Strain into chilled glass.
Float 1 oz Cream on top.

WIDOW'S KISS
Fill glass with ice.
1 oz Brandy
1/2 oz Benedictine
1/2 oz Yellow Chartreuse
Dash of Bitters
Shake.
Strain into chilled glass.

WILD FLING
Fill glass with ice.
2 oz Wildberry Schnapps
Splash of Cranberry Juice
Fill with Pineapple Juice.
Stir.

WILD IRISH ROSE
Fill glass with ice.
1 1/2 oz Irish Whiskey
1 1/2 tsp Grenadine
1/2 oz Lime Juice
Stir.
Fill with Soda Water.

WILD THING
Fill glass with ice.
1 oz Vodka
1/2 oz Rum
1/2 oz Triple Sec
Dash of Lime Juice
Dash of Sour Mix
Shake.
Fill with Cranberry Juice.

WILL ROGERS
Fill glass with ice.
1 1/2 oz Gin
1/2 oz Dry Vermouth
Dash of Triple Sec
1 Tbsp Orange Juice
Shake.
Strain into chilled glass.

WIND JAMMER
Fill glass with ice.
1 oz Dark Rum
1/2 oz White Creme De Cacao
2 oz Pineapple Juice
1 oz Cream
Shake.
Garnish with Pineapple.

WINDEX
Fill glass with ice.
1 1/2 oz Vodka
1/4 oz Blue Curacao
Strain into shot glass.
Splash with Soda Water.

WINDEX 2
Fill glass with ice.
1 oz Vodka
1 oz Rum
1/2 oz Blue Curacao
Dash of Lime Juice
Fill with Lemon-Lime Soda
Use paper towel as coaster.

WINDY CITY
Fill glass with ice.
1 1/4 oz Whiskey
Dash of Triple Sec
2 oz water
Garnish with Lemon Twist.

WINE COOLER
Fill glass 3/4 with ice.
Fill 3/4 with desired Wine.
Fill with Ginger Ale
or Lemon-Lime Soda.
Garnish with Lime.

WINE SPRITZER
Fill glass 3/4 with ice.
Fill 3/4 with desired Wine.
Fill with Soda Water.
Garnish with Lime.

W

WINTER FROST (frozen)
In Blender:
1/2 cup of Ice
3/4 oz Brandy
3/4 oz White Creme De Cacao
3/4 oz White Creme De Menthe
Scoop of Vanilla Ice Cream
Blend until smooth.

WITCHES' BREW
Fill glass with ice.
2 oz Spiced Rum
Fill with equal parts Pineapple,
Cranberry and Orange Juice.
Top with 1/2 oz Melon Liqueur.
Jody Martin

WOLFHOUND
Fill glass with ice.
1 oz Irish Whiskey
3/4 oz Dark Creme De Cacao
1 oz Milk or Cream
Shake.
Top with 1 oz Soda Water.

WOMBAT
Pulverize 6 oz of Fresh Watermelon
(minus seeds) in glass.
2 oz Dark Rum
1/2 oz Strawberry Liqueur
3 oz Orange Juice
3 oz Pineapple Juice
Shake well.

WOO WOO aka
SILK PANTIES 2
Fill glass with ice.
1 1/2 oz Vodka
1/2 oz Peach Schnapps
2 oz Cranberry Juice
Stir.
Serve or strain into chilled glass.

WOODEN SHOE
2 oz Vandermint
Fill with Hot Chocolate.
Top with Whipped Cream.
Drizzle Chocolate Syrup on top.

W. W. II
Fill glass with ice.
1 oz Vodka
1 oz Triple Sec
1 oz Melon Liqueur
Dash of Lime Juice
Fill with Pineapple Juice.
Shake.

WYOMING SWING
COCKTAIL
Fill glass with ice.
1 1/2 oz Sweet Vermouth
1 1/2 oz Dry Vermouth
3 oz Orange Juice
1/2 oz Sugar Syrup
Shake.

WYOOTER HOOTER
Fill glass with ice.
2 oz Bourbon
Dash of Grenadine
Fill with Lemon-Lime Soda.

XALAPA PUNCH
In Sauce Pan over low heat:
2 cups of Hot Black Tea
Add rind of two Oranges (use carrot
peeler or cheese grater)
Heat for 5 minutes.
Let cool.
Add 1 cup of Honey or Sugar (stir
until dissolved)
Pour into punch bowl with ice.
Add:
1 Quart Amber Rum
1 Quart Apple Brandy
1 Quart Dry Red Wine
Diced Orange and Lemon
Serves 40

XANADU (floater)
1/2 oz Galliano (bottom)
1/2 oz Orange Liqueur
1/2 oz Amaretto (top)

XANGO
Fill glass with ice.
1 1/2 oz Rum
1/2 oz Triple Sec
1 oz Grapefruit Juice
Shake.
Strain into chilled glass.

XANTHIA
Fill glass with ice.
3/4 oz Gin
3/4 oz Cherry Brandy
3/4 oz Yellow Chartreuse
Shake.
Serve or strain into chilled glass.

XAVIER
Fill glass with ice.
3/4 oz Coffee Liqueur
3/4 oz Creme De Nouyax
3/4 oz Orange Liqueur
Fill with Milk or Cream.
Shake.

XERES
Fill glass with ice.
2 oz Dry Sherry
Dash of Orange Bitters
Stir.
Strain into chilled glass.

XYLOPHONE (frozen)
In Blender:
1/2 cup of Ice
1 1/2 oz Tequila
1 oz White Creme De Cacao
1 oz Sugar Syrup
Scoop of Vanilla Ice Cream
Blend until smooth.
If too thick add milk or cream.
If too thin add ice or ice cream.

XYZ
Fill glass with ice.
1 1/2 oz Rum
1/2 oz Triple Sec
1/2 oz Lemon Juice
Shake.
Strain into chilled glass.

Y. I.
Fill glass with ice.
1/2 oz Vodka
1/2 oz Coconut Rum
1/2 oz Melon Liqueur
1/2 oz Black Raspberry Liqueur
Dash of Pineapple and Cranberry
Juice
Shake.
Strain into shot glass.

YALE COCKTAIL
Fill glass with ice.
1 1/2 oz Gin
1/2 oz Dry Vermouth
1 tsp Blue Curacao
or Cherry Brandy
Dash of Bitters
Stir.

YARD OF FLANNEL
In sauce pan over low heat:
2 pints of Ale (do not boil)
Blend in a separate bowl:
4 oz Amber Rum
3 oz Super Fine Sugar
1/2 tsp ground Nutmeg
4 Eggs
1/2 tsp Ginger or Cinnamon
Beat well.
Pour mixture in heated pitcher.
Slowly add hot ale.
Stir constantly.
Serves 4.

YASHMAK
Fill glass with ice.
1 1/2 oz Rye Whiskey
3/4 oz Dry Vermouth
1/2 oz Pernod
3 dashes of Bitters
1/2 tsp Sugar Syrup
Shake.

YELLOW BIRD
Fill glass with ice.
3/4 oz Vodka
3/4 oz White Creme De Cacao
3/4 oz Orange Juice
3/4 oz Cream
1/2 oz Galliano
Shake.
Strain into chilled glass.

YELLOW BIRD (frozen)
In Blender:
1 cup of Ice
1 oz Rum
1/2 oz Coffee Liqueur
1/2 oz Banana Liqueur
2 tbsp Cream of Coconut
1/2 cup fresh or canned Pineapple
Blend until smooth.

YELLOW FEVER
Fill glass with ice.
2 oz Vodka
Fill with Lemonade.
Stir.
Garnish with Lemon.

YELLOW JACKET aka
KENTUCKY SCREWDRIVER
Fill glass with ice.
2 oz Bourbon
Fill with Orange Juice.

YELLOW JACKET 2
Fill glass with ice.
1/2 oz Jaegermeister
1/2 oz Bärenjägur
1/2 oz Coffee Liqueur
Stir.
Strain into chilled glass.

YELLOW PARROT
Fill glass with ice.
1 oz Apricot Brandy
1 oz Pernod
1 oz Yellow Chartreuse
Shake.
Strain into chilled glass.

YELLOW RATTLER
Fill glass with ice.
1 oz Gin
1 oz Dry Vermouth
1 oz Sweet Vermouth
3 oz Orange Juice
Shake.
Strain into chilled glass.

YELLOW RUSSIAN aka
JUNGLE JIM
Fill glass with ice.
1 oz Vodka
1 oz Banana Liqueur
Fill with Milk or Cream.
Shake.

W
X
Y

YELLOW SUBMARINE
Fill glass with ice.
1 oz Peach Schnapps
1 oz Banana Liqueur
Fill with equal parts Orange and
Pineapple Juice.
Shake.

YODEL
Fill glass with ice.
2 oz Fernet Branca
2 oz Orange Juice
Stir.
Fill with Soda Water.
Garnish with Orange.

YOG
Fill glass with ice.
2 oz Yukon Jack
Fill with equal parts Orange and
Grapefruit Juice.
Shake.

ZAMBOANGA HUMMER
Fill glass with ice.
1/2 oz Amber Rum
1/2 oz Gin
1/2 oz Brandy
1/2 oz Curacao or Triple Sec
2 oz Orange Juice
2 oz Pineapple Juice
1/2 oz Lemon Juice
1 tsp Brown Sugar
Shake.

ZANZIBAR
Fill glass with ice.
2 1/2 oz Dry Vermouth
1 oz Gin
1/2 oz Lemon Juice
1 tsp Sugar Syrup
3 dashes of Bitters
Shake.
Strain into chilled glass.
Garnish with a Lemon Twist.

ZAZA
Fill glass with ice.
1 1/2 oz Gin
1 1/2 oz Dubonnet
1/2 oz Triple Sec
2 oz Orange Juice
Shake.
Strain into chilled glass.

ZAZARAC
Fill glass with ice.
1 oz Whiskey
1/4 oz Rum
1/4 oz Anisette
1/4 oz Sugar Syrup
3 dashes of Bitters
1 oz Water
Stir.
Garnish with Lemon.

ZHIVAGO STANDARD
Fill glass with ice.
1 1/2 oz Vodka
1/2 oz Kummel
1/2 oz Lime Juice
Stir.
Strain into chilled glass.
Garnish with Olive.

ZIPPER HEAD
Fill glass with ice.
1 1/2 oz Vodka
1/2 oz Black Raspberry Liqueur
Fill with Soda Water.

ZOMBIE
Fill glass with ice.
1 oz Light Rum
1 oz Dark Rum
1/2 oz Triple Sec or Curacao or
Apricot Brandy
Dash of Creme De Nouyax
or Grenadine
2 oz Orange Juice
2 oz Sour Mix
or Pineapple Juice
Shake.
Top with 1/2 oz 151-Proof Rum.
Garnish with Lemon, Orange and
Cherry.

ZONKER
Fill glass with ice.
1 oz Vodka
1 oz Triple Sec
1 oz Amaretto
1 oz Cranberry Juice
Shake.
Strain into chilled glass.

ZOO
Fill glass with ice.
1/2 oz Gin
1/2 oz Rum
1/2 oz Tequila
1/2 oz Bourbon
Dash of Grenadine
Fill with equal parts Orange and
Pineapple Juice.
Shake.

ZOOM
Fill glass with ice.
1 1/2 oz Brandy
1/4 oz Honey
1/2 oz Cream
Shake.
Strain into chilled glass.

ZUMA BUMA
Fill glass with ice.
1 1/2 oz Citrus Vodka
1/2 oz Black Raspberry Liqueur
Fill with Orange Juice.
Splash of Cranberry Juice

Serving Wines
Temperature
   Whites and Rose'- 40-55
   Reds- 55-65 (exception: Red Beaujolais 40-55)
Note: When room temperature is suggested, it means European room temperature (approximately 60).
If you enjoy white wines warm and red wines chilled by all means, serve it as you like it.

Opening
   There are two methods of getting at the cork.
      1. Using a knife, cut around the top of the bottle above the raised lip, but below the mouth.
      2. Using a knife, remove the foil capsule leaving the neck naked.
Note: The latter is favored because of lead toxins which can occur if the foil contains lead, and dripped wine sits for any length of time in the minute crevice created by using step one. (Newer wine foils do not contain lead).
Before uncorking insure the top of the cork and lip of the bottle are free of mildew which commonly occurs. Wipe with clean damp cloth.

Removing the cork
Place bottle on flat surface. Insert tip of corkscrew slightly off center, so that spiral will penetrate the center of the cork. Insure the spirals completely penetrate the cork, lessening chance of breaking cork.

Opening Champagne
Remove foil to expose wire fastener. Take a clean cloth and grip cork and fastener firmly and untwist fastener. Slowly twist cork and bottle in separate directions. Cork may want to rifle out of bottle, but control cork so it releases slowly.

Types of Wines

Beaujolais-(Bow-show-lay) (primarily red) (France, U.S.)
Should be drunk young, and served chilled.

Bordeaux-(Bore-doe) (primarily red) (France)
Many types exist. All wines from this seaport are entitled to the name.

Burgundy-(Bur-gun-dee) (red, white and rosé) (France, U.S.)
True French ones are better than average wines. Americans use the name as a word meaning generic red wine.

Cabernet Savignon-(Cab-air-nay So-veen-yaw) (red) (France, U.S.)
A superb grape. Took very well to American soil. A kaleidoscope of flavors, undertones, and nuances.

Chablis-(Shab-lee) (white) (France, U.S.)
In France it is strictly made with Chardonnay grapes by a certain process. In the U.S. it's name is used as a term for any white wine.

Champagne-(Sham-pain) (white) (France, U.S.)
Made from a mixture of different grapes. Before final bottling, sugar, wine and even Brandy are added for flavor. Brut means up to 1 1/2% added. Dry means up to 4% added.

Chardonnay-(Shar-doe-nay) (white) (France, U.S.)
Probably the best U.S. grown white table wines. Globally considered one of the finest white grapes.

Chateauneuf-du-Pape-(Shot-toe-nuff-dew Pop) (primarily red) (France)
A mixture of different grapes. Best between 5 and 10 years old.

Chenin Blanc-(Shay-nan Blaw) (white) (France, U.S.)
A grape of excellent quality. The grape transplanted to American soil took very well.

Chianti-(Key-ahnt-tee) (red) (Italy)
Properly drunk young. The elegant straw wrapped bottles are often worth more money than the contents, although the contents are sometimes excellent.

Cotes-du-Rhone-(Coat dew Rone) (primarily red) (France)
Moderately priced, fair to good table wine from the Rhone Valley.

Dubonnet-(Due-bawn-nay) (red, white) (France, U.S.)
Wine laced with herbs, and quinine. Usualy served as an apertif.

Fume' Blanc-(Foo-may-Blaw) (white) (France, U.S.)
A dry, crisp, popular wine. Made with Sauvignon grapes.

Gewurztraminer-(Ge-vertz-tram-mener) (white, pink) (Germany, France, U.S.)
A spicy, highly prized, heavy scented wine.

Graves-(Grahv) (red, white) (France)
The reds age very well. The best whites come from Leognan.

Liebfraumilch-(Leeb-frau-milsh) (white) (Germany)
"Milk of the Blessed Mother". Almost always Rhine wine.

Madeira-(Ma-day-rah) (red) (Portugal)
Made world famous by American settlers. In modern day it is primarily used as cooking wine.

Marsala-(Mar-sahl-la) (red, amber) (Italy)
High alcohol content due to the fact it is fortified with high proof brandy. Popular for cooking.

Medoc-(May-dawk) (red) (France)
A superior red, even the lesser of the Medocs.

Merlot-(Mair-lo) (red) (U.S., Italy, Switzerland)
Much like a Cabernet in taste, but simpler and fruitier. It is a short lived wine.

Muscadet-(Mus-cad-day) (white) (France, U.S.)
An agreeable, fresh, fruity early maturing wine.

Muscatel-(Mus-cat-tel) (red, white) (U.S., Portugal, Spain, France, Italy)
Range from poor to excellent quality.

Petite Sirah-(Peh-teet See-rah) (red) (U.S.)
An American wine made from Syrah grapes transplanted from the Rhone Valley.

Piesport-(Peas-port) (white) (Germany)
From one of the most famous yet smallest wine producing villages.

Pinot Blanc-(Pee-no Blaw) (white) (U.S., Italy)
A light white.

Pinot Noir-(Pee-no Nwahr) (red) (U.S. France)
One of the main grapes of Champagne. A mainstay of Burgundies.

Pommard-(Po-mar) (red) (France)
Probably the most popular Burgundy. It is soft, well-balanced and fruity.

Port-(Port) (red, tawny, white) (Portugal, U.S.)
Fortified with Brandy. The most celebrated dessert wine.

Pouilly Fuisse-(Poo-ye Fwee-say) (white) (France)
Made from the Chardonnay grape. It does not improve past the age of 3 years.

Rhine-(Rine) (white) (Germany, U.S.)
Means the Rhine Valley. Americans can call any wine from any grape Rhine wine.

Riesling-(Reece-ling) (white) (Italy, Switzerland, Chile, Austria, Germany, U.S.)
There are many types with many flavors. It is probably the most famous grape in the world.

Rosé-(Ro-zay) (pink) (France, Italy, U.S.)
It should be chilled and drunk young. Excellent domestic ones are available.

St. Emilion-(Sant A-me-lee-aw) (red) (France)
This wine is primarily Merlot.

Saké-(Sa-kay) (beer) (Japan)
Made from fermented rice and served warm. It is actually a beer and not a wine.

Sauvignon Blanc-(So-veen-yaw Blaw) (white) (France, U.S.)
This is the same wine as Fume' Blanc. A dry, crisp popular wine.

Semillon-(Say-me-yaw) (white) (France, U.S.)
A prominent grape in white Bordeaux.

Sherry-(Shar-ee) (red) (Spain, U.S., Australia, South Africa)
The finest apertif as well as an excellent dessert wine. Made from
raisin or table grapes, and fortified with Brandy.

Soave-(So-ah-veh) (white) (Italy)
This wine should be drunk 3 to 4 years old.

Spumante-(Spoo-mahn-teh) (white) (Italy)
This is a sparkling or foaming wine.

Valpolicella-(Vahl-po-lee-chel-la) (red) (Italy)
Should be drunk 4 to 7 years old.

Vermouth-(Ver-mooth) (red, white) (France, Argentina, Italy, U.S.)
Wine fortified with herbs, barks, seeds and spices.

Vouvray-(Voo-vray) (white) (France)
Made from Chenin Blanc grapes, it is a long-lived white.

White Zinfandel-(Whyt Zin-fan-dell) (pink) (U.S.)
An American original, originally made by mistake.

Zinfandel-(Zin-fan-dell) (red) (U.S.)
Best drunk young. It is full bodied and peppery.

Wine and Food
Matching of wine and food is an individual's choice. For a rule of
thumb, try to match food with wine of similar flavor or try matching
food with wine of a contrasting flavor.

If a dish has a brown sauce or a red wine sauce, red wine is
suggested.

If a dish has a white sauce or a cream sauce, white wine is
suggested.

ALES

ALE: A fermented beverage containing malt and hops, similar to but heavier than beer. Ale can vary from blond to black in color.

ALT: Means "old" in German and refers to a traditional brewing process.

BITTER: A hoppy flavored light bodied ale.

LAMBIC: Originating from Belgium, made with wheat mash and flavored with a wide range of fruits.

STOUT: A very dark or black ale, with a bittersweet flavor.

INDIAN PALE ALE: Brewed originally in Britain with extra hops to survive the voyage to India. It has a very unique hoppy flavor.

WHEAT BEER: Made with wheat malt and brewed originally in Germany. Many are fruity and tart. Traditionally served with lemon.

PORTER: A darker ale, rather bitter and malty.

LAGERS

LAGER: Bottom fermented beer from the German word "to store." It is aged at cool temperatures which gives it a smooth refined taste.

PILSNER: A kind of lager originating from Pilsner, Czechoslovakia.

DRY BEER: Brewed with enzymal additives which convert more of the malt into alcohol, making a drier tasting beer.

BOCK: Traditionally brewed in Germany in the spring. It is a stronger lager with a malty finish.

LIGHT BEER: An American term suggesting a watered down, low calorie brew.

ICE BEER: A lager filtered through an ice chamber. Ice is removed from the brew leaving a higher alcohol content.

MALT LIQUOR: An American term for a strong lager.

147

GLOSSARY

Akvavit or Aquavit: A Scandinavian liqueur made with rye and caraway.

Aperitif: An alcoholic liquor or wine drunk to stimulate the appetite before a meal.

Ale: A fermented beverage containing malt and hops similar but heavier than Beer.

Amaretto: Originally from Italy, made from apricot pits and herbs. With an almond and vanilla taste.

Amer Picon: A French cordial with a bitter orange flavor.

Anisette: A very sweet liqueur made from anise seed. Tastes like black licorice.

Beer: An alcoholic beverage brewed from malt and flavored by hops.

Benedictine: A liqueur produced by monks, with a secret formula.

Bitters: A bitter tasting alcoholic liquid made from herbs and roots.

Black Raspberry Liqueur: Chambord is by far the most popular Black Raspberry Liqueur.

Blended Whiskey: A whiskey made by blending 2 or more straight whiskeys. Some Scotch as well as Canadian and iced in the Dutch West Indies.

Bourbon: Solely American made. Aged 4 years or more. Named after Bourbon County Kentucky

Brandy: An alcoholic liquor distilled from wine or from fermented fruit.

Campari: A bitter Italian apertif.

Canadian Whiskey: Made under strict government regulations. With a lighter taste and color than other whiskeys.

Chambord: A French black raspberry liqueur.

Chartreuse: An herb liqueur. Developed by Carthusian monks in 1605.

Coffee Liqueur: The most popular brands are Kahlua from Mexico and Tia Maria from Jamaica.

Cognac: Basically cognac is brandy from the Cognac region of France.

Cointreau: An up-scale, French orange liqueur, in the Curacao family.

Cordial: A straight liqueur drink to stimulate or enhance a warm or friendly situation.

Cream of Coconut: A coconut base or syrup used for many exotic drinks the most popular being the Piña Colada.

Creme De Cassis: A liqueur made from European Black Currants (berries).

Creme De Cacao: A liqueur which comes in either dark or white (clear) form. Made from cacao and vanilla beans.

Creme De Menthe: A liqueur which comes in either green or white (clear). Made from peppermint.

Creme De Nouyax: A brilliant red liqueur made from almonds.

Curacao: A liqueur made from orange peels. Produced in the Dutch West Indies.

Dash: Approximately 1/4 teaspoon.

Drambuie: A liqueur made from Scotch whiskey and honey.

Dry Vermouth: A white wine flavored with herbs and spices.

Dubonnet: An aromatic wine from France. Usually kept refrigerated.

Falernum: A spicy sweetener from Barbados, with almond and ginger undertones.

Forbidden Fruit: A liqueur made with brandy and shaddock (grapefruit).

Framboise: A raspberry liqueur.

Frangelico: A hazelnut liqueur.

Galliano: An Italian liqueur named after Major Giuseppe Galliano. Sweet and spicy.

Garnish: A garnish is no more than a decoration, sometimes functional, either eaten or squeezed into drink.

Gin: A liquor made by distilling rye or other grains with juniper berries.

Goldschlager: High proof cinnamon Schnapps with floating flecks of gold leaf.

Grand Marnier: A highly prized cognac-based triple orange liqueur.

Grappa: Unaged Italian Brandy

Grenadine: A sweet, red syrup made from pomegranates. Essential for children's drinks as well as adult drinks.

Hazelnut Liqueur: There are many different brands. Frangelico is considered the best.

Irish Cream: A liqueur made from Irish whiskey and cream.

Irish Mist: A liqueur made with Irish whiskey as a base, and heather honey as well.

Irish Whiskey: A blend containing barley whiskeys and grain whiskeys.

Jaegermeister: Considered a form of bitters. It is made of 56 herbs, roots, and fruits.

Kahlua: A coffee liqueur, one of Mexico's most popular exports.

Kirsch: A clear liqueur distilled from black cherries.

Kummel: A liqueur made from caraway and anise.

Lager: A bottom fermented beer.

Liqueur: A syrupy alcoholic beverage often with a Brandy base.

Licor 43: A Spanish brandy-based liqueur with 43 ingredients, with a prominent vanilla flavor.

Liquor: An alcoholic beverage made by distillation.

Lillet: A french apertif wine. It comes in red and white.

Madeira: A blended and fortified Portuguese wine.

Maraschino: A Yugoslavian liqueur made from cherries.

Marsala: A full bodied fortified red wine from Sicily.

Metaxa: A sweetened Greek brandy.

Midori: A melon- flavored liqueur from the Japanese house of Suntory.

Mist: Is a term meaning "On the rocks" (preferably with shaved or crushed ice). Coming from the fact that certain clear liqueurs cloud or mist when poured onto ice.

Muddle: Meaning to mix together or mash.

Neat: Is another way to say straight, no ice, not mixed.

Orange Liqueur: The most common are Triple Sec and Curacao. The best are Grand Marnier and Cointreau.

Orgeat: An almond flavored sweetener.

Ouzo: An anise flavored Greek liqueur.

Passion Fruit Liqueur: A Hawaiian liqueur flavored with peaches and mangos.

Pilsner: A light bodied beer.

Peppermint Schnapps: A rather light mint based liqueur.

Pernod: A French absinthe type liqueur.

Pony: Means 1 ounce. Also refers to a certain glass.

Port: A rich, sweet fortified wine. Originally from Portugal.

Pousse-Café: Refers to either layered drinks, or an alcoholic drink taken with coffee.

Proof: A term to tell alcohol content. 80-proof liquor would be 40% alcohol, meaning 40% of the contents of the bottle would be pure alcohol. Bottled wine at 12% alcohol by volume would be 24 proof.

Rum: A liquor made from fermented molasses or sugarcane. Aged 2-10 years.

Rye: A whiskey made from at least 51 percent rye.

Sabra: An orange-chocolate liqueur from Israel.

Sake: Made from re-fermented rice. It is actually a type of beer.

Sambuca: An Italian liqueur with an anise-like flavor.

Schnapps: Refers to light-bodied, flavorful liqueurs. It has many other meanings globally.

Scotch: A liquor from Scotland. They can be either single malts or blends.

Shot: A pour between 1 and 2 ounces

Sloe Gin: A very sweet liqueur made from sloe berries and steeped in gin.

Soda Water: Carbonated water, sometimes coming in flavors.

Sour Mix: They come in powder and liquid form. Essential at bars. It can be made fresh. Blend 12oz. lemon juice, 18oz. water, 1/3 cup sugar and an egg white.

Southern Comfort: A liqueur made from bourbon and peach liqueur.

Splash: Approximately 1/2 teaspoon.

Strega: An Italian liqueur made from herbs and spices.

Stout: A very dark and strong ale.

Sugar Syrup: Basically liquefied sugar. Simply mix sugar to water 2 to 1.

Sweet Vermouth: A red wine flavored with herbs and spices.

Swedish Punch: A Scandinavian liqueur made from rum, tea and lemon.

Tequila: An alcoholic beverage distilled from the Central American Century plant.

Tia Maria: A coffee liqueur from Jamaica.

Tonic Water: A carbonated quinine-flavored beverage.

Top: Means to add ingredient to top of drink, approximately 1 teaspoon, if alcoholic. Approximately 2 tablespoons if referring to whipped cream. Approximately 1 oz if referring to non-alcoholic ingredient.

Triple Sec: A light-bodied, orange-flavored liqueur.

Tuaca: An Italian brandy-based liqueur, flavored with citrus, nuts, vanilla and milk.

Vandermint: A Dutch chocolate-mint liqueur.

Vermouth: A wine flavored with herbs and spices. Comes in sweet and dry, and is primarily used as an ingredient in cocktails.

Vodka: A liquor originally distilled from wheat. Now made from rye, corn or potatoes.

Whiskey: A liquor distilled from grains such as corn, rye or barley.

Wine: A fermented juice of any various kinds of grapes or other fruit.

Yukon Jack: Liqueur made from Canadian whiskey.

INDEX OF DRINKS LISTED
BY INGREDIENT

Use this index to find all of the drinks listed in this book by the ingredients they contain. The ingredients and the drinks are listed in alphabetical order.

• AMARETTO

Abby Road
Abby Road Coffee
ABC
Alabama Slammer
Almond Enjoy
Almond Kiss
Almond Mocha Coffee
Amaretto Sour
Amarist
Ambush Coffee
August Moon
B-54
B-57
Bahama Mama
Banana Frost
Beach Hut Madness
Bend Me Over
Black Magic
Black Tie
Bocci Ball
Boss
Boston Iced Tea
Boston Massacre
Brain Eraser
Brandy Almond Mocha
Brown Squirrel
Bubble Gum
Bungee Jumper
Burnt Almond
Cactus Juice
Café Amore
Café Magic
Café Venitzio
Cherry Life-Savor
Chocolate Covered Cherry
Chocolate Squirrel
Climax
Coca Lady
Cocoetto
Cool Aid
Cuddler
Cupid's Potion
DC-10
Dr. P.
Dr. P. From Hell
Dreamsicle
East Side
Electric Cool Aid
F.E.D.X.
Fern Gully
Ferrari
57 Chevy
57 T-Bird
Filby
Foxy Lady
French Connection
French Connection Coffee
Full Moon
Gandy Dancer
Gilligan's Isle
Godchild
Godfather
Godmother
Golden Torpedo
Grand Alliance
Gumdrop
Hammerhead
Hasta La Vista Baby
Hawaiian
Hawaiian Punched
Heart Throb
Homecoming
Hooter
Hurricane
Irish Headlock
Italian Coffee
Italian Delight
Italian Iced Coffee
Jackalope
Jaeger Monster
Killer Cool Aid
King's Cup
Komaniwanalaya

Lake Street Lemonade
Latin Lover
Lazer Beam
Lethal Injection
Lobotomy
Marlon Brando
Midway Rat
Milano Coffee
Mongolian Mother
Monkey Wrench
Moonbeam
Mooseberry
Mountain Red Punch
Nutcracker
Nutty Colada
Old Groaner
Old Groaner's Wife
Orgasm
Outrigger
Panda Bear
Paranoia
Peckerhead
Persuader
Pimlico Special
Pineapple Bomb
Pineapple Bomber
Pink Almond
Pink Paradise
Pop-sicle
Pterodactyl
Purple Matador
Rasbaretta
Red Death
Red Ruby
Rigor Mortis
Ritz Fizz
Roasted Toasted Almond
Roman Candle
Roman Holiday
Roman Iced Tea
Roxanne
Royal Canadian
Royal Sheet Coffee
Russian Quwaylude
Screaming O.
Seventh Avenue
Seventh Heaven
Sex At My House
Sex In The Woods
Sicilian Coffee
Sicilian Kiss
Silver Cloud
S. O. M. F.
Skinny Dipping
Spanish Fly
Sperm Whale At The Barn
Spilt Milk
Stiletto
Sweet Tart
Tangerine
Tawney Russian
T-Bird
Tennessee Mud
Terminator
Test-Tube Babe
Toasted Almond
Toasted Marshmallow
Top Gun
Tree Climber
Trophy Room Coffee
Tropical Moon
Ugly Ducking
Universal
Vanity Fair
Verona
Watermelon
White Swan
Xanadu
Zonker

• ANISETTE

Angel Face
Apple Margarita
Apple Pie

Apres Ski
Bartman
Candy Apple
Corpse Reviver
Cranapple Cooler
Deauville
Depth Bomb
Diki Diki
Dream Cocktail
Good And Plent-e
Grand Apple
Green Apple
Happy Jack
Hole In One
Honeymoon
Hot Apple Pie
Hot Apple Toddy
Ichbien
Indian Summer
Jack Rose
Jack-In-The-Box
Jelly Bean
Johnnie
Joll-e Rancher
Ladies
Liberty Cocktail
Licorice Stick
Luger
Marconi Wireless
Moonlight
Mule's Hind Leg
Narragansett
Oom Paul
Pernod Frappe
Princess Mary's Pride
Prince's Smile
Royal Smile
Saturn's Ring
Saucy Sue
Savoy Tango
Sex At The Beach
Shanghai
Sharky Punch
Sledgehammer
Snowball
Special Rough
Star
Steeple Jack
Stone Fence
Third Rail
Tic Tac
Torpedo
Tulip
Turf
Tuxedo
Vanity Fair
Very Joll-e Rancher
Warday's Cocktail
Week On The Beach
Wembly
Xalapa Punch
Zazarac

• APRICOT BRANDY

Angel Face
Antiquan Kiss
Apricot Frappe
Apricot Sour
Babbie's Special
Black Witch
Bossa Nova
Cruise Control
Darb
Devil's Tail
Elmer Fudpucker
Father Sherman
Favorite
Festival
Fifth Avenue
Flamingo
Frankenjack
Golden Dawn
Golden Daze

- **BLACK RASPBERRY LIQUEUR**
(continued)
Elysee Palace
F.E.D.X.
Frankenberry
French Dream
French Martini
French Summer
Frosted Romance
F. Loop
Gloomlifter
Grape Crush
Greatful D.
Happy Feller
Hollywood
Hootie
Hot Raspberry Dream
Hot Tub
Indian Summer Hummer
Key West
Killer Cool Aid
Kir Royale
Left Bank
Little Purple Men
Lobotomy
Macaroon
Mad Max
Madtown Milkshake
Menage a Trios
Midnight Dream
Mocha Berry Frappe
Nervous Breakdown
Nuts And Berries
Panabraitor
Paris Match
Passionate Screw
Peanut Butter And Jelly
Phantom
Purple Dream
Purple Haze
Purple Hooter
Purple Matador
Purple Nipple
Purple Rain
Purple Russian
Raspberry Colada
Raspberry Gimlet
Raspberry Kiss
Raspberry Lime Rickey
Raspberry Margarita
Raspberry Sherbet
Raspberry Smash
Raspberry Soda
Raspberry Sombrero
Raspberry Torte
Razzle Dazzle
Restoration
Riviera
Royal Spritzer
Saint Moritz
Scarlet Letter
Sex At My House
Sex In A Hot Tub
Sex On The Beach
Sour Grapes
Sovereign Coffee
Sweet Tart
Tara
38th Parallel Coffee
Traveling Wild Berries
Wadkins Glen
Wet Dream
White Ghost
Y. I.
Zipper Head
Zuma Buma

- **BLACK SAMBUCA**

Creature From The Black
    Lagoon
Dark Secret
Dragoon

Eclipse
Phantom
Slippery Black Nipple
Starlight

- **BLUE CURACAO**

Adios Mother
Alaskan Iced Tea
Anti-Freeze
Bimini Ice-T
Blue Bayou
Blue Bijou
Blue Hawaiian
Blue Kamikaze
Blue Lady
Blue Lemonade
Blue Margarita
Blue Shark
Blue Tail Fly
Blue Valium
Blue Whale
Champagne Super Nova
Chi-Chi
Code Blue
Deep Sea
Desert Sunrise
Dirty Ashtray
Flaming Blue J.
Frostbite
Gangrene
Go-Go Juice
Grape Sour Ball
Green Eyes
Hog Snort
Kentucky Swampwater
L.A.P.D.
Leprechaun
Malibu Wave
Moody Blue
Neon
Ninja Turtle
Oil Slick
Out Of The Blue
Pousse Café
Purple Armadillo
Purple Flirt
Purple Margarita
Purple Rain
Purple Thunder
Ritz Fizz
Save The Planet
Shark Attack
Smurf P.
Stars And Stripes
Swamp Water
Terminator
Tiny Bowl
Wall Street Lizard
Whale's Tail
Windex
Yale Cocktail

- **BOURBON**

American Sour
Bambini Aruba
Beehive
Bible Belt
Black-Eyed Susan
Bomb
Boss
Bourbon Manhattan
Bourbon Old Fashion
Bourbon Satin
Brass Knuckles
Buffalo Sweat
Cowboy
Deathwish
Fedora
Fiji Fizz
Forester
French 95
Ground Zero
Happy Jack
Hawaiian Eye
H. D. Rider

Hot Milk Punch
Huntress Cocktail
Italian Stallion
J. Off
Jackarita
Jackhammer
Jamaican Milk Shake
Kentucky Cocktail
Kentucky Coffee
Kentucky Colonel
Kentucky Cooler
Kentucky Orange Blossom
Kentucky Screwdriver
Kentucky Swampwater
Lazer Beam
Long Hot Night
Lynchburg Lemonade
Man O'War
Mexican Blackjack
Millionaire
Mint Condition
Mint Julep
Mule Skinner
Narragansett
Nevins
No Tell Motel
Nocturnal
Ozark Mountain Punch
Pair Of Jacks
Quickie
Quwaylude
Reverend
Rumplestiltskin
Sazerac
Screaming Viking
Skyscraper
Snakebite
Snowshoe Grog
Southside
Stock Market Zoo
Tahitian Itch
Tennessee Lemonade
Tennessee Mud
Tennessee Tea
Three Amigos
Three Wise Men
Tivoli
Trilby
Trolley
Turkey Shoot
Uncle Sam
Waldorf
Whirlaway
Wyooter Hooter
Yellow Jacket
Zoo

- **BRANDY**

Acapulco
Alexander The Great
Ambrosia
Angel Wing
Apple Cooler
Apres Ski
Apricot Frappe
Aunt Jemima
B & B
B-57
BBC
Betsy Ross
Between The Sheets
Black Iced Tea
Black Lady
Blackjack
Blast
Blizzard
Bosom Caresser
Brandy Alexander
Brandy Almond Mocha
Brandy Gump
Brandy Milk Punch
Brazilian Coffee
Bull's Milk
Café Diablo
Café Royale
Café Venitzio

• CHARTREUSE

(continued)
Save The Planet
Screamer
Swampwater
Tipperary
Warday's Cocktail
Whiskey Daisy
Widow's Kiss
Xanthia
Yellow Parrot

• CHERRY BRANDY

Ankle Breaker
Black Cat
Blood And Sand
Busted Cherry
Candy Cane
Casablanca
Cherry Blossom
Cherry Cola
Cherry Screw
Cherry Swizzle
Chinese Cocktail
Chocolate Covered Cherry
Copenhagen Pousse Café
Double-D
Dr. Funk
Electric Cool Aid
Fantasio
Fiji Fizz
Fireball
Forester
Harlem Cocktail
Hawaiian Nights
Honolulu
Hudson Bay
Hunter's Cocktail
Huntress Cocktail
Ideal
Kiss
Kiss In The Dark
Ladyfinger
Lawhill
Merry Widow
Mojo
Mon Cherie
Mountain Red Punch
Night Train
No Problem
Orange Oasis
Pancho Villa
Polynesian
Porch Climber
Purple Bunny
San Juan Sunset
Singapore Sling
Summer Solstice Sunrise
Swedish Lullaby
Tiki Bowl
Top Hat
Tropical Storm
Vanderbilt
Vanity Fair
Vodka Sling
Volga Boatman
Wedding Belle
Weep No More
White Rose
Xanthia
Yale Cocktail

• CINNAMON SCHNAPPS

Afterburner
Apple Pie
Beverly Hill
Canadian Cider
Candy Apple
Fahrenheit 5
Fireball
Gingerbread Man
Gold Rush
Hot Tamale
911
Peach Cobbler
Pumpkin Pie
Oatmeal Cookie
Red Death
Sugar Daddy
24 Karat Nightmare
When Hell Freezes Over

• COFFEE

Abby Road Coffee
After Road Coffee
Almond Mocha Coffee
Ambush Coffee
Aspen Coffee
Aspen Hummer
B-52 Coffee
Bailey's And Coffee
BBC
Black Rose
Brandy Almond Mocha
Brazilian Coffee
Café Amore
Café Diablo
Café Foster
Café Gates
Café Italia
Café Magic
Café Marseilles
Café Orleans
Café Reggae
Café Royale
Café Theatre
Café Venitzio
Cajun Coffee
Calypso Coffee
Canadian Coffee
Caribbean Dream Coffee
Coffee Alexander
Curley's Delight Coffee
Dublin Coffee
Dutch Coffee
French Coffee
French Connection Coffee
French Iced Coffee
Greek Coffee
Gun Runner Coffee
Heather Coffee
Highland Coffee
Irish Coffee
Irish Coffee Royale
Irish Gentleman
Irish Iced Coffee
Irish Maiden Coffee
Irish Mocha Cooler
Irish Money Coffee
Irish Monk Coffee
Irish Skipper Coffee
Israeli Coffee
Italian Coffee
Italian Iced Coffee
Jamaican Coffee
Kahlua Coffee
Kentucky Coffee
Keoke Coffee
King Kong Coffee
Kingston Coffee
Lebanese Coffee
Mediterranean Coffee
Mexican Coffee
Milano Coffee
Millionaire's Coffee
Mississippi Mud
Monk's Coffee
Monte Cristo Coffee
Montego Bay Coffee
Northern Lights
Nutty Irish Cooler
Nutty Irishman Coffee
Orient Express
Roman Cappuccino
Roman Coffee
Roman Rasta Coffee
Royal Sheet Coffee
Russian Coffee
Rusty Nail Coffee
Scottish Coffee
Shot In The Dark
Sicilian Coffee
Sovereign Coffee
Spanish Coffee
Spanish Coffee
Spanish Coffee
Spanish Iced Coffee
Super Coffee
Tennessee Mud
38th Parallel Coffee
Trappist Monk
Trophy Room Coffee
Vatican Coffee
Venetian Coffee
Watergate Coffee

• COFFEE LIQUEUR

Abby Road
Abby Road Coffee
Afterburner
After Eight
After Five
After Five Coffee
Aggravation
Alice In Wonderland
Amigo
Apres Ski
Aspen Coffee
Aspen Hummer
Avalanche
B-51
B-52
B-52 Coffee
B-52 On A Mission
B-52 With Bombay Doors
B-54
B-57
Banana Sandwich
Banana Split
Beam Me Up Scottie
Bearhug
Bikini Line
Black Forest
Black Jamaican
Black Lady
Black Magic
Black Rose
Black Russian
Black Watch
Blizzard
B. J.
Bob Marley
Boston Iced Tea
Boston Massacre
Brahma Bull
Brain
Brain Eraser
Brave Bull
Brave Cow
Brazilian Coffee
Bulldog
Bumble Bee
Burnt Almond
Bushwacker
Busted Cherry
Café Gates
Café Magic
Café Marseilles
Café Orleans
Café Reggae
California Mother
California Root Beer
Calypso Coffee
Cancun
Cartel Buster
Cerebral Hemorrhage
Chocolate Covered Cherry
Chocolate Kiss
Climax
Cloudy Night
Cobra
Coca Lady
Cocopuff

DRINKS LISTED IN ALPHABETICAL ORDER

• CREME DE CACAO
(continued)
57 Chevy
Flying Grasshopper
Fox River
Foxy Lady
Frost Bite
Frosted Romance
Fruitbar
Fudgesicle
Funky Monkey
Golden Caddie
Golden Gate
Gorilla
Grand Occasion
Grasshopper
Gumdrop
H. Bar
Hot Peppermint Patty
Hot Raspberry Dream
Houndstooth
Irish Angel
Irish Mocha Cooler
Irish Monkey Coffee
Irish Skipper Coffee
Jackalope
Jelly Fish
Jockey Club
Keoke Cappuccino
Keoke Coffee
Kremlin Cocktail
Kretchma
Layer Cake
Liebfraumilch
Love Potion #9
Maxim
Mocha Berry Frappe
Mocha Mint
Mon Cherie
Moonbeam
Mound Bar
Mudslide
Night Train
Ninja
Ninotchka
Nocturnal
Oil Slick
OR-E-OH Cookie
Orgasm
Pago Pago
Panama
Panda Bear
Peach Alexander
Peach Velvet
Pearl Necklace
Peppermint Pattie
Peppermint Patty
Pimlico Special
Pink Squirrel
Pousse Café
Purple Bunny
Purple Dream
Pussy Galore
Quwaylude
Rainbow
Raspberry Kiss
Rocky Road
Russian
Russian Banana
Russian Bear
Savannah
Savoy Hotel
Screaming Banshee
Screaming Yellow Monkey
Silver Cloud
Skull Cracker
Snicker
Snowball
Sovereign Coffee
Sperm Whale At the Bank
Strawberry Blonde
Swedish Bear
Tennessee Tea
38th Parallel Coffee
Tia Tia

Tootsie
Toreador
Tree Climber
Tropical Cocktail
Tumbleweed
Velvet hammer
Vodka Grasshopper
Whippet
Whisper
White Cadillac
White Death
White Elephant
White Ghost
White Heart
White Out
White Witch
Wind Jammer
Winter Frost
Wolfhound
Xylophone
Yellow Bird

• CREME DE MENTHE
(White And Green)

After Eight
Alexander's Sister
Anti-Freeze
Around The World
Barbary Coast
Bleacher Creature
B-Sting
Clouds Over Scotland
Cricket
Fallen Angel
Flaming Noriega
Florida
Flying Grasshopper
Fu Manchu
Grasshopper
Green Hornet
Green Spider
Hot Peppermint Patty
Irish Angel
Irish Stinger
Jade
Lady Be Good
London Stinger
Maggot
Midnight Snowstorm
Minstrel Frappe
Mocha Mint
Mockingbird
Ocean View Special
Pall Mall
Panda Bear
Peppermint Pattie
Pink Whispers
Point
Port And Starboard
Silver Bullet
Silver Spider
Sneaky Pete
Snowball
Spanish Moss
Stinger
Tarnished Bullet
Tequila Stinger
Traffic Light
Turkey Shoot
Velvet Glove
Virgin
Vodka Grasshopper
Vodka Stinger
Wandering Minstrel
White Mink
White Minnesota
White Spider
Winter Frost

• CURACAO

American Sour
Bosom Caresser
Chicago

Diamond Head
East India
Fair And Warmer
Fare-Thee-Well
Hammerhead
Honeymoon
Ichbien
Il Magnifico
Jade
Johnnie
Kiss Me Quick
London Sour
Maiden's Blush
Man O'War
Marmalade
McClelland
Mexican Blackjack
Millionaire
Morning
Morning Glory
Newbury
Nightingale
Olympic
Orange Julius
Parisian Blonde
Park Avenue
Pegu Club
Pineapple Passion
Platinum Blonde
Presidente
Prince Of Wales
Ramos Fizz
Rhett Butler
Sangria
Sherry Twist
Sir Walter
Southern Bride
Suffering Bastard
Tango
Temptation
Tiger's Tail
Velvet Hammer
Vulcan Mind Probe
Whip Cocktail
Whirlaway
Zamboanga Hummer
Zombie

• DRAMBUIE

Black Tie
Crankin' Wanker
Depth Charge
Dundee
Golden Nail
Heather Coffee
Hot Nail
Hot Scotch
Inverted Nail
Jolly Roger
L. S. D.
Point
Prince Edward
Russian Roulette
Rusty Nail
Rusty Nail Coffee
Scottish Coffee
Seventh Avenue
White Knight

• DUBONNET

Dubonnet Cocktail
Dubonnet Manhattan
Mary Garden
Napoleon
Oom Paul
Opera
Phoebe Snow
Princess Mary's Pride
Sanctuary
Silken Veil
Soul Kiss
Temptation
Trois Rivieres
Vancouver

DRINKS LISTED IN ALPHABETICAL ORDER

• GIN (Continued)

Singapore Sling
Skip and Go Naked
Sledgehammer
Sloe Ball
Snowball
Snowblower
Southern Bride
Sphinx
Spy's Demise
Stock Market Zoo
Straight Law
Strega Sour
Stump Buster
Sweet Patootie
Tangerine
Tango
Terminal Iced Tea
Thanksgiving
Third Degree
Three Mile Island
Three Stripes
Tidal Wave
Tidbit
Tom Collins
Tropical Storm
Turf
Twin Six
Typhoon
Ulanda
Union Jack
Union League
Velvet Kiss
Verona
Victor
Virgin
Vulcan
Vulcan Mind Probe
Wall Street Lizard
Warday's Cocktail
Wedding Belle
Wembly
White Baby
White Cargo
White Heat
White Lady
White Lily
White Out
White Rose
Why Not
Will Rogers
Xanthia
Yale Cocktail
Yellow Rattler
Zamboagna Hummer
Zanzibar
Zaza
Zoo

• GRAIN ALCOHOL

Cherry Bomb
Eat The Cherry
Hairy Mary

• HAZELNUT LIQUEUR

Aspen Coffee
Beam Me Up Scotti
Boston Massacre
Café Marseilles
Café Theatre
Chocolate Squirrel
Cream Dream
El Salavador
F-16
Friar Tuck
Irish Monk
Irish Monk Coffee
Mad Monk
Madtown Milkshake
Menage a Trios
Millionaire's Coffee
Mississippi Mud
Monk Juice

Monk Slide
Ninja
Nut and Honey
Nutcracker
Nuts and Berries
Nutty Chinaman
Nutty Irish Cooler
Nutty Irishman
Nutty Irishman Coffee
Nutty Jamaican
Nutty Russian
Peanut Butter and Jelly
Quwaylude
Rocky Road
Russian Quwaylude
747
Simply Exquisite
S. O. M. F.
Snicker
Snicker At The Bar
Trappist Frappe
Trappist Monk
Tumbleweed
Vatican Coffee
White Ghost

• HOT CHOCOLATE

Adult Hot Chocolate
Almond Kiss
Black Magic
Brandy Almond Mocha
Chocolate Irish Raspberry
Chocolate Kiss
Coconapps
Cocoetto
Cocopuff
Dutch Treat
Hot Peppermint Patty
Mad Monk
Midnight Snowstorm
Mound Bar
Mudsling
Peppermint Kiss
Snuggler
Wooden Shoe

• ICE CREAM

B-52
Banana Colada
Banana Cow
Banana Cream Pie
Banana Frost
Banana Popsicle
Banana Split
Banshee
Bit Of Honey
Black Cow
Black Forest
Black Russian
Blizzard
Boston Massacre
Brandy Alexander
Brown Squirrel
Burnt Almond
Cancun
Chi-Chi
Chocolate Banana Freeze
Chocolate Covered Cherry
Coffee Colada
Cookies And Cream
Creamsicle
Dirty Monkey
Dusty Road
Fat Cat
Flying Grasshopper
Flying Kangaroo
French Iced Coffee
Frosted Romance
Fudgesicle
Funky Monkey
G. S. Cookie
Golden Caddie
Good and Plent-e

Grasshopper
Harvey Wallbanger
H. Bar
Hummer
Jamaican Milk Shake
Kappa Colada
Key Largo
Las Brisas
Love Potion #9
Madtown Milkshake
Meister-Bation
Melon Colada
Mocha Berry Frappe
Monkey Special
Moose Milk
Mudslide
Night Train
Nut and Honey
Nutcracker
Nutty Colada
Orange Julius
Orange Margarita
Orange Whip
OR-E-OH Cookie
Orsini
Panda Bear
Parfait
Peach Alexander
Peach Colada
Peach Velvet
Peanut Butter and Jelly
Pearl Harbor
Piña Colada
Rasbaretta
Raspberry Colada
Roasted Toasted Almond
Roman Cappuccino
Root Beer Float
Russian Quwaylude
Snicker At The Bar
Strawberry Blonde
Strawberry Colada
Strawberry Shortcake
Tidal Wave
Tidbit
Toasted Almond
Tropical Breeze
Tropical Moon
Tumbleweed
Velvet Hammer
Virgin Piña Colada
Whisper
White Cargo
White Russian
Winter Frost
Xylophone

• IRISH CREAM

ABC
After Eight
After Five
After Five Coffee
Angel Wing
Apple Pie
Aspen Coffee
B-51
B-52
B-52 Coffee
B-52 On A Mission
B-52 With Bombay Doors
B-54
Bailey's And Coffee
Bailey's Comet
Bailey's Fizz
Banana Cream Pie
BBC
Beach Hut Madness
Beam Me Up Scotti
Beautiful Thing
Berlin Wall
Black Forest
Black Magic
Blizzard
Bloody Brain

• MELON LIQUEUR
(continued)
Mexican Flag
Miami Melon
Neon
Nesi
Ninja
Ninja Turtle
Nuclear Meltdown
Pearl Harbor
Puccini
Rainbow
Rainforest
Save The Planet
Sex On The Beach
Shady Lady
Slimeball
Spats
Tara
Three Mile Island
Three Story House On Fire
Time Bomb
Torque Wrench
Traffic Light
Traveling Wild Berries
Tropical Hooter
Universal
Vulcan Mind Probe
Wall Street Lizard
Watermelon
Witches Brew
W. W. II
Y. I.

• MENTHOLATED SCHNAPPS

Anti-Freeze
Cough Drop
Doctor's Elixir
Dr. J.
Fuel-Injection
Guillotine
No Tell Motel

• MILK OR CREAM

Aggravation
Alexander
Alexander The Great
Alexander's Sister
Almond Joy
Amigo
Angel Kiss
Angel Wing
Angel's Tit
Atomic Waste
Babbie's Special
Banana Sombrero
Banana Split
Banshee
Black Cow
Black Rose
BlackJack
Blue Tail Fly
Blood Clot
B. J.
Bob Marley
Boston Massacre
Bourbon Satin
Brandy Alexander
Brandy Milk Punch
Brown Cow
Brown Squirrel
Bubble Gum
Bull's Milk
Bulldog
Bumble Bee
Bungee Jumper
Burnt Almond
Bushwacker
Busted Cherry
Buttafinger
Cadiz

California Cool Aid
California Mother
Candy Cane
Canyon Quake
Capri
Chiquita
Chocolate Colada
Chocolate Squirrel
Climax
Coca Lady
Coconut Cream Frappe
Coffee Sombrero
Colorado Bulldog
Colorado Mother
Cowboy
Cream Dream
Creamsicle
Cricket
Dire Straits
Dirty Banana
Dirty Bird
Dirty G. S.
Dirty M. F.
Dirty Mother
Dirty White Mother
Dreamsicle
East Side
Eggnog
Everglades Special
Festival
Fifth Avenue
Flying Grasshopper
Foxy Lady
Frostbite
Fuzzy Navel With Lint
Gentle Bull
G. S. Cookie
Golden Caddie
Golden Dream
Golden Dream
    (With Double Bumpers)
Golden Torpedo
Grasshopper
Green Russian
Head
Henry Morgan's Grog
High Jamaican Wind
Hot Milk Punch
Hot Raspberry Dream
Huntress Cocktail
Ichbien
Il Magnifco
Irish Angel
Irish Cow
Italian Delight
Jamaican Kiss
Jungle Jim
King Alphonse
King's Cup
Kioloa
Kiss
Kremlin Cocktail
Layer Cake
Leaf
Licorice Stick
Liebfraumilch
Marlon Brando
Melon Sombrero
Menage a Trios
Metal Helmet
Miami Melon
Midnight Dream
Mon Cherie
Monk Juice
Moon Beam
Moose Milk
Mound Bar
Mount Fuji
Mudslide
Niagara Falls
Nightingale
Nocturnal
Nuts and Berries
Nutty Irishman
Nutty Russian
Oatmeal Cookie

Oil Slick
Old Groaner's Wife
Orgasm
Pacific Pacifier
Panama
Panty Dropper
Paradise Punch
Parisian Blonde
Parisian Frappe
Peach Alexander
Peach Blow Fizz
Peach Fuzz
Peaches and Cream
Pearl Necklace
Peppermint Patty
Pernod Flip
Pink Lady
Pink Rose
Pink Squirrel
Platinum Blonde
Pop-Sicle
Purple Bunny
Purple Dream
Quiet Nun
Quwaylude
Ramos Fizz
Raspberry Kiss
Raspberry Sombrero
Red Russian
Renaissance Cocktail
Roasted Toasted Almond
Rocky Road
Roman Holiday
Root Beer Float
Ruptured Duck
Russian Banana
Russian Bear
Russian Quwaylude
Saint Moritz
Screaming Banshee
Screaming O.
Screaming Yellow Monkey
Separator
Seventh Avenue
Sex At The Beach
Sexy
Silver Cloud
Silver Fizz
Simply Exquisite
Smith and Kerns
Snicker
Snowball
Snowberry
Sombrero
Southern Bulldog
Spilt Milk
Stars And Stripes
Steel Helmet
Sugar Daddy
Swedish Bear
Tam-O-Shanter
Teacher's Pet
Tiger's Milk
Tijuana Bulldog
Toasted Almond
Toasted Marshmallow
Tom and Jerry
Toreador
Toxic Waste
Trade Wind
Tree Climber
Tumbleweed
Ugly Duckling
Velvet Glove
Velvet Hammer
Velvet Kiss
Vodka Grasshopper
West Indies Yellow Bird
Wet Dream
White Baby
White Bull
White Cadillac
White Elephant
White Ghost
White Heart
White Jamaican

DRINKS LISTED IN ALPHABETICAL ORDER

- ## PEPPERMINT SCHNAPPS
(Continued)
Slippery Nipple
Snakebite
Snowball
Snowblower
Snowshoe Grog
Snuggler
Stumbling F.
Thunder and Lightning
Tic Tac
24 Karat Nightmare
Urinalysis
Whippet

- ## ROOT BEER SCHNAPPS

Head
Root Beer Float

- ## RUM (AMBER)

Acapulco Gold
Bahama Mama
Barracuda
Black Witch
B. M. P.
Bossa Nova
Grog
Hammerhead
Happy Summer
Havana
Hurricane
Jamaican Delight
Jamaican Kiss
Kioloa
Moonpie
Pago Pago
Paradise Punch
Passionate Point
Pink Gator
Pink Veranda
Planters Punch
Poker
Port Antonio
Purple Flirt
Purple Thunder
Ranch Valencia Rum Punch
Red Rum Sonic
San Juan
Stupid Cube
Tahiti Club
Tiger's Milk
Trade winds
Tropical Storm
Urine Sample
Xalapa Punch
Yard Of Flannel
Zamboanga Hummer

RUM (COCONUT)

Alien Secretion
Artificial Intelligence
Bad Attitude
Bahama Mama
Banana Boat
Bart Simpson
Beacon Hill Blizzard
East Side
F. Loop
Guana Grabber
Hammerhead
Hog Snort
Hooter
Itchy Bitchy Smelly Nelly
Las Brisas
Lethal Injection
Life-Savor
Luau
Malibu Driver
Malibu Sunset
Mound Bar

Mount Vesuvius
Ninja Turtle
No Problem
Paranoia
Passionate Screw
Pink Paradise
Pink Slip
P. M. S.
Rock Lobster
Shark Bite
Shipwreck
Sledgehammer
Spring Break
Starboard Tack
Suntan
Surfer Taking A Trip
Tara
Terminator
Tidal Wave
Time Bomb
Top Gun
Tropical Hooter
Tropical Moon
Tropical Storm
Vulcan
Vulcan Mind Probe
Wanna Probe Ya
Y. I.

- ## RUM (DARK)

American Graffiti
Antiquan Kiss
Antiquan Smile
Apple Cooler
Artificial Intelligence
Bahama Mama
Banana Cow
Beacon Hill Blizzard
Big Bamboo
Black Barracuda
Black Iced Tea
Black Witch
Blizzard
Boardwalk Breezer
Bob Marley
Bomb
Bos'n Mate
Bull's Milk
Bushwacker
Café Foster
Café Reggae
Caribbean Dream Coffee
Chinese Cocktail
Coco Loco
Dark and Stormy
Designer Jeans
Dr. Funk
Dutch Pirate
Eggnog
Fascination
Fedora
Fern Gully
Fiji Fizz
Fireside
Fish House Punch
.44 Magnum
Fu Manchu
Goombay Smash
Guana Grabber
Heatwave
Henry Morgan's Grog
High Jamaican Wind
Hot Buttered Rum
Hummer
Hurricane
Indian Summer Hummer
Jackalope
Jade
Jamaica Cooler
Jamaica Me Crazy
Jamaican
Jamaican Dust
Jamaican Milk Shake
Jamaican Pine
Jamaican Wind

Jolly Roger
Jump Up And Kiss Me
Kentucky Cooler
Key Largo
Key West
Kingston Coffee
Komaniwanalaya
Lethal Injection
Mai Tai
Modern
Monga Monga
Monkey Juice
Monkey Special
Montego Bay Coffee
Moose Milk
Navy Grog
Nutty Jamaican
Oil Slick
Open Grave
Outrigger
Panama
Paradise Punch
Parisian Blonde
Parisian Frappe
Pilot Boat
Pink Veranda
Planter's Punch
Port Antonio
Rainforest
Ranch Valencia Rum Punch
Robson
Rock Lobster
Rockaway Beach
Roman Rasta Coffee
Root Beer Float
Rose Hall
Rumball
Rum Runner
Rum-Laced Cider
Santiago
Scorpion
Sevilla
Shanghai
Shark Bite
Shark's Tooth
Sledgehammer
Spleef
Stonewall
Stupid Cube
Suffering Bastard
Tai Tia
Tiger's Milk
Tiki Bowl
Tokyo Express
Tom And Jerry
Top Gun
Trophy Room Coffee
Tropical Moon
Tropical Storm
Voo Doo
Wind Jammer
Wombat
Zombie

- ## RUM (LIGHT)

Adios Mother
Alaskan Iced Tea
American Graffiti
Antiquan Kiss
Apple Cooler
Artificial Intelligence
Bacardi Cocktail
Bahama Mama
Bambini Aruba
Banana Colada
Banana Daiquiri
Banana Split
Banana Strawberry Daiquiri
Barbary Coast
Barracuda
Bartman
Bat Bite
Bee's Knees
Between The Sheets
Bimini Ice-T

DRINKS LISTED IN ALPHABETICAL ORDER

• RUM (151 PROOF)
(continued)
Hummer
Firecracker
Flaming Blue J.
Flaming Noriega
Fuzzy Mother
Golden Gate
Green Lizard
Hand Grenade
Harbor Lights
Hogback Growler
Komaniwanalaya
Light House
Liquid Coca
Look Out Below
Mongolian Mother
Mount Vesuvius
Open Grave
Ozark Mountain Punch
Razorback Hogcaller
Red Death
Rocket
Rum Runner
San Juan
Shipwreck
S. O. B.
Speedy Gonzalas
Storm Cloud
Stumbling F.
Suffering Bastard
Three Story House On Fire
Thunder And Lightning
Volcano
Voo Doo
Vulcan Mind Melt
Zombie

• RUM (SPICED)
Bad Attitude
Banging The Captain 3
Ways
    On The Comforter
Bermuda Triangle
Cactus Juice
Captain Mariner
Firecracker
Gangrene
Hammerhead
Lethal Injection
Pineapple Bomber
Rum-Laced Cider
Starboard Tack
Stupid Cube
Sugar Apple
Tidal Wave
Wanna Probe Ya
Whale's Tail
Witches' Brew

• SAMBUCA
Barbarella
Beach Hut Madness
Bearhug
Café Diablo
Cancun
Fire-In-The-Hole
Freddy Kruger
Glass Tower
Hammer
La Mosca
Little Green Men
Little Purple Men
Roman Candle
Roman Cappuccino
Roman Coffee
Roman Holiday
Roman Rasta Coffee
Shanghai
Silk Panties
Sledgehammer
Slippery Nipple
Snowball
Tic Tac

Typhoon
Via Veneto
Vulcan Mind Melt
White Cloud
White Heart
White Roman

• SCOTCH
Aggravation
Barbary Coast
Bit Of Honey
Black Tie
Black Watch
Blood and Sand
Bloody Josephine
Bomb
Dry Rob Roy
Dude
Dundee
Flying Scott
Gail Warning
Godfather
Heather Coffee
Highland Coffee
Highland Fling
Hoot Man
Hot Nail
Hot Scotch
Inverted Nail
Italian Stallion
Joe Collins
Jolly Roger
London Sour
L. S. D.
Mamie Taylor
Marlon Brando
Miami Beach
Mike Collins
Modern
Morning Glory
Paisley Martini
Polly's Special
Prince Edward
Purple Heather
Rob Roy
Rusty Nail
Rusty Nail Coffee
Scotch Collins
Scotch Sour
Scottish Coffee
Stone Fence
Teacher's Pet
Thistle
Three Wise Men
Whiskey Fix
White Cadillac
White Knight

• SLOE GIN
Alabama Slammer
American Graffiti
Black Hawk
Chaos
Eclipse
Empire State Slammer
Firecracker
Hawaiian Garden's Sling
Hawaiian Punched
Johnnie
Kiss The Boys Goodbye
Lemonade (Modern)
Love
McClelland
Mexican Flag
Mich
Modern
Moll
Monogolian Mother
Moulin Rouge
New York Slammer
Panty Dropper
Pink Floyd
Purple Margarita
Red Death

Ruby Fizz
San Francisco
Savoy Tango
Singapore Sling
Sloe Ball
Sloe Boat To China
Sloe Brandy
Sloe Comfortable Screw
Sloe Comfortable Screw
    Against The Wall
Sloe Dog
Sloe Gin Fizz
Sloe Poke
Sloe Screw
Sloe Tequila
Spats
Spring Action
Spy's Demise
Sweet Release
Traffic Light
Union Jack
Velvet Glove
Watermelon

• SOUTHERN COMFORT
Alabama Slammer
American Graffiti
Apple Polisher
Avalanche
Banging The Captain 3
Ways
    On The Comforter
Bible Belt
Bubble Gum
Bucking Bronco
Coca
Cool Aid
Crankin' Wanker
Double-D
Electric Cool Aid
57 Chevy
57 T-Bird
Flaming Blue J.
Green Meany
Halley's Comfort
Hammerhead
Harbor Lights
Hawaiian
Hawaiian Punched
Jelly Bean
Lazer Beam
Lion Tamer
Memphis Belle
Missouri Mule
Mongolian Mother
Open Grave
Oxbend
Panabraitor
Pineapple Bomber
Pop-Sicle
Pterodactyl
Quwaylude
Rattlesnake
Red Death
Rhett Buttler
Saturn's Ring
Scarlet O'Hara
Sex At The Beach
Sicilian Coffee
Sicilian Kiss
Sloe Comfortable Screw
Sloe Comfortable Screw
    Against The Wall
S. O. B.
Southern Belle
Southern Bulldog
Southern Comfort
Manhattan
Southern Comfort Old
Fashion
Spring Action
Star Wars
Sunny Day Dream
Test-Tube Babe

• TRIPLE SEC
(continued)

Life-Savor
Little Devil
London Sour
Long Beach Iced Tea
Long Island Iced Tea
Long Island Lemonade
Love Potion
Lynchburg Lemonade
Maiden's Blush
Maiden's Prayer
Mainbrace
Malibu Wave
Margarita
Martinez
McClelland
Mexican Blackjack
Millionaire
Mimosa
Mississippi Mud
Mongolian Mother
Monmarte
Morning
Mount Vesuvius
Netherland
Nuclear Meltdown
Odd McIntre
Olympic
Orange Julius
Orange Krush
Orange Margarita
Oriental
Orgasm
Orsini
Pacific Pacifier
Panabraitor
Panama Red
Parisian Blonde
Pernod Flip
Petrifier
Platinum Blonde
Polly's Special
Pop-Sicle
Pterodactyl
Purple Rain
Quickie
Quiet Nun
Ramos Fizz
Rattler
Red Death
Roman Iced Tea
Run, Skip And Go Naked
Samari
San Sebastian
Sangria
Santiago
Sherry Twist
Sidecar
Silver Spider
Singapore Sling
S. O. M. F.
Sloppy Joe
Sloppy Joe's
S. O. B.
Southern Bride
Spanish Dynamite
Spring Fling
Strawberry Margarita
Suffering Bastard
Sunburst
Sundowner
Sweet Patootie
Tango
Temptation
Texas Tea
Three Mile Island
Tiger's Tail
Top Gun
Trois Rivieres
Tropical Storm
Ulanda
Upside Down Margarita
Velvet Hammer

Venetian Coffee
Venetian Frappe
Vulcan Mind Probe
Whip Cocktail
White Baby
White Cadillac
White Heat
White Lady
White Lily
White Mink
White Water
White Witch
Wild Thing
Will Rogers
Wind City
W. W. II
Xango
XYZ
Zamboanga Hummer
Zaza
Zombie
Zonker

• TUACA

Café Italia
Hot Apple Pie
Il Magnifico
Lemon Frappe
Puccini
Stuffed Toilet
Thumper
Tiger's Milk
Tuaca Cocktail

• VANDERMINT

Black Cow
Dutch Coffee
Dutch Pirate
Trophy Room Coffee
Wooden Shoe

• VODKA

Adios Mother
Agent O.
Alabama Slammer
Alaskan Iced Tea
Anna's Banana
Anti-Freeze
Apple Pie
Atomic Waste
Bailey's Comet
Balalaika
Bambini Aruba
Banana Cream Pie
Banana Popsicle
Banana Split
Bart Simpson
Bay Breeze
Beam Me Up Scottie
Beer Buster
Bend Me Over
Berlin Wall
Bikini Line
Bimini Ice-T
Black Cat
Black Cow
Black Eye
Black Forest
Black Magic
Black Russian
Bleacher Creature
Blizzard
Bloody Brew
Bloody Bull
Bloody Caesar
Bloody Mary
B. J.
Blue Bayou
Blue Hawaiian
Blue Kamikaze
Blue Shark
Bocci Ball

Boston Iced Tea
Brain Eraser
Brain Wave
Brass Monkey
Brown Derby
Bubble Gum
Bull Shot
Bulldog
Bullfrog
Burnt Almond
Buttafinger
Butter Shot
California Breeze
California Driver
California Iced Tea
California Lemonade
Cape Codder
Champagne Super Nova
Cheap Shades
Cheap Sunglasses
Cherry Bomb
Chi-Chi
China Beach
Chocolate Banana Freeze
Chocolate Covered Cherry
Chocolate Thunder
Clam Digger
Climax
Cloudy Night
Coca
Coca Lady
Coco Loco
Code Blue
Colorado Bulldog
Colorado Mother
Cookies and Cream
Cool Aid
Cool Breeze
Copperhead
Cosmopolitan
Cranapple Cooler
Cranes Beach Punch
Crankin' Wanker
Dark Eyes
Deep Throat
Devil's Tail
Dirty Ashtray
Dirty Bird
Dirty G. S.
Dirty Monkey
Dirty Mother
Downeaster
Dry Martini
Dubonnet Cocktail
Dutch Pirate
Dying Nazi From Hell
Eat The Cherry
Ecstacy
Eden
Egghead
Electric Watermelon
Elmer Fudpucker
Elvira
E. T.
Express
Face Eraser
57 Chevy
57 T-Bird
Fireball
Firefly
Flamingo
Florida Iced Tea
Flying Grasshopper
Flying Kangaroo
Flying Madras
.44 Magnum
Freddy Kruger
French Martini
Frog-In-A-Blender
Frozen Bikini
F. Loop
Fudgesicle
Fuzzy Guppie
Fuzzy Kamikaze
Fuzzy Navel
Fuzzy Navel With Lint

DRINKS LISTED IN ALPHABETICAL ORDER

• VODKA (continued)

Very Joll-e Rancher
Visitor
Vodka Collins
Vodka Cooler
Vodka Gibson
Vodka Gimlet
Vodka Grand Marnier
Vodka Grasshopper
Vodka Martini
Vodka Saketini
Vodka Sling
Vodka Soda
Vodka Sonic
Vodka Sour
Vodka Stinger
Vodka Tonic
Volga Boatman
Vulcan
Vulcan Mind Probe
Wadkins Glen
Wall Street Lizard
Waltzing Matilda
Wandering Minstrel
Warsaw
Watermelon
Well Red Rhino
Wet Dream
Whale's Tail
White Death
White Elephant
White Mink
White Russian
White Spider
Wild Thing
Windex
Woo Woo
W. W. II
Y. I.
Yellow Bird
Yellow Fever
Yellow Russian
Zhivago Standard
Zipper Head
Zonker

• VODKA (CITRUS)

Blue Lemonade
Lemon Drop
Neon
Pink Lemonade
Salty Dogitron
Samurai
Zuma Buma

• VODKA (PEPPERED)

Afterburner
Cajun Martini
Creole Martini
Fahrenheit 5
Firebird
Holy Hail Rosemary
Hot Dog
Louisiana Shooter
Oyster Shooter
Peppar Martini
Sparks

• WHISKEY

Alabama Slammer
Algonquin
Bend Me Over
Black Hawk
Blinker
Blue Valium
Boilermaker
Bop The Princess
Cablegram
California Lemonade
Canada Cocktail
Canadian Cider
Depth Charge

De Rigueur
Dog Sled
Dry Manhattan
Dubonnet Manhattan
Duck Fart
Eden Roc Fizz
Empire State Slammer
Fox River
Frisco Sour
Gloomlifter
Hawaiian
Heartbreak
Henry Morgan's Grog
Highball
Horse's Neck
Hot Apple Toddy
Hot Toddy
Hunter's Cocktail
Ink Street
Japanese Fizz
John Collins
Klondike Cooler
Ladies
Lawhill
Linstead
Los Angeles Cocktail
Madeira Cocktail
Manhasset
Manhattan
Maple Leaf
Mexican Blackjack
Monte Carlo
Mother Love
New World
New York Cocktail
New York Slammer
Niagara Falls
Oh, Henry
Old Fashion
Old Groaner
Old Groaner's Wife
Opening
Oriental
Perfect Manhattan
Pink Almond
Prairie Oyster
Preakness
Press
Quebec
Raspberry Lime Rickey
Rattlesnake
Royal Canadian
Seven And Seven
Seventh Heaven
Sharkey Punch
Snake Bite
Soul Kiss
Spilt Milk
Temptation
Tennessee
Tom Mix High
Trois Rivieres
Twin Hills
Vancouver
Ward Eight
Whippet
Whiskey And Water
Whiskey Collins
Whiskey Daisy
Whiskey Fix
Whiskey Highball
Whiskey Rickey
Whiskey Sour
Wind City
Yashmak
Zazarac

• WINE (RED)

Appetizer
Cranes Beach Punch
Drunken Waiter
Gluewein
Mountain Red Punch
Port In A Storm
Prince Of Wales

Red Wine Cooler
Restoration
Sangria
Spritzer
Wine Cooler
Wine Spritzer
Xalapa Punch

• WINE (WHITE)

Fuzzy Guppie
Hawaiian Cocktail
Kir
Leslie
Quaker City Cooler
Scorpion
Spritzer
Tear Drop
White Cargo
White Water
Wine Cooler
Wine Spritzer

• YUKON JACK

.SCanadian Coffee
Frostbite
Gandy Dancer
H. D. Rider
Mackenzie Gold
Northern Lights
Pair Of Jacks
Panama Jack
Peckerhead
Pineapple Bomber
Rattlesnake
Red Death
Rocket
Shot In The Dark
Snake Bite
Spring Thaw
Sweaty Mexican
Lumberjack
Terminator
Yog

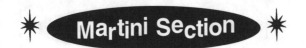

Martini Section

AMBER MARTINI
Fill glass with ice.
1 oz Vodka
1/2 oz Amaretto
1/2 oz Hazelnut Liqueur
Stir.
Strain into chilled glass.

BLACK MARTINI
Fill glass with ice.
2 oz Vodka or Gin
1/2 oz Blackberry Brandy or
Black Raspberry Liqueur
Stir.
Strain into chilled glass.

BLACK AND BLUE MARTINI
(Caution: DRY usually means
less Vermouth than usual.
EXTRA DRY can mean even
less Vermouth than usual or
no Vermouth at all.)
1 oz Top Shelf Gin
1 oz Top Shelf Vodka
1/2 oz Dry Vermouth
Stir.
Strain into chilled glass or
pour contents (with ice) into
short glass.
Garnish with Lemon Twist
or Olives.

CAJUN MARTINI aka
CREOLE MARTINI
Fill glass with ice.
2 oz Peppered Vodka
1/2 oz Dry Vermouth
Stir.
Strain into chilled glass.
Garnish with a Jalapeno Pepper.

CHOCOLATE MARTINI
Fill glass with ice.
2 oz Vodka
1/2 oz Creme de Cacao or
Chocolate Liqueur
Dash of Orange Liqueur (optional)
Stir.
Strain into chilled glass or pour
contents (with ice) into short glass.
Garnish with Chocolate-covered
Cherry or small Chocolate.

COSMOPOLITAN
Fill glass with ice.
2 oz Vodka
1/2 oz Triple Sec
1/2 oz Lime Juice
Dash of Cranberry Juice
Stir.
Strain into chilled glass.
Garnish with Lime.

DIAMOND HEAD
Fill glass with ice.
1 1/2 oz Gin
1/2 oz Curacao or Triple Sec
2 oz Pineapple Juice
1 tsp Sweet Vermouth
Shake.
Strain into chilled glass.
Garnish with Pineapple.

FIDEL'S MARTINI
Fill glass with ice.
1 1/2 oz Russian Vodka
1/2 oz Banana Liqueur
Stir.
Strain into chilled glass.
Garnish with Banana.

FRENCH MARTINI
Fill glass with ice.
1 oz Vodka
1/2 oz Black Raspberry Liqueur
1/2 oz Peach Schnapps
Shake.
Strain into chilled glass.
Garnish with Cherry.

GIBSON

(Caution: DRY usually means less
Vermouth than usual.
Extra DRY can mean even less
Vermouth than usual, or no
Vermouth at all.)
Fill glass with ice.
2 oz Gin
1/2 oz Dry Vermouth
Stir.
Strain into chilled glass or
pour contents (with ice)
into short glass.
Garnish with Cocktail Onions.

GIMLET

Fill glass with ice.
2 oz Gin or Vodka
1 oz Lime Juice
Stir
Strain into chilled glass or pour
contents (with ice) into short
glass.
Garnish with Lime.

HOLLYWOOD MARTINI

Fill glass with ice.
2 oz Vodka
1/2 oz Black Raspberry Liqueur
Dash of Pineapple Juice
Shake.
Strain into chilled glass.

HOUNDSTOOTH

Fill glass with ice.
1 oz Vodka
1/2 oz White Creme De Cacao
1/2 oz Blackberry Brandy
Stir.
Serve or strain into chilled glass.

KEY LIME SHOOTER

Fill glass with ice.
1 oz Rum or Vodka
1 oz Licor 43
Dash of Sour Mix
Dash of Cream
Dash of Orange Juice
Dash of Lime Juice
Shake
Strain into chilled glass.

KYOTO

Fill glass with ice.
1 1/2 oz Gin
1/2 oz Dry Vermouth
1/2 oz Melon Liqueur or Apricot
Brandy
1/2 oz Triple Sec
Dash of Lemon Juice (optional)
Shake
Strain into chilled glass.

LEMON DROP

Moisten inside of shot glass with
Lemon Juice.
Coat inside of glass with sugar.
Fill shot glass with chilled Vodka.

METROPOLIS MARTINI

Fill glass with ice.
1 1/2 oz Vodka
1/2 oz Strawberry Liqueur
Stir.
Strain into chilled glass.
Top with 1 oz Champagne.
Garnish with Strawberry.

MIDNIGHT MARTINI

Fill glass with ice.
2 oz Vodka
1/4 oz Coffee Liqueur or Coffee
Brandy
Stir.
Strain into chilled glass or pour
contents (with ice) into short
glass.
Garnish with Lemon Twist.

PURPLE KAMIKAZE

Fill glass with ice.
2 oz Vodka
1/2 oz Black Rasberry Liqueur
1/2 oz Lime Juice
Stir.
Strain into shot glass.

QUEEN

Muddle 1/2 cup Pineapple in
glass.
Fill glass with ice.
1 1/2 oz Gin
1/2 oz Dry Vermouth
Stir.
Strain into chilled glass.

SAKETINI

Fill glass with ice.
2 oz Gin
1/2 oz Sake
Stir.
Strain into chilled glass or pour contents (with ice) into short glass.
Garnish with Lemon Twist or Olives.

SAMARI

Fill glass with ice.
1 1/2 oz Citrus Vodka
1/2 oz Triple Sec
Stir.
Garnish with Lemon

VELVET KISS

Fill glass with ice.
1 oz Gin
1/2 oz Banana Liqueur
1/2 oz Pineapple Juice
1 oz Cream
Dash of Grenadine (optional)
Shake.
Strain into chilled glass.

WHITE HEAT

Fill glass with ice.
1 oz Gin
1/2 oz Triple Sec
1/2 oz Dry Vermouth
1 oz Pineapple Juice
Shake.

WOO WOO

Fill glass with ice.
1 1/2 oz Vodka
1/2 oz Peach Schnapps
1/2 oz Cranberry Juice
Stir
Serve or strain into chilled glass

OTHER MARTINI FAVORITES

Below is an index of other Martini recipes which can be found in alphabetical order in this book.

KISS IN THE DARK

KNICKERBOCKER

LEAP YEAR

LONE TREE

MAIDEN'S BLUSH

MAIDEN'S PRAYER

MAURICE

MAXIM

MOLL

MONTMARTE

NAPOLEON

NEGRONI

NEWBURY

NINETEEN

NINOTCHKA

OLIVER TWIST

OPERA

PAISLEY MARTINI

PARADISE

PARISIAN

PARK AVENUE

PEPPER MARTINI

PINK GIN

PINK PANTHER

PLAZA

POLLYANNA

POLO

PRINCE'S SMILE

PRINCETON

PURPLE RUSSIAN

RACQUET CLUB

RENDEZVOUS

SELF-STARTER

SOUTHERN BRIDE

SPHINX

TANGO

TEQUILA MARTINI

THANKSGIVING

THIRD DEGREE

THREE STRIPES

TURF

TWIN SIX

ULANDA

UNION JACK

VERONA

VICTOR

VIRGIN

VOLGA BOATMAN

WARSAW

WEMBLEY

WHY NOT

WILL ROGERS

YALE COCKTAIL

YELLOW RATTLER

ZANZIBAR